# Pragmatism, Technology, and the Persistence of the Postmodern

# Pragmatism, Technology, and the Persistence of the Postmodern

Andrew Wells Garnar

LEXINGTON BOOKS
*Lanham • Boulder • New York • London*

Published by Lexington Books
An imprint of The Rowman & Littlefield Publishing Group, Inc.
4501 Forbes Boulevard, Suite 200, Lanham, Maryland 20706
www.rowman.com

6 Tinworth Street, London SE11 5AL, United Kingdom

Copyright © 2020 The Rowman & Littlefield Publishing Group, Inc.

*All rights reserved.* No part of this book may be reproduced in any form or by any electronic or mechanical means, including information storage and retrieval systems, without written permission from the publisher, except by a reviewer who may quote passages in a review.

British Library Cataloguing in Publication Information Available

**Library of Congress Cataloging-in-Publication Data**

Library of Congress Control Number: 2020940122

ISBN 978-1-4985-9759-3 (cloth)
ISBN 978-1-4985-9761-6 (pbk)
ISBN 978-1-4985-9760-9 (electronic)

*To Mary Ann and Bill*

# Contents

| | | |
|---|---|---|
| Acknowledgments | | ix |
| Introduction | | xi |
| 1 | Technology and the Postmodern Condition | 1 |
| 2 | The Continuing Necessity of Jean-François Lyotard | 25 |
| 3 | Taking the Attitude of the Other in Communication Networks | 47 |
| 4 | Proliferating Realities | 67 |
| 5 | How to Reconstruct "Timeless Time" | 89 |
| 6 | Pragmatism and the Garden | 109 |
| Conclusion | | 135 |
| Bibliography | | 149 |
| Index | | 159 |
| About the Author | | 165 |

# Acknowledgments

Portions of chapter 2 were published in *Techne: Research in Philosophy and Technology*, 16(3) (Fall 2012): 231–251 as "Hickman, Technology, and the Postmodern Condition."

The support and advice from the editors at Lexington Books, Jana and Sydney, is really appreciated. My thanks to the feedback from the anonymous reviewer for helping to strengthen the book. Writing this book would have been impossible without the encouragement and friendship of many people, including Dick Burian, Jim Garrison, Ivan Guajardo, Ashley Shew, Tom Staley, and everyone at Clemson; the discussions with Nikeetha Dsouza, Matt Duncan, and Justin Williams; Daniel Brunson, Brian Butler, Tom Burke, Judith Green, Gordon Hull, Phillip McReynolds, Robert Rosenberger, Seth Vannatta, Dylan Wittkower, and David Woods for their comments to different parts of the project; Joe Pitt and Bill Maker for reading various stages of the manuscript; Jason Turner for being so generous after we moved to Tucson; the residents of 2409; and the input from my feline overlords (Who, Doctor, and Caty) and the other two who stayed clear (Lexie and Monty). I also want to thank the students who participated in my seminars on Nietzsche, information technologies, post/post/modernism, and American pragmatism. All of those seminars were invaluable for preparing this book. Lastly, Tracy, for her love, feedback, editorial suggestions, and general putting up with me.

# Introduction

In an attempt to make sense of what makes postmodernity distinct from modernity at a conceptual level, consider the opening of H. P. Lovecraft's classic "The Call of Cthulhu":

> The most merciful thing in the world, I think, is the inability of the human mind to correlate all its contents. We live on a placid island of ignorance in the midst of black seas of infinity, and it was not meant that we should voyage far. The sciences, each straining in its own direction, have hitherto harmed us little; but some day the piecing together of dissociated knowledge will open up such terrifying vistas of reality, and of our frightful position therein, that we shall either go mad from the revelation or flee from the light into the peace and safety of a new dark age. (Lovecraft 1982, 76)

A dominant assumption of modernism was that the "out there," "the other," could be conquered. For Lovecraft, what lurks in the spaces that we do not yet know will destroy humanity. So long as the human mind remains ignorant, the true horror of the universe will remain unknown. Yet, if humans go too deep in exploring the universe, put the pieces together, and begin to fill in the puzzle, we will come to realize that this is a mistake and begin to catch glimpses of the horror the universe contains. It is not for humans to understand everything within the universe because the forces of the universe either are indifferent to us or will destroy us. The horror Lovecraft depicts is that of the infinite universe, all the while ignoring the evils of his own racism, anti-Semitism, and sexism. Lovecraft inverts both sources of optimism embodied in Star Trek, both that "Space [was] The Final Frontier," there for humans to explore and conquer, and the possibility of a society rid of divisions based on gender, ethnicity, class, or religion.

If exploration of the unknown, the conquest of the beyond, gave an image for modernity's universe, William Gibson's cyberspace does much the same for postmodernity.[1] Present-day Information and Communication Technologies (ICTs) are not quite the virtual reality anticipated by Gibson's seminal novel *Neuromancer*: "Cyberspace. A consensual hallucination experienced daily by billions of legitimate operators in every nation . . . " (Gibson 1984, 51) where one can "jack in" and become fully immersed. However, there are definite echoes (Floridi 2013, 10–13). One "surfs" the Internet, messages friends across the globe, and wanders through alternate realities in video games. This is a very different sense of exploration than that which dominated modernity. My wanderings on the Internet do not involve going into some uncharted, unknown environment. Cyberspace is a human-generated world. Whereas the world of imperialist, exploratory fantasies was partially human produced and partially natural, cyberspace is wholly human produced. It is not some distant land, like Australia, New Jersey, or Kadath, that I might find "over there." Yet, it is not clearly "in here," in the sense of being in an ICT. If I am online, it is produced through the interaction of many computers, distributed (at least potentially) throughout the globe. Echoing Fredric Jameson, postmodernity "is what you have when the modernization process is complete and nature is gone for good. It is a more fully human world than the older one, but one in which 'culture' has become a veritable 'second nature'" (Jameson 1991, ix). It is a world closed in on itself, where there is no longer an outside. Lovecraft's intended horror relied on a great beyond from which the unimaginable ushered forth. Gibson's cyberspace is not "out there," but instead fully contained within a world, fractal-like.

I start with this juxtaposition as a way into making plausible the claim that the concept of "postmodernity" remains relevant. The suggestion is that Gibson's artificial, closed in cyberspace comes closer to the mark in depicting the topology of contemporary thought than either Lovercraft or the original Star Trek. This is in contrast to a growing number of scholars who would agree with Giles Lipovetsky's statement that "the time of disenchantment with postmodernity itself has arrived—the time of the demythification of life lived in the present, now that it is forced to face the rising tide of insecurity" (Lipovetsky 2005, 40). Lipovetsky captures a common sentiment that the significance of the postmodern is now exhausted. This disenchantment has led to an exploration of what lies beyond postmodernism, including possibilities like "digimodernism," (Kirby 2009) "hypermodernism," (Lipovetsky 2005) "metamodernism" (Vermeulen and van den Akker 2010; van den Akker, Gibbons, and Vermeulen 2017), "perfomatism" (Eshelman 2008), and "post-postmodernism" (Nealon 2012). While these successors can go in different directions from each, there is agreement on the following: talk of "postmodernism," "postmodernity," and "the postmodern" should be relegated to the history of ideas rather than being seen as a Jamesian living option to believe in.

In his *Pragmatism as Post-Postmodernism*, first published in 2004 (later reprinted in 2007), Larry Hickman ends ups in a similar place. The crux of Hickman's argument is that if postmodernism amounts to a rejection of traditional metaphysics and it is associated with quest for certainty, then pragmatism has much in common with postmodernism. Beginning with Charles Sanders Peirce and culminating with John Dewey, pragmatism pioneered this sort of critique of modernist philosophy. The reason why pragmatism should be understood as *post*-postmodern is that pragmatism is fundamentally reconstructive. This allows pragmatists to avoid many of the aporias that postmodern philosophers find themselves trapped in like relativism, nihilism, and ludism. In essence, pragmatism provides a way to retain the most significant aspects of postmodern thought, specifically the critique of traditional metaphysics and epistemology, while circumventing the relativism usually associated with postmodernism. Unlike the post-postmodern theorists alluded to a moment ago, Hickman seeks to revitalize pragmatism's voice in the present rather than constructing a new theoretical framework. But like those theorists, he ends up downplaying the contemporary relevance of postmodernism.

## AFTER POSTMODERNISM?

It is this terrain of postmodernism and pragmatism that this book operates within. Against both Hickman and post-postmodern theorists, I will defend the continued significance of the concept of the postmodern. This involves both the concept of postmodernity and that of postmodernism. These two concepts get run together both in the literature mentioned above and in other critiques of postmodernism, which is something of a problem because, following Steven Best and Douglas Kellner, if one wants "to avoid conceptual confusion . . . use the term 'postmodernity' to describe the supposed epoch that follows modernity, and 'postmodernism' to describe movements and artifacts in the cultural field that can be distinguished from modernist movements, texts, and practices" (Best and Kellner 1991, 5). Post-postmodern theorists make important cases that postmodernism, especially postmodernism as an aesthetic movement, is no longer as relevant as it was during the 1980s and 1990s. Yet, a number use this as a way into making stronger claims that the epoch of postmodernity is either over or never started. How to conceptualize or periodize the present epoch is a matter of intense debate, but there is a common assumption that the present is no longer postmodern.

Take as an example Alan Kirby, who is among the most well known of the recent heralds of the death of postmodernism. His 2006 article in *Philosophy*

*Now*, "The Death of Postmodernism and Beyond," remains among one of the most widely read statements of the subject.[2] What he offered in that article was a sense of what came after postmodernism, what he labeled there as "pseudo-modernism." Three years later, Kirby made good on the ideas introduced in "Death" in his book *Digimodernism*. There are several theses that Kirby defends here. First, that postmodernism is dead. Second, he does not think postmodernity could be over because he implies, with reference to Habermas, that there really was no such epoch to begin with. Instead, all of this is a continuation of modernity. Third, that is, in the rise of certain information technologies, like Web 2.0, lies the heart of what comes after postmodernism. It is the last of these theses that explains the incorporation of "digi" into "digi-modernism." Here I will emphasize how Kirby describes the fundamentals of digimodernism and its social implications. I will return to many of these points in chapter 1, providing a rather different interpretation of them there.

Kirby proposes two features that can make digimodern texts different from postmodern texts: (a) the degree to which the digimodern text is defined by its use, and (b) their interactivity. Despite the claims postmodernists made about the death of the author, the author was still in control with postmodern texts. This is not the case with digimodernism. The apparent center of gravity with these is the user. In some cases, these objects are designed to be used for particular ends, like dance music being made with the express purpose of being danced to. Others objects create open-ended, interactive experiences for the user, like various Web 2.0 applications (social media, chat rooms) and video games. Whether it is a Social Networking Site (SNS) like Facebook or a video game like Fortnite, these exist to be used and to be engaged with. This interactivity can also be seen in reality television shows like *The Voice* or *Dancing with the Stars*, in which viewers can shape the show through voting. Although postmodern texts talked a good game about undecidability, the basic structure of these texts remained tied to linearity and authorial intent. Paradigmatic digimodern texts like video games and SNSs allow for a much greater degree of interactivity. For example, with online video games, the players (either as allies or as antagonists) are not limited by physical proximity. While the maps and terrain the players use in a shooter-style online game do not change from session to session, each session is a unique experience because different people participate each time. With online roleplaying games, through player interactions, stories and friendships can develop beyond that initially provided by the game.

The references here to reality TV and video games illustrate the extent to which digimodernism relies on a rather distinct aesthetic from postmodernism. First off, there is what might be referred to as an "infantilization" of aesthetics. In particular, many of the traits identified as definitive of children's entertainment (predemocratic, preliterate, ignoring reality, etc.) appear both in productions geared to children and beyond. This appears both in many mainstream TV shows, video games, and films (like the recent spate of comic book movies). Alongside this is a rise of the "apparently" real. Unlike the postmodern problematization of reality, digimodernism tends to create "realities." Which is to say that it creates things that imitate the real, whether this is reality television (whether it be about famous people, competitions, following "everyday" people, or other variations), attempts to mimic realism (like the documentary-style of *The Blair Witch Project* or *The Office*), or the fabrication of reality through the use of CGI. This tendency to create something that appears real, but without problematizing the real, illustrates the demise of irony within digimodernism. Kirby, with reason, takes irony as one of the definitive traits of postmodernism. And it is this irony that is almost wholly lacking in digimodernism, replaced with a certain earnestness (this will become significant in some strands of metamodernism as well). Lastly, as mentioned above, is the phenomenon of endlessness. Digimodern artifacts either aim at endlessness or come close to achieving this. This takes digimodernism back to a certain Homeric quality because "the *Odyssey* is 'endless' in the sense that it can be renarrated by selecting and reorganizing or shortening or extending its components: these are detachable, can be recombined (as by Joyce and Kubrick), and vary in importance" (Kirby 2009, 157–58). Different aspects of this endlessness can be seen in *Harry Potter*, reality TV, and video games, where the product can be constantly added to or revamped for each new iteration. This is not the openness or endlessness of postmodern literature. That was about endless interpretation. This is about endless production of a product.

A tension runs throughout Kirby's analysis of digimodernism. On the one hand, he expresses a hesitancy to engage in periodization, to speak of epochs, eras, and the like. On the other, he is well aware that he is describing something like an epochal shift. Specifically, that profound social ramifications follow from the information technologies that allow for so many of the aesthetic possibilities of digimodernism. Kirby identifies three ways in which society is becoming increasingly digimodern. The first he refers to as the "invention of autism." The concern here is not one of the "social construction" of autism, especially in a sense that implies autism does not actually exist. Rather, he points to the increased frequency of diagnoses of autism and what this means socially. Autism comes to have a particular meaning, specifically that it is "is the ready-made antithesis of the peculiarities of today's world; it is the mark of that which our society despises, marginalizes, and makes impossible, and is produced as the exact contrary of hegemonic social forces in a variety of contexts" (Kirby 2009, 231). Autism understood in this way is a mark of passive resistance to digimodern society inasmuch as it involves a shutting off from the frenetic, endless activity information technologies foster. Next, Kirby argues that "poisonous" metanarratives, assumed dead within postmodernity, return in digimodernism (a full presentation of metanarratives will wait until chapter 2). He points to two particular sorts of metanarratives that supposedly died under postmodernism, but seem surprisingly healthy currently. The first are religious metanarratives, which play a more much more prominent role in digimodernist texts than in postmodernism, whether this role is positively or negatively. The other metanarrative is that of free market capitalism and the related triumph of the practice of consumerism. Kirby finds the metanarrative of neoliberalism to be utterly inescapable, though he never clearly nails down the exact relationship between it and digimodernism. Lastly, he proposes that we are now witnessing the degradation of competence. This involves three strands: "the evacuation of the value of competence in public fields it previously dominated . . . the withering away of the expectations of competence in personal fields where it was previously and rightly taken for granted . . . [and] the diminished social valorization and economic reward of technical competence" (Kirby 2009, 240). The more that these trends take hold, the more difficult it is to achieve meaningful politics and social engagement.

Kirby's proposed response to this situation is "an Enlightenment rightly revamped, rewritten, and renewed by postmodernism, and a restored family structure rightly critiqued and renewed by feminism. No politics today wants it either: it wants consumerism, which would destroy both" (Kirby 2009, 245). He offers little more than a sketch of what this rekindled Enlightenment would involve, but he finds it necessary in order to answer the questions he concludes *Digimodernism* with "Who does digimodernism belong to? What is it for? What are we to do with it?" (Kirby 2009, 247). That he concludes the work this way serves to reinforce two themes within it. First, the outlines of digimodernism are only beginning to take shape, so much so that he anticipates there will be "high" and then "late" digimodernism (thus relegating postmodernism to a footnote between modernism and digimodernism). Second, that unlike much postmodern thought and theory, the answers to the questions Kirby poses in *Digimodernism* are open. By this, I mean that Kirby suggests that the answers are up to us, whoever us might be, and that our answers will shape the development of postmodernism. This sort of open-endedness is in striking contrast to the talk of "exhaustion" and "the end of history" in postmodernism, which make this sort of human-shaped future difficult.

Kirby proves useful for a few reasons. He clearly articulates how the aesthetics of digimodernism differ from postmodernism, although as I suggested above arguably underplaying the continuity between them. As I will return to later, Kirby's arguments about the distinctiveness of digimodernism can actually be used to support my point that postmodernity remains a relevant concept. On a different front, he isolates an important, yet underappreciated, strain in these discussions: technology. As the subtitle of *Digimodernism* makes plain, "How New Technologies Dismantle the Postmodern and Reconfigure Our Culture," technologies play a central role in his story. Although I will be critical of Kirby in a number of places, he is right to pay attention to technology. Looking to the role of technology is decisive for understanding the present. The lesson I will defend inverts his. Rather than dismantling the postmodern, I argue that examining technology through the lens of pragmatism reveals the persistence of the postmodern. Specifically, this will demonstrate why the present should continue to be characterized as "postmodernity," rather than searching for some new term. One consequence of this is that postmodern philosophy then continues to provide invaluable tools for making sense of the present moment. While Kirby is correct that there is much about postmodernism that no longer holds the same, elements of postmodern philosophy remain an important wellspring for interpreting the contemporary world. The first step in making this case is better defining both modernity and postmodernity.

## A PROJECT AND A CHALLENGE

One fruitful way to describe postmodernity is as a challenge. The challenge is this: What does one do after modernity? Postmodernity is a particular condition in that, as the term implies, comes after modernity. Specifically, I take this to mean that the hallmarks of the modern undergo a mutation. This then raises the question: What is the modern?

Especially in terms of philosophy, modernism is best conceived of as a project. It was an attempt to make the world in a particular image. One associated with reason, science, emancipation, and so on. Modern*ism* grew up as a response to emergence of modern*ity*. Modernity, very roughly 1600 to the late 1900s, was a period defined by the growth of capitalism, the development of science, colonialism, and imperialism, and so forth. Legitimation underwent a profound change because of the pressures of modernity. Unlike earlier epochs, in which tradition was sufficient to justify practices, modernity created conditions in which, officially, rational modes of legitimation needed to be employed (Habermas 1975, 1987). A core part of the project of modernism involved producing such legitimation for new institutions that broke with tradition, like capitalism, democracy, or modern science. The demise of the project of legitimation is one important barometer of the shift from modernity to postmodernity. That the would-be traditional tools for legitimating discourses no longer functioned properly indicated that something had changed within modernity. To be clear, the demise of this sort of legitimation did not cause this mutation but is a sign of the deeper transformations that produced postmodernity. Along with this shift, many of the basic expectations associated with modernity are also transformed. Modernity, as expressed through trends in modernist philosophy, invoked assumptions about the possibility of the domination of the world (at least the natural world, if not control over the human as well), sovereignty of reason (especially as exemplified by science), the incredible capacities of the individual, and a time-consciousness radically oriented toward the future and the related claim of progress (scientific and material, as well as moral and political). This is most clearly illustrated by the Enlightenment modernist Immanuel Kant, but more subtle variations on such themes can be seen in nineteenth- and early twentieth-century philosophies, including Marxism and pragmatism. These later modernists worked within a modernist framework, but tempered its excesses (usually through incorporating elements of romanticism). Postmodernity is the situation in which all of these are fundamentally called into question. Hence, the challenge of postmodernity: how to live when modern assumptions no longer hold?

## THE BOUNDED INFINITE

In order to better capture what this challenge involves I will follow a clue that comes out of the topology of Gibson's cyberspace. To begin, contrast a static circle and one that expands. With the former, quite obviously, there is a limited area. Only so much can occupy the space inside it. With the latter, the area contained within the expanding circle increases as a function of its growing radius. It covers more and more space, and more and more can be contained within it. This latter circle illustrates one conception of infinity, in the sense that the circle expands without end. If taken to the limit, it would be an unbounded infinite. That is, something that would possess a radius of unlimited length, as well as containing an endless number of objects. I suspect that this concept of the unbounded infinite is what most nonmathematicians have in mind when they think of "infinity." Put colloquially, something that goes indefinitely or possesses an unlimited number of objects. Yet, it is possible to conceive of different sorts of infinities. For example, those who have worked through set theory know about smaller and larger infinite sets. What I am concerned with is one of the stranger sorts of infinities, one that lies between the static circle and the unbounded infinite. I will refer to it as a "bounded infinite," and it comes from Henri Poincaré's model of hyperbolic geometry (Poincaré 1952, 64–68; also Trudeau 1987, 235–44).

The purpose of Poincaré's model was to demonstrate the consistency of non-Euclidian geometry by relying on the assumed consistency of Euclidean geometry. Given the familiarity of Euclid, this makes the ideas of non-Euclidian geometry a bit more approachable (Trudeau 1987, 236). Poincaré asks the reader to imagine two-dimensional people existing within circle within a

Euclidian plane. A quirk of the circle is that it "is filled with a funny gas that causes meter-sticks (sticks one meter long when placed at the center . . . ) to shrink as they move away from the center" (Trudeau 1987, 236). This shrinking happens according the formula: Length of a meter-stick at distance $r = 1-r2/R2$ meters, where $R$ is the diameter of the circle (Trudeau 1987, 236). As seen in figure 0.1, the pattern within the circle repeats in accordance with this shrinking, such that the further the figure gets from the circle, the smaller it becomes.[3] "All triangles and heptagons are of the same hyperbolic size, but the size of their Euclidean representations exponentially decreases as a function of the distance from the center, while their number exponentially increases" (Krioukov et al., 2010, 036106-2). This introduces another quirk: everything inside the circle "experiences a corresponding variation of linear dimension, [so] it follows that no insider is aware of these strange goings-on" (Trudeau 1987, 236). The observer outside of the circle is well aware of the way in which the meter-stick, the person holding it and everything else shrinks as it

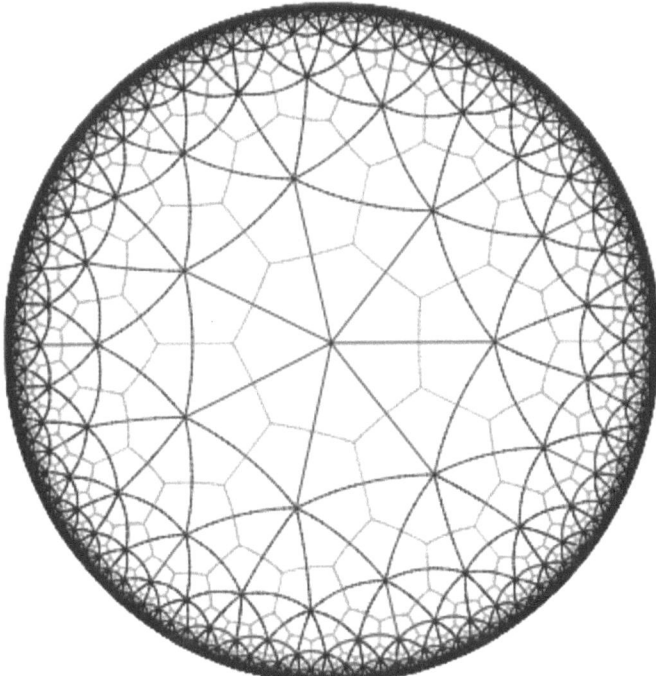

**Figure 0.1  Illustration of the Poincaré Model.** Reprinted figure with permission from Krioukov, Dmitri, Fragkiskos Papadopoulos, Maksim Kitsak, Amin Vahdat, and Marián Boguñá, Physical Review E, 82, 036106, 2010. Copyright 2010 by the American Physical Society. DOI:10.1103/PhysRevE.82.036106.

gets closer to the edge of the circle, but for those inside, everything appears to operate in a conventionally Euclidian manner. In this way, there is an infinitude contained within the circle, even if it ultimately only has a radius of *R*. Hence, the contents of the circle are at once bounded and infinite.[4]

I take this excursion through geometry in order to come away with an image to illustrate an important difference between modernity and postmodernity. The conceptual world of postmodernity shared many features in common with this sort of hyperbolic geometry. The world has become bounded. In this way, the conceptual world of postmodernity shares more in common with the how ancient Greeks and medieval Europeans conceived of their world. Whether the heavens themselves were infinite is another matter, and probably one not for mortals to know. Regardless, the world that humans lived within was clearly of finite size (Lindberg 1992, 244–61). This is in sharp contrast to the world of modernity. The world as reimagined through the Scientific Revolution in effect shattered the very space of the Aristotelian cosmos, replacing it with an "infinite universe" to use Alexander Koyré's (1957) phrase. As Koyré demonstrates in *From Closed World to the Infinite Universe*, the shift from one worldview to the other was difficult and marked with controversy about the meaning of the transformation at almost every step. Yet, by the end of the journey, a new world emerged in which: "[t]he infinite Universe of the New Cosmology, infinite in Duration as well as in Extension, in which eternal matter in accordance with eternal and necessary laws moves endlessly and aimlessly in eternal space, inherited all the ontological attributes of Divinity. Yet only those—all the others the departed God took with Him" (Koyré 1957, 276). The medieval world was cozy, a world in which everything had its proper place (Heidegger 1993, 283–88). Within the modern world, the only vestige of God that remains is the infinitude of Space and Time. Even once the broad concept of the infinitude of the universe become established, much needs to be determined about what exactly this entails, which takes over two hundred more years with discoveries like the birth of stars and the expansion of the universe.

While the concept of place falls by the wayside within the infinite universe, it is replaced by a world, geographically and conceptually, that can be discovered, explored, and expanded into. There was always something further, beyond the horizon. Modernity was marked by periodic revolutions, dramatic transformations from one state to another. Politically, there were the American and French Revolutions. Economics saw the Industrial Revolution, never mind the rise of capitalism. Intellectually, there are the revolutions in science, like with Copernicus, Galileo, and Newton, and later Darwin, Freud, and Turing (Floridi 2014). This sense of endless expansion and revolution was also echoed in modernism. Especially within the arts and literature from late nineteenth to the mid-twentieth century, modernism was the province of the avant-garde. The arts at this time were driven by a relentless, almost violent, succession of styles, each more radically reimagining what art should be. Albeit more slowly, a similar radicalization occurs within philosophy in their modern period, beginning with Descartes's use of doubt to secure certain knowledge and Kant's attempt to determine on what grounds knowledge is even possible, to Nietzsche's unmasking of all this as inherently nihilistic. This period was also marked as an "Age of Exploration" in which Europe exerted itself increasingly across the rest of the globe, in terms of exploration and representation (Haraway 1991, 203-30; Harding 1994; Harvey 1990, 240-59). Conceptually and otherwise (politically, economically, and geographically), modernity was an era of exploration.

The postmodern condition involves a return to a closed world, but in a way illustrated by image created by Poincaré's Model. Conceptually, it is akin to the sublunary medieval world, bounded, possessing a finite radius. But the postmodern bounded infinite is different from the medieval Earth in two ways. First, unlike the closed medieval cosmos, the postmodern world is not cradled by the heavens. It possesses no "outside," no superlunary realm. Everything that is, is contained within the bounded infinite. Where things diverge from Poincaré's Model is while those living within his circle still act as if they operate in Euclidian space, an unbounded infinite, they might well be aware that they do not. Such a realization will be crucial below. Following Koyré's reasoning, if the modern worldview stripped away all Divine attributes except infinite Extension and Duration, then these last vestiges of God also fall away because neither remains infinite in the sense of being unlimited (the case about duration will be made in chapter 5). Second, the universe is at once limited, but contains an infinite amount within itself. In contrast with modernity, the conceptual universe of postmodernity is closed off, yet remains infinite nonetheless. The number of objects contained in the world is still endless, but unlike an unbounded infinity there are limits. The modern world was infinite in the sense of being endless at least, and there is a case to be made that it contained innumerable objects. The postmodern world contains innumerable objects, but as illustrated by Escher, in a rather limited space. Since the modern universe was infinite in terms of its radius, more objects could be added, or incorporated, into it. This is no longer the case in postmodernity, where no more can be added to the bound infinite. Instead, only its contents can be rearranged.

A telling illustration of this comes from Kirby's analysis of rock music in *Digimodernism* (2009, 206-18). He argues there that Radiohead's *OK Computer* (1997) was "the last great art-album ever made . . . as beautifully formed as anything in rock" (Kirby 2009, 211). This album marked the effective termination of rock music. Instead of there being new styles to be developed, after *OK Computer* rock and pop would largely involve reconfiguring old styles and melding them together in new ways. This is ultimately different from the history of rock from 1950s up to that point, where wholly new styles evolved out of previous styles of music, usually with a fair bit of cross-pollenization between genres. Two examples include (a) the decisive innovation of early Beatles consisted of playing pop very well, with hints of R&B and Country and Western. Their nigh flawless execution of this style then allowed their music to evolve into their middle and later period; (b) all those bands, usually British (like The Rolling Stones, Led Zeppelin, or Black Sabbath), that took American blues and added other techniques and/or instrumentation, which produced the archetypes of rock, hard rock, and heavy metal. As much as all these groups were indebted to earlier performers, their music evolved into something clearly new. The punch line of Kirby's argument is that this style of evolution is over. Rock music has reached what amounts to an evolutionary dead end. No new genres, like heavy metal, punk, or hip-hop, are likely to emerge. Rather, much like contemporary jazz and, more arguably, classical music, two things will occur. First, we will continue to see an ever-increasing refinement of genres, which might produce exemplars that perfect the genre or sub-genre but most of it is thoroughly derivative. Second, we will continue to see the continued combination of disparate styles, sometimes to interesting effect. But unlike what occurred in the earlier history of rock, these combinations will not open up new spaces for genres per se. Instead, they will produce a possibly endless number of subgenres within and between genres. The building blocks out of which popular music will be formed have been laid out and will not change. Furthermore, if Kirby is correct, this has been the case for almost two decades. What we are left with is recombining those pieces in new and temporarily interesting ways. Kirby's analysis here is quite perceptive even if the overall conclusion of *Digimodernism* is that this, and many other examples, demonstrate the demise of postmodernism. My suggestion here is that rather than marking a sharp ending to the postmodern, this change in musical style is an extension of trends already existing within postmodernity.

Talk of "hyperspace" is not new when considering postmodernity. In Jameson's analysis of the Bonaventure Hotel in Los Angeles, his arguments rest on the hotel being a hyperspace where the assumptions of Euclidian geometry break down (Jameson 1991, 39–45). The hyperspace becomes emblematic of how postmodernism creates a fundamental experience of space and time. While Jameson's analysis might come off as a bit airy at points, the suggestion that space and time mutate within postmodernity is borne out through the empirical investigations of David Harvey (1990) and Manuel Castells (2010a, 2010b, 2013). Such mutations will reappear in later chapters, but my use of the bounded infinite is not simply in reference to ideas of hyperspace. Instead, my primary purpose is to provide an image for making sense of the shape of the conceptual universe of postmodernity. The expectation, the general way in which modernism, reflecting the outlines of modernity, conceived of itself was as the unbounded infinite. There was a limitlessness to the world and how the moderns conceived of it and their place in within it. Because postmodernity is defined by the bounded infinite, such limitlessness falls away.

## THE POSTMODERN AND PRAGMATISM

The challenge of postmodernity can now be stated more specifically: How should one live within the bounded infinite? As I hint at here, and will articulate throughout, although there may be the same number of objects within the conceptual universe of postmodernity, the shift from an unbounded to a bounded world has serious implications. For example, if the "out there," the beyond, is cut off, then the standard modernist form of legitimation can no longer function. This transition also reshapes the experience of temporality, which is of note because of the necessity of a linear conception of history for modernists' narratives to operate. These postmodern motifs continue to define the present and should be understood as part of the wider postmodern condition. This is why retaining both the concept of the postmodern and postmodern philosophy is important. Both continue to illuminate the contemporary world, the latter inasmuch as it serves as a diagnosis of the former.

In order to make this case, I will examine an underappreciated aspect of the postmodern: technology. One reason for this is simply that technology is rarely used as an explicit theme for understanding postmodernity, so by doing so I will reveal an underappreciated dimension. More importantly, technology illustrates and exemplifies a number of important postmodern motifs. In particular, the contemporary usage of ICTs reflects the flexibility, heterogeneity, playfulness, and, at points, relativism, commonly associated with postmodern thought. Furthermore, these technologies reshape social interactions, and in turn society, in ways that echo the thought of postmodern philosophers like Lyotard, and further entrench the distinctively postmodern sense of temporality. Without arguing that postmodernity is reducible to technology, technologies provide a valuable way to see why postmodernity persists.

In making the argument that pragmatism is ideally suited to aid in reconstructing the postmodern present, I will incorporate the writings of the major, male classical pragmatists: C. S. Peirce, William James, John Dewey, and George Herbert Mead. While Mead receives more explicit attention than the others, the goal is to work from a generally pragmatic perspective, rather than following out the logic of a particular pragmatist. Each of the classical pragmatists brings distinctive concepts that illuminate the present. I borrow from Peirce his critique of Cartesian philosophy and the basic pattern of inquiry, both of which mark a crucial break with modern philosophy and an important extension of it. From James, I draw upon the concept of meliorism. Given the role of Hickman in my argument, much of what is appropriated from Dewey comes from Hickman's writings. What is not taken directly from Hickman centers on democracy. Lastly, I draw on Mead's work on the social self, symbols, and his unfinished writings on temporality. My purpose here is to work with the spirit of classical pragmatism and demonstrate the fruitfulness of these divergent concepts as a response to the postmodern condition, rather than to attempt anything systematic. The hope is that by taking such an approach, I can show the breadth of classical pragmatism.

After an initial exploration of the roles technologies play within postmodernity, I turn to the writings of Jean-François Lyotard as a way to understand this epoch. Although *The Postmodern Condition* was published forty years ago, both in terms of its analyses of modernity and postmodernity, it continues to provide among the most accurate roadmaps of the epoch. His now-classic definition of the postmodern, "incredulity towards metanarratives" (Lyotard 1984, xxiv), remains crucial for making sense of how science and other discourses are legitimated. I argue that what is important now is how societies' responses to this situation have changed, rather than the fundamental situation itself (what I refer to as "postmodernity") has changed. This definition continues to illuminate many of the challenges certain societies face with respect to knowledge and authority, especially when the definition is wedded to his prescient account of how computerization transforms society. As I demonstrate, Lyotard can provide a unified vision of postmodernity, one that can both account for many of those motifs typically associated with both postmodernism and postmodernity and how and why these remain relevant into the present. I will also wrestle with other postmodern theorists such as Roland Barthes, Albert Borgmann, and Manuel Castells, but Lyotard occupies the central place. With both the pragmatists and postmodernists, my selection is not motivated by exhaustively analyzing every relevant text, since the relevant literatures are vast. Rather my goal is to make my case by working with texts that are representative of particular ideas. This better facilitates the overall goal of the work, which is to make connections between several relatively separate areas.

## NOTES

1. For those who would like to remain within the horror genre, an exquisite postmodern parallel to Lovecraft is the "Ring" trilogy by Koji Suzuki. Without spoiling the series, unlike Lovecraft where the source of horror is almost always from somewhere beyond, Suzuki locates the source of horror firmly within the world that

humans constructed, which Suzuki makes more complicated in each iteration through intensifying the degree to which the horror depends on human constructions like the media and virtual reality.

2. As of July 2, 2019, Kirby's article still appears in the top ten Google search results for "post-postmodernism" and until 2015 remained among the top five most read articles on the *Philosophy Now* website.

3. Among the clearest illustrations of my usage of the bounded infinite is seen in M. C. Escher's "Circle Limit" Series. All of the prints in the series illustrate hyperbolic geometry through the repetition of the basic figure. What is most important here is the way in which Escher repeats the figure, at least in principle, an infinite number of times within the circle. Obviously, Escher bumped up against physical limits when drawing this, but the implication is clear enough and can be seen by examining the geometry behind the series (Coxeter 1979; Trudeau 1987).

4. There are thorny questions about the sort of infinity the bounded infinite is besides it being bounded. For example, are the contents of the circle countable or not? Either way its objects can be infinite, but if they are not countable, then this would be a larger infinity than if they are countable. Given the argument here, the objects contained in the bounded infinite should be countable. Whether this is the case for the unbounded infinite that I allege underlies modernity is an altogether more difficult question. There is reason to think, especially in light of what follows, that modernity was conceptually an unbounded infinity consisting of an uncountable number of objects, but this might depend on whose image of modernity is being considered. Given the difficulties here, I will ignore further discussions of the question because it takes me too far afield from the important thing here which is the *image* of the bounded infinite.

*Chapter 1*

# Technology and the Postmodern Condition

For as useful as it might be, the image of the bounded infinite provides only a conceptual way into understanding postmodernity. What has not been addressed is what is involved with this epoch in terms of material and social practices. Speaking very generally, these levels of postmodernity involves the transformation in the mode of production and consumption (from Fordism to post-Fordism/"flexible accumulation"/"just-in-time" capitalism), time-space compression, globalization, decolonization, reverse colonialism, changes to social hierarchies, the emergence of what Cornel West (1993, 3–31) calls "the new politics of difference," among others. None of these phenomena are particularly new. Links between capitalism and modernity are as well documented as they are contradictory. For Marx, the emergence of capitalism is the principle driver of modernity, whereas Weber ties modernity to rationalization and disenchantment, which in turn drives the development of capitalism. As early as Karl Marx, the "annihilation of space and time" was discussed (Harvey 1990, esp. 201–323). Depending on what one means by the term, "globalization" is either old or quite old. What marks postmodernity as distinctive is the way in which these phenomena have not merely persisted, but intensified (oftentimes feeding into each other). Following Harvey, the previous stage of modern capitalism was Fordism, the rise of the assembly line enabling mass production and consumption. As he argues, the move to "flexible accumulation," postmodern capitalism, is not a wholly different mode of production, but rather continues the trajectory of Fordism through more targeted mass production and consumption (what he refers to as "just-in-time" production). Furthermore, capitalism has always been global in scope, and this remains the case. What is new is the speed at which this globalization of markets occurs, along with capital being far more globally mobile than in previous eras. This gives some sense of the variety of social phenomena with which postmodernity is bound up with (much more could be added).

This chapter will demonstrate the interrelationships between these different postmodern phenomena in something of a novel way. While building on the work of scholars like Best and Kellner (1991, 1997, 2001), Ebert (1996), Harvey (1990), Jameson (1991), and Lyotard (1984), my focus will be on technology, because this is an important, yet underappreciated, dimension of postmodernity. As I show, technology is woven throughout postmodernity. It enables the sorts of communication distinctive to "network societies," creates new modes of aesthetic expression, and can recapitulate a number of postmodern motifs. The latter will allow me to demonstrate the way in which the postmodern continues to play out in contemporary life. Specifically, postmodern philosophy offers a way to make sense of the technological practices underlying the present. I make this case by returning to Albert Borgmann's work on postmodernism and technology, then routing this through Hickman's philosophy of technology.

## TECHNOLOGY AND THE POSTMODERN

While there has not been a great deal of scholarship using technology as a way to understand the postmodern, there are many resonances. Lyotard makes technology a central theme in his thought, starting with *The Postmodern Condition*, Michel Foucault begins to phrase his thought in terms of technology beginning with *Discipline and Punish* (1975), and Jacques Derrida remained fascinated by "tele-technics" throughout his career (see Derrida 1994 and 1998 as examples). Bruno Latour goes so far to state that, when it comes to technology, postmoderns "relish its completely naked, sleek, ahuman aspect" (Latour, quoted in Hickman 2007, 19). The clearest celebrations of the ahuman dimensions of technology appear in postmodern science fiction, both more highbrow (such as the *Ghost in the Shell* franchise) and summer blockbusters (*Transformers*). Jean Baudrillard, especially in *Simulation and Simulacra* (1994), and certain interpretations of Donna Haraway make this point reasonably well in terms of philosophy. Such motifs underlie various sorts of transhumanist and extopian writings, like those of Ray Kurzweil. In these examples, we see illustrations of Latour's observation that postmodernists can fetishize certain sort of technologies.

Beyond these depictions of technology in postmodernism, we can also point to ways in which technology helps constitute postmodernity generally. This can be seen in the relationships between technologies and the arts. Usually, when telling the story of the emergence of postmodern architecture, it is framed as an expression of the exhaustion and tedium of the modernist style. For example, Harvey is attentive to both the rejection of modernism for this reason, as well as the pressures of political economy, in his analysis of postmodern architecture, but makes no mention of technology per se (Harvey 1990, 66–98). This sort of analysis is no doubt true and necessary, but not sufficient, for explaining postmodern architecture. It is plausible to think that this story is another about the rise of new architectural materials, construction methods, and design techniques. The horror of late modernist architecture like Le Corbusier and Mies van der Rohe is important to understand, but what these technologies allowed for might also help to make sense of why the architecture developed as it did.

A more specific story can be told with respect to music. As the composer John Adams writes from his own experience, much of his music can be understood as an interaction with new ways of creating music, going from amps to tape recorders to digital keyboards (Adams 2008, 194–209). Alan Kirby links the end of rock music's dynamism to the digitization of music (Kirby 2009, 206–14). The development of industrial music is shot through with changes in technology. In its early phases, the 1970s and the 1980s, recording tape played an important role. For example, bands like Throbbing Gristle and Cabaret Voltaire spliced tape together in order to create sounds to either create otherwise impossible sounds, or augment their traditional instrumentation. By recording music on blank cassette tapes and circulating them through a vast, informal mail network, the music could be exposed to a much wider audience. There are also the more obvious ways in how innovations in keyboard, drum machines, and sequencers, along with drops in prices, allowed for the emergence of industrial dance music with distinctive recognizable beats, in part because, "the music these machines made was always in a 4/4 time signature. . . . This scheme . . . enforced through its colors a four-beat pattern, visually dissuading even a syncopated clavé rhythm" (Reed 2013, 132). The ubiquity of these instruments, in part because only a few models were inexpensive, fostered a particular subgenre (Reed 2013). These examples of architecture and music show how the aesthetics of postmodernism rely on technological innovations, in addition to responding to and building upon the works of earlier musicians and architects.

This suggests that technology is useful for understanding some aspects of the postmodern, and it is this idea that the chapter will pursue by examining the relationship between Information and Communication Technologies (ICTs) and postmodernity. This class of technology plays a pivotal role both in terms of lived experience and self-conception in the present, both in terms of individuals and society. The massification of computing, the Internet and World Wide Web, and smartphones, along with less glamorous examples like photocopiers, fax machines, satellite and cable TV, VCRs, and DVD players, produce transformations of everyday life, sometimes in profound ways. Generally speaking, these should be called "postmodern" technologies in that they decenter the user, are anti-hierarchical, encourage heterogeneity, and so forth (Dreyfus and Spinosa 1997). When these technologies are framed in this way, I will demonstrate that key motifs of postmodern thought take on a new significance, whether in terms of economics, society, or culture.

Realizing that periodizing technologies is always approximate, I can note a few salient features of "postmodern" technologies with the example of listening to music on iTunes or Apple Music. In this case, there is a tendency to deemphasize materiality. Viewed from the consumer's side, iTunes requires little in terms of embodied connections: just the iTunes program, a device to run the program and the listener. So long as I have access to my music library, I have an effectively endless amount of music available. Whereas older sorts of media storage (LPs, cassettes, CDs) were bulky in various ways, iTunes allows for a large amount of data to be retained in a small space. The fact that the music is now disengaged from older forms of storage which facilitated distinct sorts of listening experiences, encourages new ways to relate to music (including how it is acquired). ICTs also have a profound effect on libraries. A library which emphasizes on-line tools and texts is structured quite differently from traditional ones based on the physicality of books. For example, the culture of the traditional library will put a premium on carefully selecting editions to make sure they are accurate and authoritative. These editions will usually be classified based upon disciplines and once established this will remain stable. The collection is also expected to be permanent, but allow for the user to effectively browse the stacks of books. On the other hand, a collection built around the concept of information-retrieval will emphasize having as many texts as possible available to the users. Access will center on user-friendliness and allowing for the following of links (both to within the space and beyond). This will allow for the "intertextual evolution" of the collection, rather than the simple adding of new editions to a permanent collection (Dreyfus and Spinosa 1997, 164). As one would anticipate, and is borne out in extensive analyses, the changes from "library cultures" to "information-retrieval cultures" involves a host of changes to reading practices, research practices, and ultimately conceptions of self and thinking (see Dempsey, Malpas, and Lavoie 2014 for an overview of some challenges). Furthermore, these transformations will illustrate a number of postmodern motifs to be discussed in the next chapter.

Before moving further, it is vitally important to be very clear on the following point: I am not claiming that postmodernity, or postmodernism, is nothing more than a technological phenomenon. Such a claim would clearly be both an overstatement and deeply troubling. Fredric Jameson points out specifically the dangers of doing this:

I want to avoid the implication that technology is in any way the "ultimately determining instance" either of our present-day social life or our cultural production: such a thesis is, of course, ultimately at one with the post-Marxist notion of a postindustrial society. Rather, I want to suggest that our faulty representations of some immense communicational and computer network are themselves but a distorted figuration of something even deeper, namely, the whole world system of a present-day multinational capitalism. The technology of contemporary society is therefore mesmerizing and fascination not so much in its own right but because it seems to offer some privileged representational shorthand for grasping a network of power and control even more difficult for our minds and imaginations to grasp: the whole new decentered global network of the third stage of capital itself. (Jameson 1991, 37)

This attempt to explain the postmodern condition as technology falls prey to two traps. One is the temptation to use essentialism, reductionism, and/or determinism to make sense of the postmodern. When such a determinist move is made, a host of troubles appear, which we will see below in Hickman's attempt to overcome the same. The trouble with reducing or essentializing postmodernism and postmodernity to technology is that it obscures other, equally significant transformations that go beyond the technological, including Jameson's wider concerns about global capitalism. The second problem at first appears to be nothing more than a Marxist terminological dispute: whether the current economic structure is best described as "late capitalism" or "postindustrial." Following Jameson, as well as Theodor Adorno (2003), the manifest danger in talk of a "postindustrial society" is the tendency to ignore labor, specifically labor struggles, in contemporary production. For this reason alone, there is reason to be cautious about terminology and "technology." Although this book is not strictly speaking "Marxist," Marxist analyses of postmodernity have been among the most penetrating, specifically because of how Jameson (1991), Harvey (1990), and Ebert (1996) account for society and culture as shaped by economics. I argue elsewhere (2009) that there is significant overlap between certain sorts of Marxism and classical pragmatism. So given the importance of Marxist interpretations of postmodernity and the resonances between the less scientific Marxists and pragmatism, it is worth following Jameson's recommendation on this point.

Instead of reducing postmodernity to technology, I claim that the postmodern condition is shot through with technology. First, as Jameson alludes to, *technology can serve as one way into sorting out the postmodern condition*, even if one must deploy other tools to ultimately make sense of the condition. Second, without consideration of the technologies involved with postmodernity, one fails to fully understand why the concept of the postmodern remains relevant to the present moment. Technologies are one element in the constellation, alongside changes to the mode of production and consumption, power structures, international relations, and so forth. Without seeking to reduce either postmodernism or postmodernity to technology, *emphasizing the place of technology helps to keep consideration of both grounded*, rather than considering issues as ethereal or playful. In this way, technology serves as a way to ground these considerations and potentially draw links between seemingly disparate parts of postmodernity.

## ASSIMILATION BY THE BORGMANN

Albert Borgmann's *Crossing the Postmodern Divide* is one of the few books that follows this possibility, exploring the deep resonances between postmodernism and technology. Mark Poster's wonderful *Mode of Information* (1990) is another, though Poster goes in a somewhat different direction by applying individual post-structuralists to particular technologies. This is not to say technology is ignored in postmodernism. It was a concern for many so-called postmodern philosophers and plays a role within Jameson's writing as well. And I would be remiss to not mention Donna Haraway and cyborg theorists following in her wake (Leitch 2004). Yet, Borgmann's work is different because he approaches the postmodern as a question for the philosophy of technology. He brings the distinctive conceptual resources of this area of philosophy, or at least those of his own distinctive neo-Heideggerian philosophy, to bear on postmodernity. By approaching the postmodern as bound up with technology, both product and producer of, he emphasizes several important features about postmodernity. First, his examination of how technologies are used illustrates the significant differences between modernity and postmodernity. Second, this approach allows Borgmann to make sense of Baudrillard's "hyperreality," though in a way less open to standard criticisms of Baudrillard because of the phenomenology that underwrites Borgmann (Best and Kellner 1991, 137–45; 1997, 110–18). Lastly, his philosophy of technology opens up the possibility of using postmodern ways of thinking to produce relationships between humans and with the natural world that goes beyond either the hyperreal or modernist exploitation. This sort of "postmodern realism" is a distinctly underappreciated facet of postmodern thought.

According to Borgmann, postmodernism is an inchoate response to modernism, so it worth saying a few words about how he defines modernism. Modernism boils down to three traits: aggressive realism, methodological universalism, and ambiguous individualism. Each of these Borgmann traces back to pivotal early modern philosophers: Francis Bacon, René Descartes, and John Locke. Bacon provides the core of aggressive realism, which emphasizes the technological domination of nature. Methodological universalism involves the application of Cartesian ordering rules ("the rules of abstraction, of dissection, of reconstruction, and of control" [Borgmann 1992, 35]) to the domination of nature and, ultimately, humans as well. From Locke (and later appropriations of him) one finds the assertion of "the sovereignty of the individual as the fundament of authority" (Borgmann 1992, 37–38), though what exactly this claim of individualism entails remains indeterminate. In addition to tracing these back to the philosophical sources, he also shows how each of these traits was manifested in technology. The Baconian aggressive realism that Borgmann finds is the domination of nature, exemplified through the American railroad project in the nineteenth century. Universalism and individualism can both be seen in various aspects of capitalism: the former in the organization of corporations; the latter in consumerism.

Postmodernism is first a critique of these modernist motifs. It begins with the general characterization of postmodernism as a critique of realism, universalism, and individualism. Though in different ways, each of these pillars of modern thought comes under scrutiny, some devastating (like that of universalism), some not so much (like individualism), within postmodernism. At this stage, postmodernism makes no positive claims about how universalism should be rethought in light of these critiques. As a critique, postmodernism is inherently ambivalent. Where one goes from this critique is open-ended. One option radicalizes realism, in the sense of finding a successor to reality. This can be seen in the realms of economics and more prominent forms of art, where Borgmann finds a move toward mimicking the world and replacing it with something far more efficient, if not perfected. The other goes in the opposite direction, not replacing the world, but rather returning humans to it. Both of these possibilities are inherent within postmodernism. The latter he refers to as "postmodern realism." As Borgmann's phrase implies, this possibility seeks to fuse realism to a postmodernist sensibility. Rather than the imperialist realism of modernism, he argues that postmodernism opens up the prospect for "focal realism." This sort of realism seeks to return to the reality of things as the core of focal practices (Borgmann 1984). Against the reductionist and individualistic tendencies of modernism and the other strain of postmodernism, this realism emphasizes patience, community, and the fullness of things. When Borgmann wrote *Crossing the Postmodern Divide*, he saw postmodernism as open-ended, capable of being shaped such that it would allow for this sort of realist return to being. While not admitting that bending postmodernism toward this, rather than embracing the worst excesses of modernism, was easy, he did see it as achievable. One gets the sense just from the title that the book that follows *Crossing*, *Holding On to Reality*, he sees the possibility of postmodern realism increasingly slipping away into something more perilous.

This more perilous possibility is what he refers to as "hypermodernism." This Borgmann finds to be far more dangerous because it moves humans further away from focal practices that are decisive for his vision of the good life. The emphasis here is clearly on the "hyper" in that it involves an increased acceleration of both life and certain modernist tendencies. With hypermodernism, we see various sorts of displacements of traditional understandings of reality, as can be seen with the central role played by "hyperreality." This concept he borrows from Baudrilliard, though Borgmann develops his own spin on it. For both, the core idea is reproducing and replacing reality with a more perfect substitute. Borgmann distinguished between instrumental and final hyperreality. Instrumental hyperreality involves building upon and the displacement of natural reality. Contemporary ICTs are a prime example of this, whether financial instruments or video games. For example, "Takeover specialists in a Wall Street law firm marshal hundreds of millions of dollars, dislocate thousands of workers, oust dozens of executives, enrich countless stockowners, beat out competitors, stay ahead of the Securities and Exchange Commission, all within a few heady and frenetic months" (Borgmann 1992, 84). If anything, this process has only accelerated in the years since this was written (Harvey 2011). What puts the legal and financial industry in a position to create new means and spaces for the production of profit is their use of instrumental hyperreal technologies. The financial instruments, once developed to a certain level, have only a tangential link back to the world of labor, instead being the product of the financial system itself (Harvey 1990, 140–97; 2011). A very different example illustrates the idea of instrumental hyperreality as effectively as anything. "Cool Whip is hyperreal whipped cream. Cool Whip does not need whipping and is free of cholesterol. Enormous efforts have been undertaken to provide us with fats and sugars devoid of calories. Nutritious foods, too, are engineered to be cheaper, more attractive and convenient, and more healthful" (Borgmann 1992, 93). Cool Whip and other instrumental hyperrealities displace traditional reality by making objects that go beyond what is "natural." That said, for as much as the hyperreal undermines more traditional conceptions of reality, instrumental hyperreality must still be wedded to natural reality. "To prosper, instrumental hyperreality must retain the shape of a centaur. The refined part must remain attached to the crude part; information processing must be intimate with research, development, and manufacturing" (Borgmann 1992, 86). To return to the financial example, even though much of the financial industry is bound up with many sorts of hyperreal instruments, it continues to be very much a part of the world of commodity production and capital. We can continue to see these sorts of instrumental hyperrealities in the present with examples like energy drinks and bars, and some styles of video games (in particular simulators like first-person shooters or flight simulators), which attempt to augment, if not replace, things in the natural world with technological devices.

Final hyperreality is different from the preceding in that it "is not constrained by a reality principle" (Borgmann 1992, 87). Instead of being something of an augmentation (albeit troubling for Borgmann) of natural reality, final hyperreality seeks to be a substitute for natural reality. "A truly brilliant hyperreality will exclude all unwanted information . . . that would betray the presence of the machinery beneath the hyperreal commodity. Technically, brilliance means absence of noise" (Borgmann 1992, 87–88). Furthermore, this sort of hyperreality can be, in a certain sense, richer than natural reality, and clearly more pliable. The former, because hyperreality can simulate particular aspects of experience far more than they usually occur, thus providing a "richer experience"; the latter because hyperreality need not be bound by the regularities of the physical world. All this said, Borgmann admits much of the hyperreality we deal with thus far is not as totalizing as he implies. Television and video games involve increasing richness, but lack the total sensory immersion that final hyperreality promises. Based on Borgmann's description, the purest form of final hyperreality would be virtual reality simulations as described in science fiction. At present, we find something of a continuum from natural reality to something approximating final hyperreality, with many strange hybrids in between.

The hyperreal opens a space for a sort of addiction to it, which Borgmann refers to "hyperactivity." The more one is engaged in hyperreality, the more the lines between reality and hyperreality become blurred. For example, as ICTs became more and more a part of labor, the line between work and relaxation, home and office, become harder to find. Borgmann then goes on to claim that "[s]ince mindless work is uniquely exhausting and debilitating, its subjects are uniquely susceptible to disburdening and diverting hyper-realities" (Borgmann 1992, 101). In this way, individuals are increasingly caught in a web of the hyperreal. Lastly, Borgmann anticipates that as these technologies, in particular ICTs, are further networked together, that they lead to "hyperintelligence." IT networks all offer something akin to human intelligence, in that they allow for data processing and transmission, memory, monitoring, and surveillance. This hyperintelligence threatens to displace traditional uses of human intelligence, like remembering things or engaging in critical thought.

Now we can draw together these various strands to get a full picture of Borgmann's account of postmodernism. It begins with the general characterization of postmodernism as a critique of realism, universalism, and individualism. This critique has several important consequences on its own for philosophy, architecture, and the economy.[1] Yet, as Borgmann rightly points out, the postmodern critique, on its own, is clearly underdeveloped. From here, two different postmodern possibilities emerge: postmodern realism on the one hand; hypermodernism on the other. While both of these of these postmodern possibilities can be seen in the present, no doubt to Borgmann's dismay, hypermodernism is the dominant mode. With hypermodernism, we see various sorts of displacements of traditional understandings of reality. Many of these involve replacing what Borgmann refers to in *Holding on to Reality* as "information *about* reality" and "information *for* reality" with "information *as* reality" (Borgmann 1999). Traditionally, information served as a means for humans to navigate the world. A natural sign like smoke might indicate fire. This provides information about reality. The score to a Bach partita instructs the musician in how to produce organized sounds that some find aesthetically pleasing, which counts as "information *for* reality." Now, instead of providing humans information about what occurs or how to make something in the world, information becomes a reality unto itself. In Borgmann's terminology, this would amount to hyperreality, a perfect, shining replacement for the nature world. "For better or worse reality will become lighter, both more transparent and less heavy" (Borgmann 1999, 216). The danger of such a world is that its very perfection obscures the necessity of contingency and resistance for a meaningful human life. For this reason, his expectation is that "with all its impending expansion, integration, organization, and innovation, the information revolution . . . will devolve into an institution as helpful and necessary as the telephone and as distracting and dispensable as television with an unhappy slippery slope between its cultural top and bottom" (Borgmann 1999, 215).

Borgmann is quite useful in mapping the large-scale connections between technology and postmodernity. His analysis of hypermodernism highlights many salient features of the use of technologies that help to make sense of why postmodernism grew up the way it. Additionally, Borgmann helps establish why the basic patterns that constitute the postmodern condition continue to shape the present, and does this through reference to many examples quite analogous to those of we saw from Kirby in the introduction. Yet, Borgmann relies on a number of assumptions that end up leading into serious problems. "Borgmann advances an American frontierman's version of . . . Heidegger" (Dreyfus and Spinosa 1997, 159). Instead of Heidegger's "Black Forest Kitsch," Borgmann frequently deploys examples from Montana and elsewhere in the American West to illustrate the challenges of technology and how to resist them. The worry about this reliance is that it obscures how those who live in more urban, and technologically suffused, areas can take on these dangers. Also, Dreyfus and Spinosa (1997) argue that Borgmann's invokes an interpretation of Heidegger that finds no possible benefit to modern and postmodern technology because these technologies fall prey to *The Danger* of the enframing (though Borgmann describes The Danger in different terms). Instead of following Dreyfus and Spinosa's path and using Heidegger to correct this, because Hickman himself provides a compelling argument that this will not succeed (Hickman 2001, 51–53), I will instead turn to Hickman's Deweyian critique of Borgmann.

## HICKMAN ON BORGMANN

In "Literacy, Media, and Technological Determinism" (2001, 115–28) Hickman offers a critique of Borgmann on the differences between various media. This argument is useful because it provides a telling example of the sort of quasi-Heideggerian logic involved with Borgmann's work and also the troubles Hickman falls into. As Hickman explains, Borgmann makes a rather sharp distinction between "traditional texts" and "technological texts." The former are things like "literary texts, printed musical scores, and architectural drawings," and the latter "includes information on tapes, disks, silicon chips, and celluloid" (Hickman 2001, 115). Borgmann goes on to argue that there is an inherent superiority to traditional texts through the ways in which they engage their user. The works of Shakespeare and Dickens are superior to any film or video game. Furthermore, traditional texts speak about reality. As seen earlier, the danger of technological texts is that they can become a reality unto themselves. These sorts of texts create a world that can estrange the user from the "real" one. Hickman resists Borgmann's dualistic approach by instead arguing that, regardless of the sort of text under consideration, the task of creative intelligence remains constant: "to generate and improve hypotheses with a view to the reform of habits" (Hickman 2001, 119). This entails a rejection of the determinist logic underlying Borgmann, that is, that a particular type of text guarantees the manner in which it will be used. For reasons developed both in this particular critique of Borgmann and throughout his work, Hickman makes the case that technological determinism fails as a hypothesis explaining technology because it falls prey to the philosophical fallacy and overlooks the variety of possibilities that arise with new technologies. Hickman's goal of moving beyond essentialism and determinism is laudable. The trouble arises when one considers his positive claims, which are more ambiguous. The sort of determinism Borgmann deploys is clearly too simple, and the essentialist move to say that some texts are always better than others is deeply problematic. Yet to simply negate both of these claims will not do. While the history of technology has done much to "open the black box" of technological development, patterns of how technologies are used still remain. While Hickman does not make this "simple negation," thus falling into a trouble constructivism, it is not quite clear where he stands on this issue.

This concern about Hickman appears again in an attempt to show the value of productive pragmatism in the implementation of what Hickman refers to as "the Information Superhighway." Hickman uses his Deweyian toolkit to provide means for constructing such technologies in ways that foster a more democratic community life. His evolutionary naturalism leads him to emphasize the ways in which these new technologies are extensions and transformations of older artifacts and organic structures. Information technologies are shot through with continuities, but he is also mindful of potential discontinuities and displacements. Examples include those excluded from using these tools (the digital divide) and a host of changes to labor practices. To facilitate the realization of a better community life, Hickman then proposes several recommendations including *not* falling back on traditional technology assessment (top-down, cost-benefit analysis), the creation of publics brought into contact with experts, an openness to fallible experimentation (as he puts it: "not so much a 'planned' society as . . . one that is continually 'planning'" [Hickman 2001, 61]), and a very serious rethinking of education practices to reflect changing social environments. While the recommendations Hickman make are clearly worth taking seriously, the worry here should concern why it is so difficult to achieve the sort of democratic social reconstruction desired here. Dystopian fears about information technologies like Big Brother from *1984* seem not to have come to pass, but we are falling short of the community life Hickman envisioned.

Much of Hickman's emphasis in his philosophy of technology is on the side of reconstruction. What he spends less time articulating is the significance of the background against which such reconstructions occur. This is something of a problem for Hickman. On the one hand, if one is to understand how to reconstruct technology in a democratic manner, the background, and my particular emphasis here is on social structures, must be brought to the table. On the other hand, many of the existing approaches to such questions in the philosophy of technology (critical theory, scientific Marxism, Ellul, Heidegger) have tended toward heavy-handed essentialism and determinism that Hickman rightly rejects. The principle issue, then, becomes the way in which to best incorporate these background concerns, without totally jettisoning the Deweyian core of Hickman's writings.

The key move in resolving this issue involves foregrounding the significant relationship between technological artifacts and habits. By emphasizing the ways in which artifacts are like habits, we begin to see how to make sense of the technologies underlying postmodernity. Postmodern technologies require new habits from their users. As we might expect from the earlier discussion, these habits and actions will be distinct from other technologies.

From the discussion thus far, one way to map these transformations is through the concept of "habit." Whereas modern technologies emphasized certain sets of habits, like rigidity and control, postmodern technologies encourage others, such as flexibility and adaptability. "On Borgmann's account, modern technology, by rigidity and control, overcame the resistance of nature and succeeded in fabricating impressive structures such as railroad bridges as well as a host of standard durable devices. *Postmodern* technology, by being flexible and adaptive, produces instead a diverse array of quality goods such as high-tech athletic shoes designed specifically for each particular athletic activity" (Dreyfus and Spinosa 1997, 162, Emphasis original). As noted above, there is a tendency with postmodern technologies to facilitate more decentered selves. No longer does the individual need to be conceived as a whole. Instead, the individual can be distributed externally (i.e., spatially) and internally (i.e., involving multiple, nonintegrated selves depending on context). Both of these sorts of decentering can be accounted for in terms of habit. External distribution implies that habits can have a much farther reach. Internally, the individual becomes a disaggregated set of habits. While Hickman himself has not explored such possibilities, both Dewey and George Herbert Mead's writings on selfhood lay the conceptual groundwork for this, which has been further developed by other contemporary pragmatists like Jim Garrison (1997). In the next chapter, I turn to Mead's writing in order to show how this plays out in ICT-based communication.

## POSTMODERN THEORY, POSTMODERN TECHNOLOGY

With this in mind, I can now fully address the central issue at stake: Why Hickman and others must not dismiss postmodernism so quickly. On the one hand, Hickman finds that the classical pragmatists anticipate the substantive conclusions of postmodern philosophy. On the other, a post-postmodernists like Kirby holds that postmodernism is now conceptually exhausted. Either way, the conclusion is the same: postmodern thought can be ignored in favor of something else. While the previous argument has made some headway in making sense of what is distinctive in postmodern technologies, I will now try to show: (a) that postmodern philosophy can also be used for this purpose, and (b) that this set of tools fits together relatively cleanly with the pragmatism articulated here. To do this, I will draw out several postmodern themes from the writings of Roland Barthes. Barthes's status as a "postmodern philosopher" can be challenged in at least two ways: (1) that he is more a literary critic than philosopher; and (2) that he marks a transition between modernism and postmodernism given his lengthy career and his tendency to dabble in various movements like structuralism and post-structuralism. That said, Hickman (2007, 29) mentions that Barthes is a postmodern philosopher, and there should be little doubt that his texts helped instruct the overall postmodern oeuvre and, especially in his post-structuralist writings, established several tropes important to postmodern theory (Best and Kellner 1991, 17–18).

I emphasize here two of Barthes's essays: "From Work to Text" and "The Death of the Author." At stake in both is an attempt to understand the changing relationships between producers and consumers of literary texts. The motif found in each text is the move away from traditional concepts of "authorial intent" and "definitive interpretations," toward much more open-ended, revisable readings of texts. For example, as Barthes explains in "From Work to Text," traditionally there was a sharp distinction between literature (the Bröntes, Balzac, Joyce and Proust) and other forms of writing. He maps this shift in order to breaks down this hierarchy. Now, any text is worth reading and pleasure can be derived from it, regardless of whether it is high literature, an airport novel, or a technical manual. Rather than a vertical hierarchy, these texts form a horizontal spectrum, all worthy of analysis and enjoyment (potential "*jouissance*," more precisely). Further, the author is no longer taken to be the genius that puts forward a work "that can be computed" (Barthes 1977, 156), and that is definitively interpreted. Instead, authors become producers of sentences and paragraphs that can be endlessly recombined and reinterpreted. The "author" occupies one moment in the production of writings, but many others also play a decisive role. Specifically, the reader now plays a much more significant part. The place of the reader is not to (somewhat) passively absorb the brilliance of the author's work, but instead actively participate in the production of the text's value and meaning. Without the reader, the text sits idle, pointless. But, because the reader now actively participates in the production of the text, the author's significance diminishes. The emphasis now is on the potential for the reader to "play" with the text: "the reader plays twice over, playing the Text as one plays a game . . . also playing the Text in the musical sense of the term" (Barthes 1977, 162). This new world of "authorless" texts opens a space for many kinds of new readings.

Although Barthes does not directly address technology in either of these essays, the account of "texts" he presented fits well with the basics of certain postmodern technologies. Coming out the discussion of music-related technologies, the tropes that Barthes introduced with reading reappear. Whereas both traditional performances of classical music and LPs emphasize experiences closer to what Barthes called "works," the more recent artifacts, in particular iTunes or Apple Music either on computer or a smartphone, encourage listening to music in a more "text-like" fashion. No longer is the listener bound by "the tyranny" of music producers, consuming particular songs in a particular order. Instead, the iTunes user can engage songs in any order they desire. If she or he does not like a particular song by a particular artist, there is no need to listen to it or even acquire it. An artifact like an LP, along with a turntable, speakers, and so forth, fostered a certain sort of negotiation between the "artist" and the listener, in which the listener needed to wrestle with the "artist's" intentions for the music.[2] iTunes does not wholly do away with this, but allow for new sorts of experiences in which the listener can play a much more active role in putting together playlists, selecting the music on iTunes, selecting the potential cacophony of the "shuffle" function, and so on. This provides a space for achieving new sorts of pleasures in listening, closer to allowing the listener to perhaps not rewrite particular songs or compositions, but at least be their own DJ. For example, do you think that the Beatles "White Album" should have been only one LP? Now, one has the opportunity to sort out the good bits from the aimless noise. In such instances, the listener is more than simply a consumer of the music. The listener now can play a more active role in its assembly, which for Barthes marks the possibilities of previously unknown pleasures. Other information technologies all allow a much more active role for those outside the industry to produce music. The relatively easy availability of remixing software, as well as Apple including GarageBand preinstalled on its devices, speaks to this.

Barthes provides tools for making sense of the changing way individuals listen to music. This approach can easily be extended out to other sorts of technologies in which the user possesses more obvious degrees of freedom. Computers offer several different examples. The most obvious concerns the ways in which the Internet allows a great many more to be content-producers, like bloggers. Also, many websites provide spaces for users to provide comments on various on-line materials, never mind the assorted uses of social networking sites like Twitter and Facebook. Lastly, there is the explosion of "wikis," which are largely user-generated. Each of these examples briefly illustrates the usefulness of Barthes's writings for understanding the changed relationship between the reader and the read. The older model emphasized a sort of subservient relationship, in which the reader was relatively passive with respect to the Work. The Text, at this point including many sorts of on-line materials, actively engages the reader. The reader participates in realizing the Text. In this way, Barthes provides valuable insights for a philosopher of technology interested in the contemporary textures of technological practices.

The same can be said of other postmodern philosophers and theorists. I will deal with some of Jean-François Lyotard's writings on technology and its implications in the following chapters. Borgmann touched on how Jean Baudrillard's postmodern writings, like *Simulation and Simulacra* (1994), illustrate how technology shatters traditional conceptions of reality. As Mark Poster (1990) demonstrates, the writings of Jacques Derrida, Gilles Deleuze, and Félix Guattari all provide very general visions of how to rethink subjectivity that go to the heart of the postmodern condition. While abstract, the webs of concepts they developed offer rich resources for making sense of shifting conceptions of human existence, including the role technologies play (like in Derrida on "the trace" and Deleuze and Guattari on "rhizomes").

## A PRAGMATIC DEFINITION OF TECHNOLOGY

With the case that (a) there are distinct features specific to contemporary technologies, and (b) postmodern philosophy provides a set of conceptual tools for understanding these contemporary technologies in mind, I can now turn to Hickman's philosophy of technology. As a way in, I start with his chapter "Tuning Up Technology" from *Philosophical Tools for Technological Culture*. This chapter provides a succinct summary of many themes from Hickman's other writings, most importantly *John Dewey's Pragmatic Technology*. The central theme throughout Hickman's writings is an attempt to understand technological naturalistically. This means that technology needs to be understood as one sort of human practice alongside many others, while at the same time technology allows humans to cope with a sometimes precarious and unstable world. With this larger goal in mind, we can now make sense of Hickman's technical definition of technology:

> Technology in its most robust sense, then, involves the *invention, development, and cognitive deployment of tools and other artifacts to bear on raw materials and intermediate stock parts, with a view to the resolution of perceived problems.* Technology in this sense is what establishes and maintains the stable technical platforms—the habitual tools, artifacts, and skills—that allow us to continue to function and flourish. (Hickman 2001, 12; emphasis original)

This definition has much going for it. First, Hickman emphasizes the knowledge-side of technology, the logos-ness. Technology is not simply an artifact, but it is relevant skills, development, and implementation, among other things. Second, habit plays a significant role here. This prevents technology from being considered apart from its "users." This also emphasizes an embodied dimension in technological practices. Third, it is naturalist in that technology is an extension of the sorts of techniques other organisms use to function and flourish. Fourth, Hickman wants to avoid both essentialist and reductionist accounts of technology. The essentialist move, including the standard reading of Heidegger's "Question Concerning Technology," aims to say that technology has some definite essence, some definitive quality that makes it technology. The reductionist move is to explain technology in terms of one basic concept, like the simple reading of the Marxist tradition. Hickman instead construes technology quite broadly, so that there is no clear essence or underlying mechanism to its development and implementation. As he notes: "Activities that are *technological* include much of what engineers, computer programmers, musicians, architects, and historians do, as well as what each of us does when we utilize tools and artifacts, whether they be concrete or abstract to address some perceived problem" (Hickman 2001, 17, emphasis original). A whole host of activities count as technological in his philosophy, though beyond some general traits like involving the solving of perceived problems, there is no overarching or deep pattern here. How technological activities are pursued will go in many different directions.

Furthermore, there is a significant normative component that runs throughout Hickman. The goal of a philosophy of technology is not simply to describe how technology operates. Rather, Hickman's end is to reconstruct, reform, human relationships to and through technology. Following Dewey's lead, any reform of technology should be done along democratic lines. This requires participation from the various publics involved with the technology. While the definition quoted above does not make this plain, Hickman firmly rejects the move toward technological determinism. Instead, his reconstruction of technology encourages moving the agency for technological decision-making to those involved with it. For this reason, no technology is in-and-of-itself good or bad. The problems emerge through human use of technology, which tends to be established in a top-down manner.

Given the concerns developed thus far about postmodern technologies, it is necessary to emphasis the significance of "habit" in Hickman's philosophy. One purpose of creative intelligence is the establishment of effective habits. Habits are decisive for an organism successfully flourishing in a given environment. The definition of technology offered above makes plain the links between habits and technology, for habit is one part of the stable technical platform allowing for human functioning and flourishing. Habits can operate through technological devices, like my typing at the keyboard. There is a temptation to reverse the claim of another Hickman article and say that we should consider "artifacts as habits" (Hickman 2007, 241–54). Given the naturalistic core of Hickman's philosophy, such a claim is not a terrible stretch in that an artifact, in its relatively finished state (not so much the raw or intermediate materials), functions as yet another extension of a human organism. Artifacts will then be one result of technological inquiry, "the invention, development, and cognitive deployment of tools and other artifacts to be bear on raw materials and intermediate stock parts, with a view to the resolution of perceived problems" (Hickman 2001, 12; emphasis removed). This then allows us to better position the relationship between habits and thinking. As Hickman argues: "Habit and thinking are thus for Dewey not polar opposites, but phases within human experience. Habit *determines* the channels within which thought operates, and thinking takes place within the fabric of habits" (Hickman 2001, 132; emphasis mine). One task of reconstruction is to use thinking to reshape habits in light of the goals described above.

This provides a sketch of the main points of Hickman's naturalistic approach to technology. While many human activities fall under the heading of "technology," not everything humans do will. A central part of his philosophy is problem solving. Clearly, not everything humans do will fall under this category.[3] As Dewey was wont to say " man is naturally more interested in consummations than he is in preparations. . . . Labor, through its structure and order, lends play its patterns and plot; play then returns the loan with interest to work" (LW1.71). One purpose of technology is to allow for the flourishing of such consummations. One strong point of Hickman's work is the way in which his naturalism draws together the variety of human activities and grounds them as extensions of the basic concept of organisms attempting to survive in environments.

To see this connection between technology and habits, I return to Hickman's discussion of information technology and will amplify several points in light of postmodern philosophy. I take it as given that he is correct in arguing that that Borgmann's determinism about texts is wrong that some media are inherently superior to others. Yet, there is something in his text-type determinism that is clearly correct: that different media foster different modes of engagement. I will not claim that Hickman disagrees with this, but he does sidestep the issue. Consider the following: The assortment of habits required to perform a music score are far more diverse than those involved with listening to it. To be able to realize a Chopin prelude well requires a vast array of habits, in particular moving one's fingers on the keys of the piano while coordinating this with reading the sheet music. Listening to music incorporates different habits depending on the medium used to hear the music. A live performance engages the audience in a different way from listening to the same music on the stereo, played from a CD. The live performance can draw the audience member's focus in the way a stereo tends not to. Yet, I can work while listening to music on the stereo in ways that tend to be frowned upon in concerts. Furthermore, there is a notable difference as well between listening to a CD through a stereo and music on an iPhone. While both consist of binary code, the CD in many respects is much closer to a LP in that it encourages, though does not require, the listener to listen to the album straight through. iTunes or Apple Music facilitates a different sort of experience by making listening to particular songs, as opposed to albums, much easier (consider the "shuffle" function). There is also a larger issue here about how iTunes and other on-line music distributers have transformed the music industry. In short, at several different levels, the habits and other elements of the music listening experience should be seen as somewhat different (though there are also obvious continuities as well). Hickman is correct to deny that one medium is necessarily superior to another, but this should not lead one to make equivalent various media. Different media will encourage, though not determine in the rigid billiard-ball sense, different modes of engagement. CDs on a stereo make certain sorts of listening experiences easier or more difficult, and the same can be said of music through iTunes listened to through headphones or attending a concert.[4]

What this discussion points toward is the rather intimate connection between technological artifacts and habits. Much like habits are established to be performed in roughly the same way in roughly the same circumstances, technological artifacts are generally designed to perform the same function over and over. As we should expect from Hickman's naturalism, habits operate through artifacts. Habit is one of the principal ways that organisms survive. Artifacts extend out human habits. This allows for new spaces in which habits and other forms of action can occur. To return to the example of music listening, the transformations that occurred from the advent of radio and sound recording through iPods, iTunes, and music downloading profoundly affects the relationship individuals and communities have with music. The habitual engagement with music changes as well as the habits that occur while listening to it.

This is not to imply that artifacts should be assimilated entirely under the heading of habit. As has been repeated here, one task of creative intelligence is the reconstruction of habit. Matters of reconstruction with artifacts can very. For example: with many "traditional" technologies, by which I mean buildings, a craft-person's tools, roads, and so forth, these artifacts can remain for quite some time. They linger. Such artifacts possess a permanence beyond most individual habits, or individual bodies for that matter. Also, in ways at times disanalogous to habits, is the issue of cooptation of artifacts in other contexts. While many useful habits are general enough so that they work in numerous contexts, since it is rare of the same situation to reoccur, the ways in which artifacts can be removed from one context and appropriated for different ends in another might not have a clear parallel.

## HABITS AND POSTMODERN TECHNOLOGIES

In this way, the concept of "habit" provides a way to connect a particular postmodern style of technology to Hickman's philosophy. Using this point, we can now draw in Hickman's wider concerns, especially about reconstruction. Given pragmatism's emphasis on habit formation, we can join Hickman in avoiding the perils of essentialism and the related concept of determinism.

As mentioned at several points, one consistent problem Hickman wrestles with is the failure to use creative intelligence when forming habits. If habits are established in an unreflective manner, then there is no guarantee that new habits will foster the sorts of democratic communal life central to Hickman's work. Instead, habits tend toward recapitulating the elements of the situation where they formed. In effect, there is a sociocultural inertia as to how habits are shaped. Particular habits are carried on into the future uncritically. This both gives the appearance that essentialism and determinism are correct, in that when unreflectively pursued, technology tends to develop in patterns very similar to before, and where those interested in transforming technology should focus, that is: on the decisions that go into technological development and implementation. As pragmatists have argued, habit formation is a relatively open-ended process. If it were otherwise, then their extensive discussions on questions of method would be futile. This provides a foil against essentialist and determinist tendencies among some philosophers of technology. While reshaping habits in such ways as to avoid whatever-it-is-that-a-given-essentialist/determinist-is-concerned-with (e.g., enframing, technique, class-based domination) is not an easy proposition, Hickman and other pragmatists sketch a way into dealing with such issues through foregrounding the role of critical intelligence. Furthermore, phrasing issue of technology use in terms of habit also avoids the specter of reductionism. First, as Hickman's definition of technology makes plain, technology cannot be summed up as just one thing. Rather, it involves techniques, devices, tools (material and cognitive), invention, innovation, development, and so on. I argue here that habit does play a significant role, but it is alongside many other aspects of technology. Also, the concept of "habit" covers a remarkably wide terrain (there are physical habits, mental habits, crossings of the two) and encourages the user of the concept to turn to specifics of habits rather than remaining at the level of gross generalities. In following this strategy, the reductionism of something like standard readings of Marxism become difficult since there is no clear common denominator to reduce technology to.

When put in this light, we can frame analyses of postmodern technologies that bring together Hickman's philosophy with what is especially useful in postmodernism. One way to capture what is distinctive about postmodern technologies is the habits they cultivate. As sketched above, information technologies make easier or more difficult certain habits, like the differences between listening to music on a LP, a CD, or iTunes. iTunes facilitates some sorts of listening experiences, like the shuffle function and allowing the user to skip between songs with ease. So if I listen to the Beatles "White Album" and want to compare the final version of "Glass Onion" with the working version included on "Anthology 3," this is a matter of a few simple motions (as opposed to the linearity of LPs or even CDs). After some time, using iTunes or Apple Music, this sort of habitual engagement with the artifact begins to reshape my engagement with, and thinking about, the music itself. Similar sorts of analyses can be performed on postmodern technologies such as computers, smart phones, and video game systems. I relate to each of these sorts of artifacts, and whatever "information" they contain, through habits. Using Hickman's language, these habits "determine" my manner of experiencing the world (at least via whatever technology). The habits set the rules of engagement in which thinking then occurs, though this will also produce feedback loops between my thinking and further habit formation and reform.

Postmodern philosophy brings to this discussion concepts that help in mapping out the specifics of the habits involved. As I argued in the discussion of Roland Barthes, his writings provide a way into understanding the aspects of the styles involved with postmodern technologies. The motif of the decentering of the author, and the rising importance of the reader, appears repeatedly in considerations of information technologies. The user of such technologies plays a more active role in realizing the significance of content. Rather than seeking to calculate, rigorously determine, the meanings involved, the user is now encouraged to "play" around. While Barthes never puts it as such, this appropriation of his concepts can be put in terms of "habits." It is fair to point out that some modern technologies share much of Barthes's author-centered works, like the classic Fordist assembly-line, and these entail corresponding, usually rather settled, habits. Postmodern technologies still involve habits for many uses, but they tend to be much more open-ended. Instead of emphasizing a top-down approach to habits and habit-formation, postmodern technologies, like many information technologies, open spaces for users to form and enact habits based upon their use of the artifact. The sensibility of the habits is more open-textured and open-ended, much like those Barthes describes when engaging a text rather than a work.

Between the discussion of Borgmann and my routing of postmodern philosophers through Hickman, the outlines of my concerns about post-postmodern theory come into better view. For Kirby, technologies undo postmodernism: the changes contemporary technologies produce cannot be accounted for in terms of either postmodern aesthetics or theory. By taking technology as one theme for understanding postmodernity, it is possible to push back on such arguments (though admittedly, part of this is done by shifting from postmodern*ism* to postmodern*ity*). Instead of undermining talk of the postmodern, technology can be used to show its vitality. Either in its instrumental or final form, Borgmann's presentation of hyperreality fits the sort of world at play with many ICTs. Video games are a relatively clear example in that they produce realities out of information that might either simulate traditional reality or produce worlds that are not constrained by traditional reality at all. HD television and 3D movies exemplify another sort of increasingly hyperreal media. Lastly, social networking sites and Web 2.0 phenomenon like Wikipedia clearly demonstrate many elements of hypermoderism. First, these produce hyperrealities through creating what amounts to worlds-unto-themselves. Furthermore, many individuals who use social networking possess behaviors that fit with Borgmann's "hyperactivity," in that these users are constantly engaging these networks. Wikipedia exemplifies many of Borgmann's worries about hyperintelligence, in that it functions as a replacement for human memory and, in some respects, thinking (Kirby 2009, 113–18 is instructive on this point). These examples, admittedly discussed too quickly, are useful for two reasons. First, Kirby introduces all of these as examples of "digimodernist" texts. In Borgmann's account, they fit quite cleanly within his interpretation of postmodernism, in part because of what Kirby argues makes them nonpostmodern (that these texts are in part constituted by their users). Additionally, Borgmann sets up how other technologies, from information-based technologies like financial products (which played a significant role in the Economic Crash of 2008, precisely through their lack of connection to "reality") to food-like artifacts (e.g., Cool Whip or Soylent) and labor organization, fall under the rubric of "postmodern technologies." That this, and the other aspects of Borgmann's "hypermodernism," can be used to make sense of contemporary technologies fairly easily suggests that rather than the postmodern condition ending, it continues to intensify.

Additionally, this illustrates why Hickman and others are too quick to move beyond postmodernism, at least when it comes to philosophy. Because postmodern philosophers, in many cases quite consciously, reflect the specifics of their contemporary world, they have an important value in highlighting what is distinctive now. Whether their contributions become exhausted in the realm of aesthetics is largely irrelevant, given their continued fecundity in making sense of the present. Hickman downplays this significance by arguing that pragmatism met the fundamental challenges postmodernism posed and went beyond them. With respect to Hickman, the argument here illustrates the overlap between classical pragmatism and postmodern philosophy and new directions for exploring the relationships between them. While postmodern thought does have a role to play in making sense of technology and other social trends, Hickman has two advantages over standard interpretations of postmodern philosophers, which should be kept in mind with an appropriation of postmodernism. First, the centrality of habit in Hickman, and pragmatists generally, keeps discussions of technology embodied. Certain postmodern philosophers like Barthes, Derrida, and Baudrillard deemphasize bodies such that the world seems to amount to nothing more than free-floating signifiers. Second, Hickman's philosophy reminds us of the ways in which such technologies are the product of many human decisions. And, as a consequence, when humans made choices that run counter to a Deweyian spirit of democratic life, it becomes necessary to reconstruct engagement with these technologies. Questions both about decision-making and democracy sometimes get lost in the excesses of postmodernism. I return to this issue in chapter 6 and the conclusion.

## NOTES

1. Though one might criticize Borgmann for running together too quickly the philosophical dimensions of the critique with the economic implications, since officially many postmodern theorists were (and those still alive still are) quite critical of late capitalism. Unofficially, if Teresa Ebert (1996) is correct, they are complicit in late capitalism's continued hegemony.

2. At this point, artist must be put in scare-quotes, in part because of concerns raised by Barthes about the death of the author, and also because of how many layers there are between artist and artifact to be consumed.

3. Also see Hickman (2001, 31–36) for a discussion on what counts and does not count as "technology" in his philosophy.

4. See Wittkower (2008) for a variety of philosophical considerations of the iPod.

*Chapter 2*

# The Continuing Necessity of Jean-François Lyotard

The previous chapter sought to explore how technologies, especially computers and other ICTs, can be understood as "postmodern." Specifically, I show how postmodern philosophy can be applied in such a way as to illuminate how these technologies function. The fruitfulness of postmodernism for this provides one line of support for the argument that the postmodern remains an important concept, especially so when put in front of the backdrop of Borgmann's analysis of postmodernity and technology. On the other hand, Hickman also tempers this argument. Hickman's philosophy of technology approaches the topic as always embodied, always part of a world that humans play a finite, definite role, in shaping. This prevents some of the metaphysical flights of fancy associated with postmodernism. Because of the embodied individual's engagement with the technology, there are limits, like with Borgmann's analysis of instrumental hyperreality. Humans remain organisms with biological requirements such as eating and sleeping. There is some plasticity with how these requirements can be met, but that plasticity is not unlimited. On the other side, technologies are not indefinitely flexible either. While most, if not all, technologies provide some interpretative flexibility, this too is not unlimited. It is conceivable that I could listen to music on LPs in the same way I do through a streaming service, but the effort to pull this off would be considerable. In this, the direction my approach to technology takes reflects a muted postmodern sensibility; it is not the infinite play of Derrida and Barthes, or that everything is endless simulacra. But play and simulacra are at work in the contemporary world, just in less exaggerated ways. That is to say that the concepts of these postmodern philosophers remain vital for making sense of the present.

One of the names most indelibly connected to postmodernism is Jean-François Lyotard, principally because of *The Postmodern Condition*.

Hickman describes Lyotard as the "master postmodernist" (Hickman 2007, 29) and Kirby proposes that Lyotard's definition of the postmodern ("incredulity toward metanarratives") provides what "might be the 'cogito ergo sum' of postmodernism" (Kirby 2009, 234). Even if these statements are a bit hyperbolic, they illustrate the importance that this strain of Lyotard's thought had in establishing postmodernism in the 1980s. Building on the previous chapter, I will begin my argument here that Lyotard's writings on the postmodern continue to relevant for understanding the present. This follows from his fascination with technology and how it shapes both knowledge and society. For example, early in *The Postmodern Condition* Lyotard states that "the status of knowledge is altered as societies enter what is known as the postindustrial age and cultures enter what is known as the postmodern age" (Lyotard 1984, 3). He takes some sort of fundamental change for granted for a number of reasons. First, the sciences have become more concerned with questions of information and communication. Additionally, scientific knowledge becomes increasingly commodified. Lyotard anticipates that "knowledge is and will be produced in order to be sold, it is and will be consumed in order to be valorized in a new production: in both cases, the goal is exchange. Knowledge ceases to be an end in itself, it loses its 'use-value'" (Lyotard 1984, 4–5). Lastly, the computerization of knowledge feeds into this change, both because of the capacity for the transmission of knowledge over computer networks and that the knowledge is translated into languages capable of being computerized (i.e., translation into digital).

The rise of information-based paradigms in physics and biology is well documented (Gleick 2011, 355–72; Haraway 1991, 203–30; Judson 1996). Information theory continues to shape scientific developments and several philosophers have begun to incorporate elements of it into their writings (Chalmers 1996, 276–310; Floridi 2011). In terms of the practice of scientific research, the use of computers has profound effects on the production, distribution, and reception of knowledge. Lastly, knowledge increasingly has become a commodity like any other. This follows in part from the increased corporatization of academic scientific research (Resnik 2007) and through the rise of "big data" (Sætra 2018). With respect to commodification, the difference here is one of degree, not kind. Since the Scientific Revolution, one is hard-pressed to find much research pursued outside of economic or political interest (Biagoli 1993; Haraway 1996, esp. 131–72; Hessen 1971). One must resist the urge to romanticize older science for being somehow more "pure" than the capitalist-driven science of today. That said, there is argument following David Resnik (2007) that this trend of commodifying science has accelerated over the last forty years. In this respect, Lyotard is correct. When "modern" science has always been bound up with power generally, and economics in particular, the pretense that science should be pursued as "an end-in-itself" increasingly falls by the wayside.

This all suggests that Lyotard pointed in a productive direction in his writings on knowledge production. Rob Wilkie goes so far to state that "Lyotard's influential analysis of the emerging technological age . . . remains one of the predominant guidebooks for thinking about the digital condition" (Wilkie 2011, 3). One justification for Wilkie's assessment can be seen by turning to Lyotard's analysis of legitimation of knowledge. This takes us into the heart of Lyotard on postmodernity. By following this thread, I will be able to further flesh out my portrait of postmodernity. This will begin again on the conceptual side, following how his analysis of knowledge feeds into wider issues about the destabilization of other cherished notions like progress, justice, or truth. From here, I will go on to demonstrate the subtilty of Lyotard's definition of the postmodern. Despite frequent criticisms, Lyotard's analysis of postmodernity can be shown to illuminate many important facets of contemporary society. The chapter concludes by taking these rather conceptual claims and demonstrating how they play in terms of the technologies discussed in chapter 1.

## LEGITIMATION, META-NARRATIVES, AND THE POSTMODERN

What I will build my presentation of Lyotard around is his (in)famous definition of the postmodern in *The Postmodern Condition*. While he is most famous in the English-speaking world for one particular definition of the postmodern ("incredulity toward meta-narratives"), this is actually only one of several that he provided. What I provide in this section is an explication of this definition that will incorporate elements of his others. The first thing to note about all of these is that he does not define the postmodern in terms of a period, but rather as an attitude, a way of thinking. There is a tendency to interpret this definition of postmodern as bound up with a particular historical moment; that this "incredulity toward metanarratives" is bound up with the entry into a chronological period called "postmodernity." Lyotard never says anything in *The Postmodern Condition* to dissuade the reader from this, and any number of passages appear to support this interpretation, like in the opening section mentioned above where he describes the effect of information technologies on knowledge since the 1950s. This surely gives an impression that his analysis of the postmodern is associated with a particular period of time. Yet, many of his later writings on the postmodern do not make his definition dependent on any time period at all. Instead, being postmodern is quite explicitly defined as a particular sort of attitude that has a long history within

Western philosophy. "The first traits of modernity can be seen to appear in the work done by Paul of Tarsis (the apostle), then by Augustine" (Lyotard 1997, 95–96). In this passage, and in the *Condition*, he points to how the postmodern is an attempt to rid oneself of the modern. The modern is clearly quite old, and given their conceptual intertwinement, the postmodern is as well. While the way Lyotard discusses the postmodern in the *Condition* might appear temporally grounded, everything he argues there is also consistent with the attitudinal definition.

Two further notes to set up Lyotard's definition. The first is his definition of "modern" since this forms one contrast class to "postmodern." In *The Postmodern Condition*, he uses "the term *modern* to designate any science that legitimates itself with reference to a meta-discourse of this kind making an explicit appeal to some grand narrative, such as the dialectics of Spirit, the hermeneutics of meaning, the emancipation of the rational or working subject, or the creation of wealth" (Lyotard 1984, xxiii, emphasis original). The motivation here is that in order for one discourse to be privileged over others, that discourse requires another discourse or narrative that plays by a different set of rules. For example, Lyotard proposes that science involves two distinct Wittgensteinian language-games. On the one hand, science relies on descriptive language-games (e.g., saying that "X results from Y in Z circumstances"). On the other, there is a normative language-game at work because only certain statements count as scientific. This game helps to establish which statements are part of the science game, hence should possess the cognitive authority of science. This second language-game is a form of legitimation. This legitimation game is necessary for if "science does not restrict itself to stating useful regularities" and instead is a pursuit of truth or something similar, then "it is obliged to legitimate its own game" (PC xxiii). If the sciences do not engage in legitimation, then scientific statements fail to possess their singular authority. That is, they are relegated to being on par with other narrative claims about the world, like myth and folk-knowledge. For this reason, if scientific knowledge is to be legitimated, it then must look beyond the scientific description of the world and produce "a discourse of legitimation with respect to its own status, a discourse called philosophy" (PC xxiii).

The second involves the role of emancipation in his postmodern writings. In the *Condition*, his analysis of metanarratives foregrounds the work they perform for legitimating science. In an essay like "A Postmodern Fable" (Lyotard 1997, 83–101), emancipation is now the goal the subjects of the metanarratives aim for. Part of the explanation of this change involves Lyotard shifting in terms of the sort of metanarratives with he is concerned. In the *Condition*, the primary concern is those metanarratives that legitimate science. His writings in the 1980s and 1990s broadened out to deal with all sorts of metanarratives, all of which are underwritten by the concept of emancipation. The reason for this expanding role of emancipation involves the basic structure of metanarratives, in which the conclusion of the story results in liberation from ignorance, political repression, poverty, oppression, tradition, and so on. The purpose of the metanarrative remains that of legitimation, but what comes to the fore in these later writings is the story itself. When "emancipation" is read in this way, Lyotard is correct in holding that it plays a significant, if not decisive, role in modern philosophy. Both Descartes and Bacon explicitly seek to liberate humans from previous errors and provide a way of establishing modern science. While there is a tendency, particular when teaching modern philosophy, to largely examine the epistemic dimensions, historical approaches to modern philosophy like Toulmin's *Cosmopolis* and Mary Midgley's *Science and Poetry* demonstrate that this is too narrow a reading. A case can be made that many of the moderns like Descartes were concerned with liberating humans from error, but as Toulmin (Toulmin 1990, 45–88) and Midgley (Midgley 2001, 30) argue, even the shift to epistemologies of certainty occur within wider sociopolitical contexts like the Thirty Years War. This concern for emancipation continues throughout much of modern philosophy, especially in the writings of the *philosophes* and in Kant's ethical and political writings like "What Is Enlightenment?" and "Perpetual Peace."

I alluded a number of times to Lyotard's most widely referenced definition of the postmodern, and now need to explain it fully. As he puts it in his Introduction to the *Condition*: "Simplifying to the extreme, I define *postmodern* as incredulity toward metanarratives" (Lyotard 1984, xxiv. Emphasis original). What motivates this incredulity involves the role metanarratives play in legitimation. At base, a metanarrative is a narrative, a story. The reason it is a "*meta*narrative" comes from the particular role the story plays. The structure of the narrative involves its subject, the protagonist, beginning in an undesirable situation and struggling to achieve a state of "redemption" in which the subject transforms the undesirable situation into one in which they are perfected (I explain the reasons for using this language in chapters 5 and 6). This core structure of the metanarrative, the subject moving from an imperfection, a lack, to perfection, remains constant across all of its variations. What varies is the content of metanarrative: who the protagonist is, what is the lack that motivates the story, what qualifies as redemption? The answers change depending on the metanarrative. The role metanarratives play is that of a legitimator of another discourse like science. In order for a metanarrative to be a legitimate discourse, it must be outside of that discourse. This creates the following trouble: the act of legitimizing scientific discourse goes beyond the basics of the descriptive language-game central to scientific research. Lyotard accepts at face value the standard interpretation of scientific statements: that they are denotative. A scientific statement seeks to describe a particular state of affairs, actual or possible. Such statements possess a truth-value, which is fundamentally cognitive. Politics and ethics are defined by making prescriptive statements: rules about what an individual or group should or should not do. The concern at play here is one of action. Legitimation is a prescriptive language-game because it involves the establishment of norms about statements (who can make them, the priority of different kinds of statements with respect to others, etc.). The difficulty with the legitimation of scientific knowledge depends on the way different language-games function. Because scientific statements are denotative, they cannot legitimate themselves because legitimation is a different language-game. So, in order to legitimate scientific knowledge, one must move outside of scientific knowledge. This is why metanarratives are necessary in order to legitimate scientific knowledge: just taken on its own, science lacks the normativity to legitimate its claims. The problem: by moving to a meta-discourse about science, one is no longer producing scientific statements. The statements of science possess a cognitive value (truth or falsity). In order to legitimate these statements, one must answer questions like who is permitted to make truth claims and why certain statements are ranked as more significant than others. These questions cannot be answered within scientific discourse, because science does not and should not play this sort of language-game. To do otherwise would undermine the cognitive value of scientific statements. This is part of why metanarratives must be held at bay. In order to rationally legitimate a science, one must no longer do science and shift to philosophy. In shifting to philosophy, one is faced with two problems. First, many find that philosophy does not seem like a legitimate science, if for no other reason than the role of proof being noticeably different than in the sciences. Second, even if philosophy itself can be legitimated, then one is either trapped in an infinite regress (where each mode of legitimation must require a different mode of legitimation) or its legitimation must be established on a metanarrative that is itself indubitable (and given the status of philosophy, this appears challenging).

This core problem with legitimation is nothing new, going back at least to Hume's *Treatise* and his analysis of the "is/ought" distinction (Hume 1978, 469–70). Given this, why should one be especially incredulous toward metanarratives *now*? Lyotard never provides one single reason for this. Instead, there is a rising tide of delegitimation. One example is the writings of Frederic Nietzsche, who turned the tools of science against science. Nietzsche demonstrated the limits of reason trying to justify itself and the failure that ensues. Other philosophers and thinkers of the late nineteenth and early twentieth century like Sigmund Freud, Max Weber, Otto Spengler, and Martin Heidegger, contribute to this tide, as do the horrors unleashed during World War I, World War II, the Holocaust, and the Soviet Union. Within the sciences themselves, a shift of some note occurs with the development of special and general relativity and quantum mechanics, never mind the rising importance of the "information" in the sciences mentioned at the beginning of the chapter. There is the rise of modernism, understood in the usual sense, in the arts. To this I can also add technological developments, both modern and postmodern, and their social implications discussed in chapter 1. All of these events shook very basic assumptions about politics, science, art and, ultimately, humanity. Taken separately, these do not explain the delegitimation of grand narratives. Taken together, they do help to undermine the confidence in the content of metanarratives and their rational defense. Although I am unaware of Lyotard putting it this way, appealing to metanarratives died by a thousand cuts. All of these events and others taken together force the issue of the impossibility of legitimation via metanarratives. Philosophers have been well aware of the challenge of using metanarratives. The structural tension between language-games was there all along. What forces the issue is the increasing pressure created by a changing historical context. Given enough pressure from different sources, it made it increasingly difficult to paper over the trouble associated with metanarratives. Not unlike the role of anomalies in Thomas Kuhn's story of scientific revolutions (Kuhn 1996, 52–65), events keep piling up which eventually make it too much of a challenge to ignore basic problems. If it was simply the changes in the arts or sciences, or world wars or other dramatic failures of (so-called) European rationality, the postmodern condition, the situation in which the demise of metanarratives becomes all but inescapable, might not have arisen. When taken all together, it created a situation in which radical skepticism toward metanarratives is an imminently sensible reaction.

Ultimately, all the various ways to compose metanarratives fall into this same trap. If Lyotard is correct that this is gap between different language-games is unbridgeable, then the process of delegitimation cannot be stopped, at least on rational grounds. Two points on this. First, metanarratives, inasmuch as they are supposed to legitimate science, should not fall back on the traditional mode of legitimation. Traditionally, narratives are legitimate only to the extent that the speaker themselves is regarded as an authority. This tends to take the form of "I am authorized to tell this narrative because someone else who was authorized said so." This is not based necessarily on rational argumentation, but instead on custom. For a properly scientific or philosophical narrative, this is unacceptable (Lyotard 1984, 23–31). Second, as discussed above, there is a disconnect between the metanarrative and what it seeks to legitimate. The language-games involved are incommensurable. When considering science, it is primarily a language-game of denotation, while legitimation is normative. There is a further consequence of this disconnect. The metanarrative by necessity must reach beyond not just the language-games of the legitimated but also its subject matter. Science produces claims about observed regularities. Without the additional story of a knowing subject becoming emancipated from ignorance, there is no mention here of talk of "truth" or "reality." So too with politics. Any sort of law can be promulgated, but if it lacks proper legitimation, then there is no rational justification to said law. Yet, if the law is to have authority beyond that of terror or force, such legitimation is necessary. This is why Habermas (1975) regards delegitimation as so problematic. In politics it appears to undermine the possibility of just societies. In epistemology, the possibility of establishing that some forms of belief are superior to others. Among other consequences, this appears to lead straight to the relativism usually associated with postmodernism.

The postmodern condition is defined in large part by this "legitimation crisis." Other elements do feed into the condition, in particular those that force delegitimation like globalization, the rise of ICTs and its social consequences, the rise of the politics of difference and identity politics, and "just-in-time" capitalism, but the demise of metanarratives is a useful way of crystalizing postmodernity. What marks postmodernity as different from other periods is the global nature of such incredulity. It is not the case that I am skeptical of a particular metanarrative because I possess a better one. This was the hallmark of modernism that leads to the constant substitution of a grand narrative with another that should be better. Rather, postmodernity, understood at a conceptual level, calls into question the very value of metanarratives. This helps to make sense of both why relativisms of different sorts are so frequently associated with postmodernism, and why there is more to postmodernism than just relativism. Regarding the former, the demise of metanarratives at a minimum makes the privileging of different knowledges or ethics over others difficult, if not impossible. Yet, as hinted at thus far and I will turn to shortly, this incredulity toward metanarratives also has other far-reaching consequences, some of which are less immediately problematic (like an increased appreciation for difference). If this schematic account drawn from Lyotard is accurate, all metanarratives were doomed to fail because of their very structure. What in effect forces the issue about metanarratives globally, as opposed to this or that particular story, is not metanarratives themselves, since the internal problems were present all along, but the context in which they were deployed. Given the social, economic, and technological context bound up with the transition from modernity to postmodernity, the trouble with metanarratives becomes increasingly difficult to avoid. In the face of this context, relying on grand narratives to legitimate science no longer appears viable. To be faced with this global situation is to be faced with the challenge of postmodernity.

## THE SUBTLETY OF LYOTARD'S DEFINITION

Now, the inevitable qualifications. First, there are two interpretations of Lyotard's analysis of metanarratives. The more common is normative: that we *should* reject the use of metanarratives. This opens Lyotard up to a fairly obvious objection, clearly articulated by Steven Best and Douglas Kellner: "His renunciation of general principles and universal criteria preclude normative positions, yet he condemns grand narratives, totalizing through, and other features of modern knowledge. This move catches him in another aporia, whereby he wants to reject general epistemological and normological positions while his critical interventions presuppose precisely such critical positions (such as the war on totality)" (Best and Kellner 1991, 172). In order for Lyotard to make his normative claims, he requires the very conceptual space he seeks to undermine. On the surface, this appears to be a fairly damning objection. Yet, whether it takes hold depends on how we interpret both Lyotard's definition of postmodernity and the entirety of the book. What motivates Best and Kellner's argument here is reading the definition as a prescriptive claim: that we *should be* incredulous of metanarratives. This is the most obvious reading of Lyotard, for which there is textual evidence to support it. Yet, it is also possible to read this definition, and much (though not all) of *The Postmodern Condition* as a set of descriptive statements about the present state of knowledge. Instead of an argument about why present societies *should be* postmodern in his sense, Lyotard presents an overview of an emerging incredulity within contemporary societies, without either endorsing or condemning this. For my purposes, this descriptive reading of *The Postmodern Condition* is far more useful. That these narratives have lost much of their hold, especially in terms of rational legitimation, in certain societies seems empirically correct. The same should be said of the consequences that can be traced from the demise of metanarratives. For this reason, my treatment of Lyotard should be understood as largely descriptive. I interpret Lyotard as rather perceptively identifying and mapping a problem, and ignore until chapter 6 those parts of his thought that advocate for a particular normative position on the problem.

Second, is it actually empirically correct that metanarratives have fallen on such hard times? For example, I mentioned back in the introduction that Alan Kirby explicitly rejects the utility of Lyotard on this point because of the persistence of two "poisonous grand narratives": religion and consumerism. Kirby proposes that these metanarratives are currently returning with a vengeance, and he is correct in this. Narratives that possess the same structure and similar content to Lyotard's metanarratives continue to remain potent, which is explicable given the general role that narrative play in legitimation (Lyotard 1984, 18–37). Defenders of neoliberalism, and in turn consumerism, have an extensive network of intellectuals distributed throughout think tanks and universities to provide just such narratives. Myth, a particular sort of narrative, plays a vital role in forming the symbolic networks of religions (Taylor 2007, 12–33). What should be noted, though, is that sometimes the use of these metanarratives is window-dressing, like using philosophical arguments to give cover for a policy. Other times, appealing to grand stories should be seen simply as the ghost of dead habits. Even if the cognitive power of metanarratives has fallen on hard times, there remains an emotional draw to their use. The stories themselves are important, if for no other reason than humans are creatures that tell stories. In this way, even if the narrative still has the appearance of a grand story, its role is not that of legitimation in the modern sense, but instead the role of a traditional narrative. Traditional narratives rely on the authority of the speaker for its legitimation. Lyotard provides the example of Cashinauhua storytellers, whose "only claim to competence for telling the story is the fact that he has heard it himself" (Lyotard 1984, 20). This hearing of the story puts the narrator in a position to be able to legitimately recount the story. What matters here is the relationship of the narrator to the weight of tradition, as opposed to any sort of philosophical argumentation. Especially when engaging with those with whom one shares a tradition, this can be a quite effective way to support a position. Otherwise, it depends on the rhetorical skill, the charisma, of the narrator to convince the narratee of the authority of the point made. These might be useful ways to use a narrative, but we have moved some distance from the rational mode of legitimation that was supposed to underwrite the use of metanarratives.

Even if one acknowledges this, there is a further point that is vital for understanding what is distinctive about neoliberalism. When stripped to its core, it is not a metanarrative in the technical sense. It still functions to legitimate late capitalism, but not using the structure or content of something like Marxist or Enlightenment-era stories. Instead, legitimation occurs through appealing to what Lyotard calls "performativity." He introduces performativity in the context of discussing the purpose of scientific proof and explains that rather than science seeking to produce truth, it now seeks to provide "the best possible input/output equation" (Lyotard 1984, 46). The value of science resides not its capacity to produce true statements, but rather than it improves efficiency. It is the practical uses that science can be put to that justifies its superiority to other sorts of knowledge. The move to legitimate science in terms of its performativity escapes many of the difficulties that faced metanarratives of emancipation. As discussed above, the trouble with modern legitimation was that it relied on two incommensurable language-games: description and prescription. Performativity attempts to collapse this distinction by subsuming both of these language-games into one: that of performance, attempting to provide the best possible solution to questions of efficiency. The older style for the legitimation, with its appeals to truth and emancipation, might still appear in defenses of science, but it is being rapidly replaced by performativity. Some American politicians continue to make appeals to science, in part as a way to use the "truth" of science to end debates, but also because it allows them to claim that they are more rational than their opponent (Mooney 2006). Yet, when it comes to government investment in science, the principle motivating interest is in what it can do for the country, especially in terms of its economic benefits. Science is important to fund because the results of its research allows for greater efficiency, health, or economic power. Science performs. This shift over to legitimation by performativity helps make sense of the 1993 funding battle over the Superconducting Super Collider. The demise of the Collider is not a simple story, as David Voss and Daniel Koshland Jr. point out in an editorial in *Science*: "Just because particle physics asks questions about the fundamental structure of matter does not give it any greater claim on taxpayer dollars than solid-state physics or molecular biology. Proponents of any project must justify the costs in relation to the scientific and social return" (Voss and Koshland 1993, 1799). Alongside problems about the relationship of the managers with funding agencies, the utility, performativity more accurately, of the knowledge generated by the Super Collider failed to justify further pursuit of the project, especially when measured against the biotechnology boom (Riordan, Hoddeson, and Kolb 2015).

The logic of performativity has also moved beyond scientific knowledge. Many aspects of the American academy are increasingly subject to it. University administrators demand that departments prove their worth to the university, oftentimes by linking this proof to external funding. Any defense for the humanities must be made on these grounds. As any number of jokes illustrate, those with degrees in the humanities are widely assumed to have worse career prospects than those in the sciences, engineering, or business. Rather than justifying either a student's pursuit of a BA in one of the humanities or the disciplines' existence as a whole (and not just as "humanist" support, like with writing and logic courses, for "real disciplines") with reference to the importance of an understanding of history, culture, and philosophy, these defenses are made on narrow technocratic grounds (Nealon 2012, 66–84, 171–94). Lyotard also shows how the logic of performativity can be applied to politics. He shows in "A Postmodern Fable" how democracy can be justified on the basis of efficiency. The virtue of democracy is that it leaves its operating system open, allowing it to be adjusted by its citizens as events warrant. In a tumultuous world, this makes democracy far more resilient than other forms of governance. Such arguments are a far cry from Fukuyama's arguments (1992) that liberal democracy won out over other forms of government because it fits best with the complexity of human nature.

The crucial difference between performativity on the one hand and traditional metanarratives on the other is that the former does not appeal to something external to society, whereas the latter do. Performativity is by definition essentially quantifiable. The final resting place of metanarratives, like a completed science or a just society, cannot be measured in the same way because these goals must lie outside of society given their role in driving the actions of the narrative's protagonist. This is of course part of the very structure of the metanarrative, since the end point of the story must be outside the system it legitimates in order to serve the role of legitimatization. At a minimum, performativity avoids this problem by working within the logic imposed by existing within the bounded infinite. Since there is no longer a conceptual outside, a space to claim transcendence from, the only way to justify the superiority of one practice or mode of knowledge over any other is an appeal to efficiency because this can be measured within.

This should not be interpreted as saying that performativity is a perfect mode of legitimation, or that it escapes all of the traps that metanarratives faces. On the former, Lyotard admits as much when he says: "The logic of maximum performance is no doubt inconsistent in many ways, particularly with respect to contradiction in the socio-economic field: it demands both less work (to lower production costs) and more (to lessen the social burden of the idle population). But our incredulity is now such that we no longer expect salvation to rise from these inconsistencies, as Marx did" (Lyotard 1984, xxiv). With the latter, there is a lingering question which performativity does not itself answer: why pursue maximum performance? Answering this question likely requires something of a metanarrative, or a combination of institutional momentum and "terror." In the case of appealing to a metanarrative, this will likely be a dead end for reasons discussed. The other possibility follows the logic of Max Weber (1930) in *The Protestant Ethic and the Spirit of Capitalism*: the metanarratives used to support maximum performance, like stories of the creation of wealth, fall by the wayside but the goal is now thoroughly baked into society such that criticizing it is all but impossible. And if one does, then the threat of terror can be used to keep those in line.

The centrality of "terror" is the third point about persistence of metanarratives, and also something many of Lyotard's critics tend to downplay. In some parts of society, the "Anything Goes" practical relativism associated with postmodernism reigns. Yet in others, the threat or actual use of force remains. This terror is the underbelly of postmodernity. The possibility of excluding individuals from language-games enforces a sort of conformity on potential players. To return to the example of the sciences, if one does not play by certain rules, then one risks a crippling lack of funding. "The decision makers' arrogance, which in principle has no equivalent in the sciences, consists in the exercise of terror. It says: 'Adapt your aspirations to our ends—or else.'" (Lyotard 1984, 64) This logic works beneath the cheerful veneer of postmodernism. Even within postmodern art, which seems to be beyond the reach of terror, harbors the following secret: "this realism of Anything Goes is the realism of money: in the absence of aesthetic criteria it is still possible and useful to measure the value of works of art by the profits they realize" (Lyotard 1993a, 8). The logic of performativity appears everywhere, backed by the threat of exclusion of those who do not play by its rules. Kirby is correct that the child of this logic, consumerism, is just as pervasive. Yet this does not speak to a "return of metanarratives" because performativity is not a metanarrative per se. It serves as a mode of legitimation, but it lacks the structure of a metanarrative, in particular the reliance on a protagonist seeking some sort of wholeness, or the appeals to some grand concept that motivates the narrative. Also, *officially*, metanarratives did not need to rely on terror. These were supposed to succeed based upon rational argumentation. Terror is necessary to keep a system working, if for no other reason, because terror can be very efficient.

As I will show, religion also avoids the charge that Kirby makes that it somehow runs counter to Lyotard's thought. Some forms of religious life fit well within a postmodernist pluralism, through the adoption of a relatively ecumenical relationship with other forms of life. This clearly is not what Kirby means. Rather, he has in mind fire and brimstone fundamentalism: "I mean religion as killing, silencing, ignorance, and fear" (Kirby 2009, 236). For those steeped in discussions of modernism and postmodernism, the continued significance of religion, and especially fundamentalist religion, can seem perplexing. Modernism at a minimum was supposed to force religion within the bounds of mere reason, if not eradicate it altogether. Postmodernism should have done the same, or opened up the possibility of ludically playing with religion. None of this has come to pass. Although religion might function differently presently than in modernity or premodernity, it remains an important social institution, especially within the United States.

There are several lines of reasoning that illuminate the continuing significance of religion within postmodernity. First, following Anthony Giddens's institutional analysis of late modernity: "New forms of religion and spirituality represent in a most basic sense a return of the repressed, since they directly address issues of the moral meaning of existence which modern institutions so thoroughly tend to dissolve" (Giddens 1991, 206). In his analysis, the institutions of modern society become increasingly disembedded from the particularities of given groups. In this way, they become more abstract and specify less about individuals' possible forms of life. This explains the pluralism often associated with modernist liberalism. The difficulty Giddens identifies is that through this process of abstraction, the moral meaning associated with life becomes utterly vacuous in order to cover competing modes of existence. Religion and spirituality speak to this in a way that modern institutions never will. Given the importance of meaningfulness, moral and otherwise, for many humans, the persistence of religion is to be expected, especially since the possibility of fundamentalism does not disappear within postmodernity, and in fact becomes easier. The same technologies that allow for the hyperspace of postmodernity also allow for the re-entrenchment of places, or at least the hyperreal simulation of them. Throughout the 1980s, alongside the creation of a globalized culture industry, there was a blossoming of the heritage industry (Harvey 1990, 85–88; Lipovetsky 2005, 57–62). As of 1990 "in Britain a museum opens every three weeks, and in Japan over 500 opened up in the last fifteen years" (Harvey 1990, 62). Although far more attention was paid by scholars to more conventional postmodern examples (visual arts, television, literature), David Harvey is correct in linking the heritage industry to postmodernity as well. Postmodern society involves the annihilation of space and time, thus loosening the attachment anything has to any place, yet this looseness creates the possibility of reproducing these very places, but not necessarily within the context that they initially grew up with. Networks allow for the circulation of meanings globally. It then becomes a matter of producing a local network to sustain particular formations of meaning. Given the size of these networks, it is also possible now to increasingly only link up to other parts of the network that one finds some affiliation with (however understood). These realities then can shut out dissenting voices, thereby reinforcing the tenets that define the fundamentalism.

Both the contemporary role of neoliberalism and religious fundamentalism do not then so much undermine Lyotard's account of postmodernity, but instead demonstrate its subtlety. Although each shows that contemporary society is not as pluralistic as sometimes asserted by readers of Lyotard, his writings on postmodernity do provide tools for accounting for phenomena like these. In fact, he anticipates such issues when notes that "Beneath the general demand for relaxation and appeasement, we hear murmurings of the desire to reinstitute terror and fulfill the phantasm of taking possession of reality" (Lyotard 1993a, 16). Albeit in rather different ways, both neoliberalism and religious fundamentalism represent this sort of grasping after reality. Both involve the assumption of procedures for dealing with what is taken as "real." In the case of neoliberalism, it is the move to reduce everything to money. With fundamentalism, it is involves taking something as fundamental, basic and beyond question, and using that to specify reality. For both, terror serves as a tool for attaining and maintaining these realities. That this sort of reaction occurs in response to the postmodern condition is not wholly surprising. The demise of metanarratives challenges basic assumptions about legitimation and emancipation. Given the historical significance of these assumptions in philosophy and beyond, wanting to return to something like the security that provided is to be expected. Yet, given the changes that Lyotard charts, any simple return to modernity's assumed safety is misguided at best. The solutions that he and other postmodern philosophers provide face serious problems, as Hickman and many others rightly argue, but at least they identify the core issues correctly.

## POSTMODERNITY AND THE SYSTEM

If modernity was marked by a reliance on grand stories of emancipation, which were used to legitimate science and other discourses, postmodernity is marked by these no longer possessing the capacity to serve this legitimation function. In the wake of this incredulity, one response is the risk of falling into, if not reveling in, relativism. This is not the only possibility. Others involve other modes of legitimation like a return to tradition or the use of terror to ensure conformity and/or efficiency. Regardless of the response, incredulity toward metanarratives follows from closing off the infinite I discussed in the introduction. Metanarratives appeal to something that goes beyond what is present in order to effectively legitimate. It should be remembered that metanarratives are stories that involve protagonists, struggles, and redemption. It is this redemption that must necessarily reach beyond the present. This redemption is the attainment of the goal that drives the story, like achievement of the full scientific description of the world or the communist utopia. Such a state is not where the story's protagonist is currently. In the shift from unbounded to bounded infinite, the possibility of appealing to something outside of infinite, even if only the sense of something over the horizon, is impossible because there is nothing outside of the infinite; there is no horizon. With this disappearance, metanarratives no longer function properly as a means to legitimate a discourse because the supposed authority that comes from the appeal to something beyond cannot be made effectively. In this way, the bounded infinite provides a simple way of integrating many of the elements that fed into the demise of metanarratives. As noted above, this closing in is conceptual and not literal. It is a way of representing the phenomena feeding into the postmodern condition, like the shift to late or "just-in-time" capitalism, globalization, the politics of difference, the massification of information and communication technologies, and so on. These are all material practices that intersect, amplify each other, and then produce the conceptual shift from an unbounded to a bounded infinite. The closed-in world of postmodernity is then one in which the utility of metanarratives dissipates.

There is a further connection between these two concepts that is important to explore because they help to explain the rise of what Lyotard refers to as "the system." What Lyotard envisions is the emergence of a global "system," in sense of the term inspired by systems theory and cybernetics, in Norbert Wiener's sense (1961) of a self-modifying feedback system that regulates the world though decentralized means. One example of this is capitalism, which "is a system structured as a regulator of growth (to speak in cybernetic terms); in principle it allows the introduction, the circulation, and the elimination of every greater quantities of energy" (Lyotard 1993b, 64). While "the system" is of cosmological importance to him, exemplifying the struggle between entropy and complexification (Lyotard 1997, 93, 98. See chapter 4 for a fuller discussion of this), its role here is to show what happens to emancipation in the bounded infinite. "Emancipation is no longer situated as an alternative to reality, as an ideal to be conquered despite reality and to be imposed from the outside. Rather, it is one of the objectives the system seeks to attain in one or another of the sectors that make it up: work, taxes, marketplace, family, sex, 'race,' school, culture, communication" (Lyotard 1997, 69). Emancipation continues to play a role in postmodernity, but because there is nothing outside of the bounded infinite, emancipation must function quite differently. It can no longer be something external that is aimed toward. Such moves become impossible with the demise of metanarratives. Instead, emancipation is simply a function of the system. "Emancipation becomes tangible. The system's real mode of functioning henceforth entails programs that are not just directed toward optimizing what exists but also *venture programs*, research efforts just 'to see,' which generate more complexity and make room for more 'flexible' institutions" (Lyotard 1997, 70. Emphasis original). Emancipation, then, operates in two ways. The first involves finding ways to improve particular parts of the system. His use of the word "optimize" here is telling because it reinforces the sense in which this is about performativity, rather a more traditional modernist appeal to ethics. As he notes elsewhere: "Postmodern politics are managerial strategies, its wars, police actions" (Lyotard 1997, 200). The concern here is what benefits the overall system in terms of its efficiency, not the objective moral value of a cause. The society is managed for optimum performance, where emancipation is one possible way of achieving this goal. This system is not static, which feeds into the second use of emancipation. The system does not simply take what programs already exist and improve them. It also generates new ones. A clear analogy exists with venture capital. In addition to more standard uses of capital (wages, reinvestment, materials, etc.), some firms will use capital to support more exploratory endeavors that are riskier than more conventional projects, but if they succeed, the return should be far greater. The system pursues the same strategy, exploring new possibilities in the hope of generating new and more effective processes. Based on the results of such venture programs, the system can then incorporate new strategies into itself that provide additional spaces for emancipation to function. This makes some sense of the recent expansion of the concept of rights-talk: "We must constantly reaffirm the rights of minorities, women, children, gays, the South, the Third World, the poor, the rights of citizenship, the right to culture and education, the rights of animals and the environment, and I'll skip over the rest" (Lyotard 1997, 68). These are all places where this new sort of tangible sense of emancipation can be brought to bear in order to improve performance. From before the American Revolution through the Civil Rights Movement, humans rights discourse played a vital role in criticizing societies, whether in the form of government, economics or both, with the aim working to transcend the then-existing social order (Hunt 2007). Now, this discourse is part and parcel of the society itself, incorporated into its functioning. It is not (just) those of the margins of power that advocate for this or that cluster of rights but also those at the center of power as well. A reasonably telling example of this phenomenon is the number of major companies that actively sponsor Gay Pride parades.[1] This speaks to the way in which support for a certain sort of liberation moves from being a check on society to working to allow society to function better. While clearly not the case for all sorts of "rights talk," some can be legitimated by its performative value, irrespective of claims to justice and the like. That is to say, rights are important precisely to the extent that they allow society to function efficiently. Lyotard goes so far as to apply this reasoning to liberal democracy at large (1997, 90). The value of liberal democracy is not its capacity to allow humans to flourish. Rather, it strikes a balance between having a firm operating system and being able to change in response to new situations. Thus, liberal democracy triumphs because of its capacity to increase its complexity in response to crises. In other words, liberal democracy is the most efficient form of government developed thus far.

Lyotard's system shows what happens when the concept of emancipation is translated into the bounded infinite. Emancipation must become a concrete end, rather than some transcendent aim, because this is the only way for it to function if there is no outside. Emancipation must operate wholly within the world. This amounts to a continual shifting of the elements contained within the bounded infinite. No further objects can be added to infinite, but the arrangements of those objects can change, like with the discussion of rock music above. Elements are combined in new and novel ways. Through this process: "The system is continually revised by its integration of winning strategies in the various domains: you could say it constructs itself. Its complexification allows it to control and exploit 'natural' and 'human' energies that were previously dispersed" (Lyotard 1997, 200). Through assessing the effectiveness of its programs, the system can find ways to integrate disparate elements of the bounded infinite, allowing the system to become more complex. It is this increased complexity that allows the system to perpetuate itself in the face of threats like rigidity or entropy while also expanding out its reach.

When intentional language is avoided in describing how the system functions, it provides a useful way for understanding how emancipation operates in postmodernity. The intentional language needs to be stripped away because the system is not aware of itself. It is simply a network of diverse elements. Instead, it functions like a cybernetic feedback system. Understood in this way, the system does explain several curious phenomena. First, even if liberal democracy faces few serious challenges presently, there is still pursuit of emancipation, especially in terms of rights. Individuals are called on to: "sign petitions, write texts, organize conferences, stand on committees, take part in electoral consultations, publish books" (Lyotard 1997, 68). Such activities make little sense in terms of simplistic interpretations of the end of history, but if there is a continual need for society to watch itself against entropy, it accounts for this practice. Second, it does some work at explaining why other elements of system support such liberatory practices. As mentioned above, in the space of fifty years, gay rights went from Stonewall to having corporate sponsorship for the New York City Pride Parade (Bruce 2016; Weiss 2018). Nike uses the "woke" Colin Kaepernick, criticized for kneeling during the National Anthem, in a series of ads. Companies regularly pull adds from television shows associated with racist, homophobic, or sexist comments. From the modernist perspective, such corporate behavior appears strange because these institutions tend to be precisely what individuals should be liberated from. From the perspective of the system, these actions are entirely sensible if they in fact help to maximize the society's efficiency.

Likewise, taking Lyotard's incredulity and the bounded infinite together can account for many features of postmodernity that remain relevant now. The same logic that undermines the utility of metanarratives as tools for rational legitimation explains the prevalence of relativism. If the conceptual universe is closed in on itself, then there is nothing outside of it that serves as way to justify one claim over another, at least without appeals to performativity or, ultimately, terror. So too with other characteristics of postmodern thought like irony, self-referentiality, anti-representationalism, and citationality. All of these are predicated on there being nothing outside of the conceptual universe. As I will return below, this makes sense of why postmodern thought tends to emphasize self-referential languages, rather than anything representational. If the bounded infinite contains all that is and can be, it is rather easy to see how it is possible to reference anything that is part of it, but making a representation that stands outside to be compared to the thing represented becomes impossible. Other important motifs like difference, pluralism, and play are best understood as resulting from the others. If metanarratives fail to legitimate and this leads to a sort of relativism, then, especially in the wake of "tangible emancipation," the prioritization of difference and pluralism follows because those tools that sought to hold everything together in a unity fail as well. Similarly, if metanarratives should no longer be treated authoritatively and no practice can be privileged over any other, merely playing with things follows quite easily. If the structures that provided global sources of meaning fall apart, permanently, finding pleasure in toying with ideas, concepts, and ultimately ourselves is a fairly straightforward way to fill the void.

## TECHNOLOGY, LANGUAGE, AND THE POSTMODERN

I conclude this chapter by drawing how Lyotard intertwines concerns about technology, language, and postmodernity in order to demonstrate how his concepts operate at the same level of material practice discussed in the previous chapter. To see this, return to *The Postmodern Condition* where Lyotard highlighted the centrality of language and information in (then) contemporary science. This serves as a barometer of the serious changes the sciences undergo in the transition from modernity to postmodernity. Talk of codes, bits, bytes, and information becomes increasingly prominent. The implication of Lyotard here is that the turn to what I referred to above "the information paradigm" echoes a particular conception of language at work in post-structuralism. What is decisive in the postmodern conception of language is that language functions as a self-reflexive system, rather than referential. Elizabeth Deeds Ermarth describes it succinctly this view holds that languages are "self-reflexive rather than referential systems—systems of differential function which are powerful but finite, and which construct and maintain meaning and value" (Ermarth 1998). One of the more startling formulations of this comes from Derrida: *"There is nothing outside of the text* [there is no outside-text; *il n'y a pas de hors-texte]"* (Derrida 1998, 158. Emphasis original). Typically, this is interpreted to mean that texts can only refer to other texts, never anything outside of the text (though staying closer to the French problematizes this reading). Understood in this way the operative conception of language echoes the bounded infinite. Language consists of an indefinite, if not infinite, number of objects, endlessly reconfigurable, but meaning is not established by words linking up to objects in the "external world." Instead, words are meaningful through reference to other words. What Lyotard implies is that the emergence of this information-based paradigm in the sciences echoes of this larger trend in thinking about language.

This conception of language comes to prominence alongside the advent of the postmodern technologies discussed earlier. This is not to say that one caused the other, but to suggest that both the technology and this conception of language are part of a wider sociocultural shift (Borgmann 1999; Hayles 1999). Lyotard himself hinted at this, but further evidence can be seen by turning to ICTs. At base, these devices work on a very simple binary code. Other languages can then be translated into and out of this code, allowing for the easy transmission of messages. This at least creates an impression of a bounded conceptual universe. First of all, binary code provides something of a *mathesis universalis*, allowing for all other languages to be captured, processed, and then re-expressed through a more fundamental, albeit artificial, language. As Borgmann (1999, 193–212) points out, through this process of translation, certain sorts of information can be lost. For example, in the move from speech and the written word, the medium that carries the message falls away, replaced by a different medium. While this might create a purer "message," in that the noise of the vocal medium is deleted, such purity need not include everything associated with message initially. The printed word (carried on paper or electronically) lacks the many of the capabilities of the spoken word, in terms of tone of voice, volume, passing, etc. There is a certain clarity the printed word possesses, but this comes at a cost of other modes of expression associated with spoken language. This makes the message more easily transmitted via computer and other sorts of networks, but without the depth associated with the voice. Lyotard suggest that the shift toward this *mathesis* reverberates throughout contemporary knowledge production. Realizing that knowledge now must be transmittable through information networks, knowledge producers now create it with this in mind.

Lyotard finds a curious consequence of such a translation is that it allows for the further commodification of knowledge. Because knowledge is translated into forms that allow for easy transmission, it also becomes easier to treat knowledge as an object to be bought and sold. This then takes us back to the some of the material conditions that increase incredulity toward metanarratives. Scientific knowledge is seen as no longer pure, objective. Rather it is delegitimated precisely to the extent that it is reduced to a commodity. The two generic metanarratives that Lyotard considers in the *Condition* that justify the production of science do not treat it as an end-unto-itself. The first of them legitimates science because of how it furthers the interest of the nation and the other because of its importance for liberation of humanity. Even admitting this, both of these metanarratives treat science as distinctly different from and superior to other human endeavors. This is a far cry from the logic of performativity. These metanarratives of legitimation serve to allow knowledge to flourish (at least officially). Performativity makes science subservient to what that knowledge can do and what it can produce.

As knowledge comes to be legitimated via performativity, it is treated more and more as a mere commodity. This undermines the supposed autonomy and objectivity of science. This chips away at metanarratives, especially so because of the once privileged place of science, the one subject legitimated by metanarratives that seems the least suspect. The shift to what the information-based paradigm and the translation (or expectation of translation) into binary code is thus another part of the waves that wash away at the rational significance of metanarratives.

This is part of the story of how technology helps to create incredulity toward metanarratives, albeit a rather abstract part. A more straightforward connection can be found by looking at the massification of communication networks mentioned in the last chapter. One immediate consequence of this massifaction is that ICTs allow for the formation of a global network (at least a global network of those who live where it is accessible and can afford to be part of it). Because of the vastness of this network and the extent to which the individual charts their own path through it, these ICTs can foster fluidity and open-ended experiences. When surfing online, one can hop from link to link to link, starting in one "place" and ending up looking at something quite different. The capacities for technologies to allow for this sort of engagement loosens, "slackens," the linear ordering at work within metanarratives (I return to the point about linearity in chapter 5). These global networks open spaces for exposure to narratives beyond that of the Euro-American sphere (although they must first be translated as described above). This potentially challenges the hegemony of traditional metanarratives because other options come into view. One response to such exposure to this might be the practical relativism I have associated with common conceptions of postmodernism. After seeing a panoply of worldviews (most of which are both different from one's own and reasonably well developed and supported), one takes something of a "live and let live" attitude to such differences. By making such a move, the importance metanarratives is eroded because such a relativism assumes that there is no need to legitimate one discourse over another. When taken together, these points help to explain the continued diminishment of metanarratives. The accelerated pace at which elements of different cultures circulate, as well as their fluidity at which they can be combined (e.g., the mechanisms through which a culture was held together as something more unified and exclusive becomes looser), makes it increasingly difficult to sustain the claim that there is any single metanarrative to rule all others. The claim of exclusivity is harder to justify, especially when one is forced to reckon with well-developed narratives from outside of one's own sphere. Of course, another possible response to this is instead to re-entrench one's own position. One option of living within the network is to simply remain within a particular cluster of nodes and fortify those, preventing alternative views for intruding. This preserves exclusivity, but at the cost of abandoning the supposed rationality of metanarratives in favor of more traditional or charismatic modes of legitimation, and the possible reliance on terror in order to ensure exclusivity.

The ways in which they serve to bring into contact different discourses makes more challenging holding on to one exclusive metanarrative. The official line, or at least the dream, is that ICTs allow individuals to explore the world without interference. In chapter 4, I will show why Lyotard finds this more complicated, but it appears that one does not need to take the word of travelers or the government to find out about other parts of the world; one can explore via the Internet. Clearly, the actual situation is far more complex, and less "free from interference," than suggested here, but there is enough truth in it to see how this might disrupt to effectiveness of metanarratives. Even if less "pure" than supposed, the exposure to different societies and cultures that ICTs allow for discourages complacency in assuming that one possesses the only means of legitimating discourses. The fluidity and anti-hierarchicality these technologies encourage also play roles here. Metanarratives serve to impose a hierarchy on discourses. It is because of the legitimation provided by a metanarrative that one discourse, say science, is taken to be superior to others. Hierarchy implies at least a minimal degree of linearity: one discourse must be positioned before another. As discussed earlier, ICTs can disrupt linearity by making the imposition of it up to the user. The user can hop from "place" to "place" online, cycle through tabs, and go from song to song at random. Linearity is imposed not by an outside force, but by users themselves. The increased commonality of such experiences chips away at the linearity implied within metanarratives. Alongside other factors mentioned above like the "pessimistic" thinkers of the late nineteenth and early twentieth century, world wars, scientific developments, and technologies help to undermine the authority that metanarratives rely upon. In this way, technology does help foster the demise of metanarratives, which help further demonstrate why Lyotard remains a valuable guide to postmodernity.

## NOTE

1. For example, MasterCard was the "Official Card Sponsor" of the 2019 New York City Pride parade. See https://www.nycpride.org/sponsors/ (accessed July 19, 2019).

*Chapter 3*

# Taking the Attitude of the Other in Communication Networks

The previous chapter made the case for the continued importance of Lyotard's description of the postmodern condition as "incredulity toward metanarratives." This provided a high-altitude view, in contrast to the emphasis in chapter 1 on the material practices associated with the postmodern. This chapter works between these material practices and Lyotard's more schematic presentation of postmodernity through first examining another concept from the Postmodern Condition: the social bond. Lyotard provides a remarkably far-sighted and abstract analysis of this emerging "network society" by describing how society is held together as a network of nodes connected irrespective of distance. This account of the social bond proves to be rather insightful as way to interpret social engagements through ICTs. From here, it is a matter of reconstructing Lyotard's analysis through the writings of George Herbert Mead. By playing Mead and Lyotard off of each other, I will be able incorporate the dynamism of Lyotard's account of the social bond into Mead, thus taking a step toward showing how his thought can play out in what Luciano Floridi refers to as "the Infosphere," which at a minimum is "the whole informational environment constituted by all informational entities . . . , their properties, interactions, processes, and mutual relations" (Floridi 2013, 6). The importance of Mead will be to show how such interactions still contain, albeit indirectly, an irreducible element of embodiment. The introduction of embodiment allows me to avoid the issues surrounding many descriptions of ICT-based sociality that treats this somehow as "weightless," without consequence.

## SOCIAL BONDS, MODERN AND POSTMODERN

Rather than the modernist account of social relations, an account that relies on an organic model of society, Lyotard starts from the assumption that social interaction occurs increasingly through communication networks, specifically computer networks. The expectation of this postmodern social bond is that it better captures the dynamics of contemporary societies. The functionalist account he criticizes is best presented in either Talcott Parsons's functionalism or the critical theory of Max Horkheimer. In Parsons, society is understood in terms of a self-regulating organism, where each individual segment of society (e.g., economics, politics) would be analogous to a particular organ of the human body. This is technocratic vision, where the principle goal is the smooth functioning of the social order (a task suited to sociologists operating within the society). For Horkheimer, the critical theorist assumes a role outside of society in order to criticize the social order. For Lyotard, both of these models of the social bond fundamentally misunderstand the extent to which society has become atomized. Skipping over the question of whether society was ever truly analogous to an organism, Lyotard argues that such a model no longer applies if one wants to adequately understand the present. Two obvious problems with the organic model are the assumptions that (a) the "organs" of society are relatively distinct and static; and (b) individuals are largely defined by their position with respect to particular organs. If one takes seriously the claim that society has become atomized, then neither assumption is warranted. With the first, while some segments of the social network are relatively isolated and/or static, the lines between institutions, organs, have, and continue to, become increasingly fluid. Lyotard's example of the university is instructive here: consider the ways in which higher education is increasingly corporatized (outsourcing, vendors, branding, sponsorship, "students as consumers," etc.). Where industry and corporations stop, and the university starts, seems less clear by the day (Nealon 2012; Resnik 2007).

A different model of the social bond is thus called for. In postmodernity, the social bond becomes atomized. Lyotard is quick to note that this does not fall into the chaotic "Brownian" motion he accuses of Jean Baudrillard. Rather, atomized individuals circulate through networks. "A *self* does not amount to much, but no self is an island; each exists in a fabric of relations that is now more complex and mobile than ever before" (Lyotard 1984, 15. Emphasis original). Individual selves are now constituted as nodes in vast networks. In the context of *The Postmodern Condition*, Lyotard argues that these networks are vast communication systems understood both as webs of language-games and as networks of ICTs. As messages flow through nodes, individuals possess certain degrees of mobility because, given the flexibility of language-games, individuals can shape the messages that pass through them. This means that no individual is entirely powerless, since they can attempt to invent new moves for the language-games they participate in. Such invention is actually necessary to prevent entropy within the system and to maximize its efficiency. So, on the one hand, any particular individual "does not amount to much," but this does not mean that any particular node is irrelevant. In light of the social bond now being interpreted in terms of networks and nodes, Lyotard can account for the fluidity, fragmentation, and eclecticism of postmodern societies. Unlike the modern bond, which emphasized an organic holism where individuals fit cleanly into their proper function, communication networks allow individuals to connect to other aspects of a large network, thus explaining why it is possible that "you listen to reggae; you watch a western; you eat McDonald's food at midday and local cuisine at night; you wear Paris perfume in Tokyo and dress retro in Hong Kong; knowledge is the stuff of TV game shows" (Lyotard 1993a, 8). Stability within these networks is reinterpreted as the atrophying of language-games. The number of moves available to individuals becomes increasingly limited. Lyotard uses this to explain the bureaucratic paralysis that underlies certain parts of the social network.

Given the centrality of a quasi-Wittgensteinian understanding of language-games to the postmodern social bond, it is worth saying a little more on them. Lyotard makes notable three points in his initial methodological discussion of language-games. "The first is that [the language-game's] rules . . . are the object of a contract, explicit or not, between players" (Lyotard 1984, 10). By engaging in the game, the rules play the role of agreement to regulate the relationships between those involved. "The second is that if there are no rules, there is no game" (Lyotard 1984, 10). The procedures that govern the acts compose the game. They are required for there to be a game. Lastly: "every utterance should be thought of as a 'move' in a game" (Lyotard 1984, 10). Since his discussion here is concerned with language-games, particular statements of the individuals involved would be the equivalent of moves in a game like chess. In an atrophied part of a network, the moves in the relevant language-games are restricted. For example, the military puts a premium on the game of commands, while deemphasizing narratives and questions (the former being the province of literature; the latter, philosophy). In more dynamic parts of the network, games play out differently. Players "use any available ammunition, changing games from one utterance to the next: questions, requests, assertions, and narratives are launched pell-mell into battle. The war is not without rules, but the rules allow and encourage the greatest possible flexibility of utterance" (Lyotard 1984, 17). By arguing that the social bond is a vast assemblage of language-games that runs the gamut from the open-ended to the bureaucratized, Lyotard provides a tool for better understanding the fluid character of postmodern societies.

By reinterpreting the bond in terms of language-games, Lyotard does not make interaction dependent on location. As Lyotard presents it, the modern social bond itself appears agnostic about questions of distance. Given its inherent "blockiness" though I am hard-pressed to see how it could capture both the dynamism and operations at a distance in Lyotard's network version of the bond. The games constituting the social bond can be played face to face, over the phone, or through computers. What matters is that the individuals are linked up through a network. As Sellars points out (1991, 341–50), a game like chess depends not on the material pieces, but on the roles that the pieces play. The same game of chess can be played with a traditional set, through the mail using code, or Texas-style (where counties are squares and Cadillacs are pieces). Regardless of the location of players with respect to each other, so long as they can connect to the network, they can play the game. The network here is defined by its capacity to connect individuals. While networks are not a phenomenon produced only through ICTs, such technologies certainly facilitate and accelerate them. Depending on the sort of network, the speed through which interaction occurs and the degree of interactivity can vary. Contemporary ICTs allow for nigh instantaneous communication between nodes, assuming those nodes are located in more privileged parts of the network.

## WEIGHTLESS ELECTRONIC PRESENTATIONS

Given the capacity of individuals to shift from linkage to linkage, game to game, like cycling through tabbed webpages, individuals circulate through a vast network. Since proximity need not matter, but the individual can potentially join any number of different games, the perceived fluidity and mobility of postmodern society can be accounted for. Returning to the example of music consumption from chapter 2, the listener can be freed from the intentions of the "artist" in favor of creating an experience all their own. If they want to listen to album all the way through, they can. But if they want to let Spotify or another streaming service determine their playlist based on their interests (which is, in turn, being determined by algorithms), or create their own playlists by themselves, entirely either through a streaming service or from their own collection, these are also possibilities. This sort of fluid freedom is at once theorized in postmodernism, and valorized and extended out to other areas like personal identity. For the strand of postmodern thought that privileged semiotics, this fluidity was assumed to be limitless. Anything or anyone could be morphed into anything else. Clearly, this is an overstatement, but exposes a common tendency to think about the usage if ICTs as "weightless." By "weightless," I intend to the capture the sense that social interactions carried on via ICTs are, in a sense, unreal because they occur over a distance and without many of the usual characteristics of embodied communication, like bodily gestures and/or voice. Given this supposed unreality, these interactions are of a lower order than traditional communication. This can be found in the popular tendency to draw sharp contrasts between what happens online and what happens in "real life." The online world should be regarded as parasitic on the "real," and when taken on par with the "real," this is a sign of pathology. Academics are not immune from this. Both Albert Borgmann and Hubert Dreyfus wrote broadsides against the increased role of computers. We saw elements of this in chapter 1 with Borgmann's writings on hyperrealism. He develops his argument for this more fully in *Holding on to Reality*, arguing that contemporary ICTs only exacerbate the world obscuring capacities of technology. For Dreyfus (1999), the use of computers in education can only play a very limited role because they allow only the most facile of engagement with a subject.

At work, most clearly in the weightless vision of ICTs is a conception of society that can be described as "an interrelational complex of the subjective mental presentations which the society's members have of one another" (Joas 1997, 111–12). Borgmann and Dreyfus would reject the accusation that they reduce *all* of society to "mental presentations." And no doubt this is correct because they want individuals to turn away from their screens and toward embodied human beings. Yet, because of their privileging of traditional engagement over ICT-based social interactions, it is an accurate statement of their positions when it comes to the latter. Although their reasoning comes from somewhat different angles, Borgmann's neo-Heideggerianism as opposed to Dreyfus's reliance on Kierkegaard in this article, the conclusion is much the same: computer interactions are a pale copy of embodied communication. The first clue that Borgmann sees ICTs as of a lower order is his constant use of the contrast in *Holding on to Reality* of "reality," the everyday world of bodies, trees, and squirrels, and "virtuality," which is represented by ICTs. For Borgmann though, the trouble with virtuality goes deeper in that "the ambiguity of cyberspace dissolves the contours of facts, of persons, and of places" (Borgmann 1999, 192). There is a fluidity and lightness to cyberspace that does allow for the exploration of possibilities, a point Dreyfus agrees with. The problem is that the fluidity means that "any choice I make does not get a grip on me so it can always be revoked. It must be constantly reconfirmed by a new choice to take the previous one seriously" (Dreyfus 1999, 18). There is a fundamental thinness to ICT-based sociality that is compounded by the fact that, unlike the constraints of traditional communication, far more facets of an individual's presentation are under their control. As the old *New Yorker* cartoon says: "On the Internet, nobody knows you're a dog." Rather than engaging with "real" humans, interaction is mediated through devices. Instead of embodied interactions involving a more robust phenomenology, individuals present themselves to each other through the use of these devices. Each individual only engages with other members of the online society through *electronic* presentations of others. Given this qualification, it is fair to say that both Borgmann and Dreyfus assume that society is, rephrasing Joas, "an interrelational complex of subjective electronic presentations." The perceived subjectivity enters here, given the fluidity of the medium. Computer-based communication allows individuals more possibilities for presenting a selective façade of themselves, and also more selectivity about with whom they engage. Given the typical set of assumptions about how ICTs are used, there is a clear appeal of this subjective conception of society. It preserves the divide between the material world and what Borgmann calls cyberspace, thus making sense of why the social bond there appears comparatively thin, weightless. All one is engaging with are electronic presentations, so all society can consist of is electronic presentations.

## IN THE EYES OF MY FRIENDS

This is not to imply that all philosophers who write on this ICTs share this assumption of weightless and the related subjective conception of society; far from it, actually. A number of philosophers and other scholars present ICT-based social interactions in much more substantial ways. There is a well-developed literature exploring the various facets of how ICT use extends out to more conventional interactions. Examples range from friendship (Kaliarnta 2016) to mourning (Brubaker, Hayes, and Dourish 2013) to virtual sexual assault (Craft 2007). As a rule, this body of literature does not hold that social engagement on Social Networking Sites (SNSs) or gaming is exactly the same as conventional sociality, but neither does it not fall into the trap of simply dismissing it. Instead, much of this work explores the similarities and differences in interaction such that ICTs allow for something of an extension into other parts of human activity. This can be seen in some of the recent work on the phenomenon of online friendships. This is a potent example because of the centrality friendship plays within philosophical conceptions of the good life, going back to Aristotle. If friendship can flourish online, then this goes a great distance toward showing how the social world of ICTs requires more serious consideration than weightlessness understanding gives it credit for.

A number of studies of online friendship find that SNSs are particularly effective in maintaining friendships (Kaliarnta 2016). An SNS like Facebook serves as a way to support preexisting friendships at a distance. Facebook becomes a platform for individuals who already know each other to contact and share items among themselves. On the one hand, this use of SNSs to maintain friendships is important, if for no other reason that this is one of the most frequent voluntary uses of ICTs (as opposed to more "involuntary" uses like checking one's work email). Checking on SNSs is something that many, if not most, ICT users do in the United States. On the other, this example does not totally undermine the claims of someone like Borgmann, precisely because this sort of maintenance begins with traditional embodied friendships and merely shifts it onto an SNS. What allows one to push back on Borgmann's point is how SNSs allow friendships to develop. Consider a problem that D. E. Wittkower worries over: posting photos of one's food. He explains this phenomenon in the following way:

> This will be ever a mystery to us as long as we believe that the point of the communication is the information it contains. The point is to invite friends to lunch. The sharer can then eat alongside his absent friends, who he knows to be experiencing the appearance of his sandwich, as if sitting across the table. The friends, for their part, have been granted this window into the life of their friend, which they may either ignore entirely, or choose to reflect upon and, in so doing, revitalize their connection. (Wittkower 2012, 25–26)

Assuming one reflects on the friend's photo, the point of the activity is reintensification of the friendship. The activity plays on the embodied phenomenon of breaking bread together, but shifted on to a networked device. It allows for something like being with the friend, even when absent. It is precisely because such moments have the capacity to bring people closer together, albeit in a "kind of asynchronous, opt-in broadcast, mediated" way (Wittkower 2012, 26), that we can see why Borgmann oversimplifies SNS-based relationships. Borgmann treats these activities as a mere supplement to more traditional human relationships. In doing so, he fails to appreciate that such engagements have the potential for growth: "Where the connections forged are superficial, they allow avenues for growth and intensification. Where the messages and posts are terse and simple, they allow for conversations and shared experiences to emerge. Where the group associations and activities are thin and basic, they allow opportunities to raise awareness and recruit others to causes that may become passionate commitments" (Wittkower 2012, 25). Seen from this perspective, this sort of use of SNSs appears to be another way of being friends, rather than something purely derivative.

The more difficult question about SNS-based friends involves those that remain wholly online. Here there is less consensus than with the situation of maintaining pre-existing friendships. Shannon Vallor (2012) argues that a site like Facebook does not fully allow for the robustness of friendships, understood in an Aristotelian virtue theoretic sense. The difficulty is that Facebook cannot allow for the depth of interaction between individuals that embodied face-to-face interactions allow for. For example, empathy is possible through SNSs, as when a friend posts about "a hangover, a bad day at work, a promotion, a serious illness, the achievement of a personal goal, the birth or the death of a loved one. Such revelations are typically followed by a flood of posts from friends offering expressions of sorrow, joy, regret, congratulations, encouragement, or offers of help and consolation" (Vallor 2012, 192). In many cases, the posts that follow such disclosures are genuinely empathetic. "Yet the role of embodiment in empathy must be considered as well. Joy and pain are not purely cognitive states; they are conditions that affect our breathing, our musculature, our digestive functions, our skin temperature, and so on" (Vallor 2012, 193). This poses a clear difficulty since expressions of empathy at a distance cannot fully convey this sort of physicality. Vallor goes on to argue that similar results are found with the other dimensions of the Aristotelian account of friendship (reciprocity, self-knowledge, and the shared life). SNSs capture something of each, but not their full complexity. Some of this is simply the limits of the technology, that humans are embodied creatures, and interactions via ICTs do not capture all of this embodiment. She also raises another, more worrisome, reason. In the context of considering shared lives, she finds that "the problem is merely a technological reification of a tendency already pervasive in our culture, a culture in which discussions of one's religion, politics, scientific beliefs or moral commitments are increasingly marginalized from public spaces—pushed out of our workplace, our dinner table, our holiday parties and our weekend picnics, lest serious questions or contentious issues mar our congenial, lighthearted exchanges" (Vallor 2012, 197). More sophisticated deliberations about the lives friends share together is absent from Facebook because it is absent from much of the rest of our lives. This problem is endemic to life in the early twenty-first century. Which is to say: life in postmodernity.

Wittkower and Vallor show, to different extents, how ICTs can at least maintain friendships. For Wittkower, as well as Sofia Kaliarnta and Nicholas Munn (2012), the argument is stronger, in that they suggest to various degrees the ICTs can actually foster friendships. Regardless of exactly the depth of friendship that SNSs can support, what I have shown here provides reason to be suspicious of the "weightless" account of such interactions. As Wittkower's analysis illuminates, even small gestures on Facebook like the posting of one's lunch or playing a game opens a space for renewing friendships. When such renewal occurs through an SNS, or individuals engage in shared activities like World of Warcraft (Munn 2012), it illustrates how the world ICTs provide is not merely, or at least not always, facile. Instead, it can serve as an extension of the everyday world of bodies in which social interactions traditionally took place. These two different spaces allow for different sorts of interactions, but this does not entail that one is inherently inferior to other. This sort of assessment necessarily involves questions about the ends and means, and what is feasible in a particular medium. Some sorts of interactions are made more difficult via an SNS, while others easier (Turkle 2011). If these are to be seen as actual interactions between individuals, they should not be considered weightless because they would not be able to affect the individuals, expect in pathological cases. Yet, much of the literature on SNSs tend to show that that there is something more substantive about these sorts of interactions.

Given the centrality of networks and ICTs in Lyotard's work, one might expect him to embrace something like the weightlessness understanding of social interaction. While something like this appears in his proposal of "paralogy," the production of new language-games for their own sake, Lyotard cannot fully embrace the weightless account of ICT-based social interaction because of the important role that agonism plays in his thought. Earlier I mentioned that in less atrophied parts of the network, participants in language-games would shift from one type of statement to another in order to confound their opponent, to "win" the game. For such agonistic interactions to be possible, contact, resistance, of one sort between participants must occur. If social engagements through SNSs were truly as weightless as Borgmann and Dreyfus imply, then agonistic engagement could not occur between individuals. Instead, it would only be the individual wrestling with themselves because no real connection could be forged with others. For this reason, Lyotard cannot rely on the subjective conception that society is nothing more than electronic presentations of others. The difficulty is that Lyotard never goes far enough in explaining how social engagement works, especially when networked. The logic of agonism, and also terror, appears obvious enough in face-to-face social interaction, but it is not immediately obvious how this applies to interaction at a distance. This difficulty is compounded by the perniciousness of "weightlessness," where one reads into Lyotard the common assumption that there is some sort of fluid unreality to these interactions. That Lyotard emphasizes fluidity further feeds into this reading, yet if one takes this weightlessness as seriously as Dreyfus or Borgmann does, then a major component of Lyotard's philosophy becomes deeply incoherent because there is not enough actual engagement for agonistic interactions to occur.

## A NETWORK AS AN OBJECTIVE ACTION-NEXUS

To avoid the difficulties that follow from the subjective conception of society, it is necessary to replace this with a conception that makes the active engagement between individuals decisive. This is precisely the concept of society that George Herbert Mead developed. As Hans Joas explains, "Mead regards society as an objective action-nexus" (Joas 1997, 111). Mead argues against the conception of society as a vast interconnected web of "mental presentations" in favor of a conception where social selves engage with one another. The actions of the Meadian individuals are "intrinsically social and takes into account the actions of the members of society" (Joas 1997, 111). It is not just that society involves individuals who act, but that society constitutes these actions. Society is the space in which multiple individuals coordinate their actions. Given that the self is only a self in virtue of its relationship to others, the actions individuals make with others will always be social. This is a far cry from a "mental presentation" account of society in which society is only comprised of a web of subjective representations. Instead, both society and its members are constituted through action.

Given many of the examples that Mead introduces in his writing, the context of the nexus is that of embodied organisms in relatively close proximity: dogs fighting, playing games and sports, and the act of buying and selling. Since Mead explains the development of the social self in naturalistic terms, and most social relations for many organisms occur in close proximity, the reliance on these sorts of examples is fitting. However, they should not undermine the further expansion of the concept of an action nexus to include other sorts of interactions. While I will return to this more fully later, of crucial importance to Mead's account of the social self is the ability to manipulate significant symbols. These symbols go beyond the gestures that other organisms use, in part because of their universality. They are not necessarily dependent on a particular context to be intelligible. Human use of significant symbols, especially with the development of writing, allows for social interaction at a distance. Mead himself makes passing reference to this with the importance of fiction in helping to educate individuals about the experience of others. Furthermore, following the argument of Filipe Carreira da Silva (2008), Mead's approach to democratic practice takes the seventeenth and eighteenth century "republic of letters" as a model. Da Silva is careful to note that Mead "refers to the concrete experience of the literate elites of the seventeenth-century Europe . . . [and] a normative ideal that transcends the boundaries of historical experience and is able to inspire the conduct of latter generations" (Da Silva 2008, 205). The concept of the "republic of letters" was more than a metaphor on one front: It was carried on through printed book and an extensive postal system (Goodman 1994, 16–20). The important point here is that such a "republic" occurred not just in the salons of the elite, but throughout Europe as a whole through the ability to communicate via letters. Although the sort of social interaction that occurs through letter-writing is noticeably different than face-to-face communication or playing games, they all fall within this broad heading for Mead. All of this is simply to make plausible the idea that SNSs and other forms of ICT-based communication can constitute an objective action-nexus. It remains to actually demonstrate this.

The first step in this argument is to explore what Mead's action-nexus involves at a general level. Here we find three things of importance for my purposes: social acts, social objects, and social control. Mead distinguishes social acts from others as follows: "A social act may be defined as one in which the occasion or stimulus which sets free an impulse is found in the character or conduct of a living form that belongs to the proper environment of the living form whose impulse it is" (Mead 1964, 279). When an organism, human or nonhuman, acts in a distinctly social manner, it involves the organism engaging with its environment. "Social acts" are thus always contextual. Mead goes on to qualify this definition by adding that "I wish, however, to restrict the social act to the class of acts which involve the cooperation of more than one individual, and whose object as defined by the act . . . is a social object" (Mead 1964, 279–80). For an act to be genuinely social, it is required not just to be performed within a context proper to the organism. It also requires that the act engage with other organisms through a "social object."

That coordination with other individuals appears in the definition of a social act and appears to follow from the usual usage of the phrase. The concept of "social object" requires a little more explanation. A social object is "one that answers to all the parts of the complex act, though these parts are found in the conduct of different individuals. The objective of the act is then found in the life-process of the group, not in those of the separate individuals alone" (Mead 1964, 279–80). Social objects exist at the intersection of different individual's actions. These acts constitute the object as social, because the different individuals respond to both the object and to each other through the object. Because of this, when an act involves a social object, this object must exist as part of the community. Individuals might act toward objects that exist independent of society. For example, a cow eating grass does not meet the criteria for a social object. Yet, when individuals engage with one another via objects, these are social objects. In "The Genesis of the Self and Social Control," Mead repeatedly uses the example of property to illustrate this. In some contexts, a book is merely a physical object. In others, it becomes a social object. If I go to a store to buy a book, I perform a social action with the seller by way of the book. The book-as-property is transferred from being the seller's to being mine. Our actions in this context respond to the book as being a certain kind of social object. What allows this sort of interaction to proceed is that each individual involved anticipates the acts of the others, what Mead refers to as "taking the attitude of the other." Although I am buying, not selling, the book, I anticipate the behavior of the seller. In being the buyer, it is necessary for me to internalize the actions involved with being a seller. This allows me to then act as a buyer because I can effectively respond to the seller, and the seller does the same with my attitudes inasmuch as I am a buyer. This attitude-taking is central to Mead's account of the social self. He goes so far as to say: "We appear as selves in our conduct insofar as we ourselves take the attitude that others take towards us, in these correlative activities" (Mead 1964, 284). When an individual acts in a social setting, both the individual and the other appear as objects in the individual's conduct.

The social objects and acts of ICT devices first appear to their users through physical objects, like a computer or a smartphone. Through the physical relationship, the user has with their device, they coordinate their acts with the social objects that populate SNSs. Engaging with ICT-based social objects raises the issue of distance, which Mead largely deals with only implicitly. With Mead, examples like playing games and sports or the exchange of property occur within relatively close proximity. The individuals involved can interact with each other directly. With Facebook, the role of distance changes. One can read posts, and follow links, of friends from across the world. Given the relative instantaneity of ICT communication, following Manuel Castells (2010a) there is an effective elimination of space and de-sequencing of time. The social acts of the users are not constrained by space in the way that Mead's examples are. Users might be engaged with the same social object but be separated by continents, or sitting on the same couch.

The previous discussion of friendship helps to illustrate these concepts and how they might occur through SNSs. The posting of a photo of a friend's meal is clearly a social object in Mead's terms. It is an object around which individuals orient their activities. The friends viewing it respond to it and, through this, to the one who posted it. The comments that might be posted about the photo add to the sociality of the object because the friends use the photo as a way to reinforce their relationship with the others in that community. Unlike sharing a meal together, this can happen asynchronously and at a distance. This entails a more careful application of Mead's concepts. In many examples, Mead's model is principally that of conversation and other engagements occurring within close proximity. Mead's analysis of communication begins first with the "conversation of gestures," and then moves to face-to-face speech via "significant symbols." It should be noted that printed written word arguably works quite differently from the spoken word, a point made forcefully by Jacques Derrida (1998) and Walter Ong (1982), though their reasoning is quite different. Furthermore, electronic communication is a different beast from either the spoken or written word, though it does bear some similarities to both. Depending on the platform used, when the word is disseminated electronically, it can take on elements of either the spoken or written word, or possibly both. Telephone calls or FaceTime simulate aspects of the spoken word. Articles posted on websites, the written word. Yet, be it an article on a news site or a post from a friend or "friend" on Facebook, there is a possibility of publicly engaging the writing through features like "commenting" or "liking." E-mailing, texting, messaging, or Facebook conversations lies somewhere in between these. There is the "deadness" of writing, including the lack of easy ways to replicate tone of voice, but there can be degrees of responsiveness that make them similar to spoken conversations.

How can Mead address these differences? The salient difference is how each of these types of communication are social acts and the social objects they involve. Communicating via FaceTime or other video conferencing programs involves social acts quite similar to more traditional forms of communication (i.e., speaking face to face). Others, like commenting on Facebook or e-mail involve more textual forms of social action. The social object involved is also textual. This would imply that communication has moved entirely from the realm of gestures to that of significant symbols and language. For Mead, significant symbols are those that "undergo further development through a process of generalization in which the individuals employ them take the attitudes not merely of specific others but of a 'generalized other' in responding to their own gestures. In this way significant symbols come to take their place in a 'universe of discourse,' a system of shared social meanings constituted by a community of individuals engaged in a common social process" (Cook 1993, 93–94). When we move to this terrain, we begin to see why some aspects of the concern about distance lose some force. The languages of the SNSs operate in this "universe of discourse," where meanings are stable because individuals coordinate with the "generalized other" rather than other particular specific individuals. What becomes important here is the degree to which ICT-based social acts become largely linguistic. Mead's writings emphasize the role of embodied social engagement, mainly working examples of face-to-face interaction, whether dogs barking at each other or a buyer purchasing a book from a seller. When carried on through ICTs, embodiment becomes less prominent, though not eliminated. It is still an embodied individual who uses their fingers to compose on a keyboard or touchscreen. There is also a genetic link, inasmuch as language and other symbols began as an extension of embodied communication. When using an SNS, communication itself is one of the principal social acts that individuals perform. Other acts will follow from communication, but the very act of communicating plays a decisive social role.

Embodiment becomes less prominent in the universe of discourse associated with computers and other ICTs. Some sort of embodied action is still required for a human to post anything on an SNS, whether it is typing or a voice command, but the symbols that appear on Facebook do not reflect such embodiment, except in the case of typos and other mistakes. At least compared to speech, this amounts to a flattening out of the universe of discourse because certain sorts of information cannot be contained within the symbol. The typed text of a Facebook post lacks the intonation, volume, and passing of speech, except when the author attempt to reflect these using various typographic techniques like changing font and background color, capitalization, spacing, punctuation, and so forth. Another mode of communication is through memes, typically comprised of text, most frequently in the font "Impact," and a picture (though the use of animated GIFs has also become increasingly popular). Memes of this sort convey meaning in ways that go beyond the "simple" use of words, through the interplay of text and image. Additionally, the text, image, or both can have a cultural salience which goes beyond what is simply said and shown, to involve a wider universe of shared meanings. So, in one sense the dimensions of these symbols might be flattened, but they clearly have expressive power that goes beyond the standard forms of speech that Mead dealt with.

This discussion illuminates how Mead establishes continuity between ICT-based engagements and other, more flesh-and-blood, forms of sociality. His analysis of "social control" continues this line of discussion and puts us in a better position to under the apparent "weightlessness" of SNS-driven sociality. Mead defines social control in the following way: "I take it that social control is bringing the act of the individual into relation with this social object. With the control of the object over the act, we are abundantly familiar. Just because the object is the form of the act, in this character it controls the expression of the act" (Mead 1964, 289). Social control operates by linking the individual's actions to a particular social object. Specific sorts of social objects will establish and channel what sorts of actions individuals can do. In principle, an individual could perform any act in response to another. That this does not typically occur is explained by the extent to which an individual allows themselves to be controlled. What allows this to play out is that "Social control . . . depend[s] upon the degree to which the individual does assume the attitudes of those in the group who are involved with him in his social activities" (Mead 1964, 290). If individuals are to effectively coordinate their acts with others, then it is necessary for them to take the attitude of the others they engage with. In this way social acts, social objects, and social control are tightly interlinked. Objects make acts possible, while social objects only exist as social in lieu of social acts. Social objects control individuals because those individuals anticipate the attitudes of other individuals. Social objects set up parameters for actions. These parameters amount to the ways that social objects direct social acts, hence, they are "social control." How objects exert control depends on the sort of object, the different ways in which individuals control their actions when exchanging property, as opposed to a court hearing.

It is when we turn to social control that we see clearly the differences between ICTs and other sorts of social objects and their related acts. The mechanisms of social control play out quite differently on the Web. The standard sorts of pressures that direct individuals to take the attitude of the other in social acts are absent. Depending on the ICT under consideration, individuals do not act with particular others per se, but rather what Mead refers to as "the generalized other." He explains the significance of the generalized other with reference to playing baseball as "their organized reactions to him has embedded in his playing of the different position, and this organized reaction becomes what I have called the 'generalized other' that accompanies and controls his conduct" (Mead 1964, 285). Here, the generalized other is simply all the other baseball players. As mentioned earlier, the generalized other can become further abstracted. Because social acts via ICTs do not need to be coordinated with specific individuals, the user can instead coordinate with respect to the generalized other. In making a Facebook post, an individual might be directed at a particular other, or others. It also could be posted with no particular other in mind. This move from a particular other to a generalized other helps account for the seeming weightlessness of ICTs. What makes ICTs distinctive from other social objects is the degree to which the individual determines control. While an individual might always have some capacity to resist control exerted by other social objects, these objects (like a court hearing) tend to have mechanisms that discourage this. These mechanisms do not uniformly appear within SNSs. In this way, we might say there is a lack of social control when it comes to ICT social acts. Because the more typical means of regulating action such that acts are effectively coordinated are missing, this allows for a wider range of social acts. Rather than being expected to take the attitude of the other, particular users determine whether they will or not. This move helps to better locate the perceived weightlessness of ICT-based social engagements. Rather than lacking in reality, sociality on SNSs is accounted for by Mead's basic concepts. What seems like lightness is explained by the lack of more traditional means of social control. Yet, Mead's concept of social control also points to ways to potentially weigh down ICT-based relations. Social control involves individuals taking the attitudes of others seriously and acting appropriately with respect to a social object. In this way, even if peculiarities of ICTs as objects make online social acts appear weightless, individuals can still control their acts to add weight to them.

## NETWORKED SOCIAL SELVES

With this analysis of how social interaction can occur through communication networks, I can now reinterpret Lyotard's postmodern social bond. There are several points of tension between Mead and Lyotard where one productively corrects the other. Where Mead will be most critical of Lyotard is the portrayal of the postmodern social bond as involved (communication) networks-connected nodes, consisting of *atomized individuals*. There is a temptation to read "atomized individuals" in one of two ways: (a) as atomic individuals (a la classic liberalism); or (b) as merely point particles defined by their position in a network. Neither of these are particularly appealing interpretations in light of Mead (though the latter is probably closer to Lyotard's intention). The former assumes the individual is only extrinsically social, and that society is no more than a collection of individuals. As seen throughout this discussion, Mead holds that the self is intrinsically social. The latter is equally problematic because it assumes that there is nothing more to the self than its position in a network. In Mead's philosophy, social individuals are the actors within an objective action-nexus (i.e., society). Individuals are not merely defined by their social relations, but are also capable of actively reshaping social relations. This requires a new interpretation of Lyotard's statement that "a self does not amount to much anymore." Instead of seeing the self as vanishingly insignificant, the emphasis must now be on the self not being as omnipotent or isolated as usually assumed. Mead's philosophy prevents the individual from being reduced to a point particle because the actions of individuals constitute society. The significance of this should not be overlooked because it introduces an element of "friction" into networks and decreasing the degree of weightlessness. While the Meadian self is a product of social relations, it does not merely lay at intersections (nodes) of different lines, being defined by these lines. The Meadian self is also creative. The self is a product of social interaction, but these interactions also shape other selves. This is why Joas describes society as an "objective action-nexus." The actions of a self transform those other selves with whom they engage. In this way, the self is not omnipotent, in that any self encounters potential resistance from other agents, but is not simply defined by the other selves that it relates to.

Lyotard can also be used to reinterpret Mead's account of the social, and also broaden it out. Mead's statements on what Lyotard refers to as the social bond lent themselves to being interpreted as assuming the organic-functionalist model. Take, for example, the following from his 1929 article "National-mindedness and International-mindedness": "But society is the interaction of these selves, and an interaction that is only possible if out of their diversity unity arises. We are indefinitely different from each other, but our difference make interaction possible. Society is unity in diversity" (Mead 1964, 359). On the one hand, Mead here does emphasize difference at the level of selves, and not simply "organs" (i.e., small groups of individuals). This definitely has a certain affinity with Lyotard and much postmodern thought. On the other, Mead's introduction of "unity" here is potentially troubling, in light of the postmodern social bond. Phrases like "unity in diversity" can be interpreted in a Hegelian manner, a move we have seen Lyotard criticizes relentlessly. Lyotard's critique of this sort of "unity" is that it does violence to incommensurable differences. Up to a certain point, Mead is aware of this violence. He notes later in "National-mindedness":

> However there is always present the danger of its miscarriage. There are two possible sources of its unity—the unity arising from interconnection of all the different selves in their self-conscious diversity and that arising from the identity of common impulses; the unity, for example of the members of a great highly organized industrial concern or of the faculties and the students of a great university and the unity of the crowd that rushes to save a child in danger for its life. (Mead 1964, 359)

Mead holds that the former is preferable, especially when it comes to nationalism, because it allows for "unity through difference," while the latter *reduces difference to* unity (though his particular example above is, in all likelihood, quite laudable). The latter for Lyotard is a clear example of violence, in which differences are forcibly reconciled. The former remains troubling for Lyotard, in particular Mead's examples of industry or universities, because with "terror" order will lie beneath the surface, where "terror" is understood as the threat of violence or repression in order to coerce agreement (e.g., play by the established rules of a language-game).

There is one last tension here between Lyotard and Mead worth noting. Joas correctly points out that Mead considers much more than conscious communicative exchanges, which is much of what I emphasized in my presentation of Lyotard. Three comments on this are as follows: (a) while Mead does expand the realm of the social beyond communication and direct, conscious action, these do play a role within the social for him; (b) Lyotard leaves it an open question in *The Postmodern Condition* as to whether all social relations are fundamentally language-games; (c) the value of Lyotard is that the postmodern social bond allows for a relatively seamless transition from embodied social to networked interactions. While social interactions that occur through ICT networks follow different patterns from other sorts of social interactions, Lyotard provides a framework for thinking of the social that smoothens out some of this. The upshot of these points is that, on the one hand, we should not read Lyotard in too reductive a manner and, on the other, we should avoid assuming that the networked communication under consideration here fully describes all social interaction.

With these points in hand, I can now turn to demonstrating how Mead's social individuals act through Lyotard's networks. The wisdom of Lyotard's move to explain the social bond in terms of language-games becomes clear when considering social interactions that occur through communication networks. These communications are largely built around the transmission of verbal or written language, yet the distance between senders and receivers of messages is basically irrelevant. This framework then allows one to account for the trans*actional* character of communication, while also downplaying the role of spatiality. The danger here is that one then slides into the "subjectivist" account of society discussed above. Interpreting the players of networked language-games in light of Mead prevents this. For Mead, verbal communication is an achievement that grows out of embodied social interactions (Mead treats the written word as largely the same as the spoken). Communication begins with a "conversation of gestures" in which individuals coordinate actions through movements and sounds. Conversations of this sort can be found in many animal species, like with dogs growling at each other. Human language develops this further, through significant symbols becoming increasingly abstract. In this way language relies on what was referred to above as a "generalized other." Once symbols involve not particular, but generalized, others, humans have the means to play networked language-games. The players then share these symbols in common so that they can engage in the complicated games that Lyotard concerns himself with. Yet, because through the process of generalization, the particularities of the embodied social individuals become less prominent while also incorporating "curled up" dimensions which permit different sorts of expressiveness, allowing for their transmission through communication networks.

For this reason, symbolically mediated communication, even at a distance, operates as an extension of embodied communication. While Lyotard's own account of the language-games that create the postmodern social bond obscures the significance of embodiment, Mead's analysis of games helps to demonstrate both embodiment and certain limits of Lyotard. Both hold that rules, procedures that govern the acts that compose a game, are necessary for there to be a game. As Mead notes: "For in a game there is a regulated procedure, and rules" (Mead 1964, 285). Where Mead goes beyond Lyotard is that to play a game requires more than just an understanding of the formal rules involved. It also requires that a player can take the role of the "generalized other," where: "The individual actor must orient himself to a goal that is valid for all the actors concerned . . ." (Joas 1997, 119) It becomes clear that in order to play a game, one needs to have what Mead describes as self-consciousness, because individuals playing games not only need to be able to take on the role of particular others but also must locate themselves with respect to the generalized other that embodies the rules, norms, and values of the group. "The orientation to a particular generalized other reproduces, certainly, on a new plane the same restriction as does the orientation to a particular concrete other" (Joas 1997, 119). Joas thus establishes continuity between particular others and a generalized other, and where discontinuity arises in networked communication. When a Meadian individual engages with others, they do so by taking the attitude of the other. By one individual taking on the perspective of the other, that individual can act successful with the other. In this way, the individual incorporates the rules of a "game" and the community's norms into their behavior. The same occurs when coordinating actions with the generalized other, which explains in part why linguistic symbols function in a "universe of discourse," which involves shared rules and norms governing the use of such symbols (Madzia 2013).

What allows language-games to play out differently in communications networks is the physical distance between individuals. Because individuals need not occupy the same space to interact, the enforcement of rules and norms (social control) becomes looser. Especially when networked interactions occur through language alone, an individual has less information available to help them determine how to take the attitude of the other. As Mead makes plain, interaction is inherently embodied. When communicating via networks, the richness of embodiment becomes abstracted down to the exchange of symbols. The standard repertoires of habits individuals rely upon for interaction become less useful, requiring the development of new habits that reflect the distinctive textures of postmodern technologies (Raines and Wellman 2012, 104–5, 125). In light of the diminished role of social control, individuals can have more freedom in determining whether they follow the rules and norms of a given interaction. In some circumstances, what Lyotard referred to as "terror" can help to restrain this freedom. In other circumstances, the play that Lyotard describes comes to the fore. Individuals can switch between the rules of different games with little fear of repercussion, with the exception of the communication ending. Furthermore, because individuals can participate in different networks, language-games, simultaneously, or at least switch between them quite rapidly, this creates the possibility of these different language-games becoming much more fluid. There is a general slackening of the rules governing certain networks, which accounts for the freedom individuals perceive while operating on SNSs. Because of the distinctive features of ICT-based sociality, it frequently is up to individual users as the degree to which social control functions (at least compared to face-to-face interactions).

There are two lessons at this stage. The first is the continuing importance of Lyotard's postmodern social bond. Although presented at a rather general level, it captures the fluid dynamism of contemporary society. Individuals operate through networks, sometimes at great distances. More commonly, this distance is rendered irrelevant because of the use of ICTs that allow for nigh instantaneous communication. Other times, different technologies like planes are used in order to physically move from place to place. As Lyotard notes, there are places where atrophy sets into part of the network, where mobility, especially in terms of switching language-games, becomes difficult. This accounts for the rigidity appearing in certain parts of the network, like with the military and government bureaucracies. There, social control, in the more usual sense, remains enforced. In this way, Lyotard describes both what is most eye-catching about society, fluid networks, while also explaining why some segments of society appear to operate along the lines of the older functionalist model. The second is that Mead's thought is able to interface with Lyotard's analysis, providing a way to reinterpret Lyotard in pragmatic terms. Mead's analysis of selfhood, including communication, begins with embodied individuals. This is something that has been frequently obscured within explorations of ICT-based social interactions. It is easy to slip into a Dreyfus- or Borgmann-like position and find the lack of embodiment to reduce such interactions to being mere copies of the "real" thing. Mead avoids this by building out from gestures toward significant symbols and other more disembodied sorts of communication. As one moves to communication via computers and other ICTs, certain aspects of embodied communication fall away, like tone of voice, but new dimensions come to the fore. This captures the distinctiveness of new modes of communication, but without treating it as wholly divergent or a lesser order of being. This is *not* to imply that ICTs do not have profound impacts on how humans live. Clearly they do, and I shall turn to the implications of this in the remaining chapters.

*Chapter 4*

# Proliferating Realities

On the one hand, the postmodern is frequently associated with openness, play, difference, fluidity, and relativism. The earlier chapters illustrated this in a number of different ways, ranging from how music is consumed through the demise of metanarratives to online interactions. This diversity of examples helps to support the suggestion that these postmodern traits are intimately bound up with changing material practices. In which case, postmodernism is both something of an *expression of* and a *guide to* postmodernity. Postmodernism can serve as a barometer of postmodernity and map for navigating it. More than this, many of the canonical postmodern theorists are interpreted as celebrating this sort of playfulness and difference, investing the concepts with an almost utopian importance (Eagleton 1996; Jameson 1991). On the other hand, the difficulty with this that Eagleton and other Marxist critics of postmodernism like Harvey (1990) and Ebert (1996) point out is that bourgeois hegemony remains ascendant, thus casting postmodern dreams of utopia centered on difference as a diversion from real politics. Regardless of whether Marxists are correct that downplaying issues involving class or capital is an actual problem, many postmodern philosophers are keenly aware of the operations of power within contemporary societies (Clegg 1989). Following this thread led Foucault to produce rather canny interrogators of power relations that demonstrate the insidiousness of its operations and the increased complexity of its contemporary forms (Foucault 1975, 1978, 1983). The exercise of power threatens to at least limit, if not wholly eliminate, the possibilities of playfulness because playfulness is, in no small part, about transgressing the boundaries imposed by power. Many postmodern theorists are well aware that calls to embrace the usual grab bag of postmodern concepts run afoul of power structures. Someone like Foucault is well aware of this and hint that reconceiving "bodies and pleasure" are a way beyond such traps (Foucault 1978, 159). For as much postmodernism has a well-deserved reputation as celebrating difference, playfulness, and the like, many of these theorists also develop penetrating analyses of the mechanisms that inhibit their flourishing.

This tension also appears within Lyotard's writings. For example, in chapter 3, I showed how the postmodern social bond emphasizes fluidity over stasis in social relations. Furthermore, at the conclusion of the *Condition*, Lyotard defends an approach to legitimation based upon what he refers to as "paralogy." Rather than legitimating science based upon its capacity to produce results, he argues that the importance of postmodern science is its production of endless hypotheses. There is no goal per se, other than the science theorizing its own the development. Examples like these exemplify the ludic dimensions of his thought. Yet, he can also be astutely aware of how power operates within postmodernity, especially through technology. "The system" is one such illustration, inasmuch as society self-regulated in a way to foster liberal democratic capitalism to the exclusion of more radical senses of liberation. Another comes from his reflections on specifically computers where he worries that, because someone else handles their programming, then end putting limits on their uses. I will return to both these points later, but for the moment, it is enough to note that this same pattern appears in his work.

Chapter 3 sought to explain that ICT-based social interactions should be regarded as an extension of other sorts of social interactions, rather than "weightless" as proposed by Borgmann and Dreyfus. My goal here is to build on that case and show how these ICT-based objects are part of the same common world as their users. What I push back against is the line of reason found in Borgmann and Baudrillard that such objects are "hyperreal," understood in a sense of being less valuable than real "reality" or even unreal. For Borgmann, reality should ground humans. By displacing the real world with hyperreal simulations, the so-called world can conform to human whims rather than the other way round. Seen from the perspective of both Lyotard and pragmatism, this talk of "displacement" and "replacement" is problematic. Instead, I will use both pragmatists and Lyotard to argue that hyperreality is better understood as part of a trend toward proliferating the contents of the world. This all deals with one side of the tension, because the malleability of the hyperreal is another expression of postmodern playfulness and fluidity. My ending point involves the other. Specifically, I will show how Lyotard's growing concern about computers and occasional references *1984* serve to constrain the ways in which reality expands. In this way, this chapter works with this fundamental tension within postmodern thought.

## ENERGY AND ENTROPY

In a number of later essays (Lyotard 1988, 8–23; 1993b, 112–23; 1997, 83–102), Lyotard explores what would be involved with humanity surviving the destruction of the Earth by the Sun. He proposes that the best option to avoid such a fate would be to transfer human brains to computers and then send those brains far enough out into the universe that they would escape the fate of the Earth when the Sun begins its late phase expansion in which it consumes much of the inner part of the solar system.[1] Lyotard puts this story to different uses depending on the context. Sometimes, like in "Can Thought Go on Without a Body?" he is concerned with showing the limits of human thought or to understand what defines thoughts (as opposed to calculation). When he makes this the fable at the heart of his "A Postmodern Fable," he deploys it in order to articulate several crucial features of postmodernity. Since I deal with those features elsewhere, I will address here a number of points Lyotard raises in his fable to take the sting out more Borgmann's critique of hyperrealism.

Although Lyotard goes to great lengths to write the fable in the third-person, passive voice, thus obscuring any notion of agency, one is tempted to say that its "hero," or at least its protagonist, is the concept of "complexity." When working in this vein, he portrays the history of the universe as a struggle between energy and entropy, where energy produces ever more complex forms that can resist, albeit only temporarily, its dissipation by entropy. This struggle begins in earnest with the origins of life. Through the operation of chance, a new, more complex order emerged out of nonliving components. This then showed that "A process contrary to entropy was therefore possible" (Lyotard 1997, 86). Life then developed new strategies that allowed it to further complexify (e.g., sexual reproduction). Eventually, a peculiar species was selected for humanity. This marked another high-water mark in the process of complexification because of their use of tools, most notably language (LW1.191-225; Burke 2005). Where Lyotard's telling differs from standard, more hagiographic, versions of this story is that humans are not its terminus. Instead, humans are simply one waystation in a very long journey. I noted above that he fully anticipates that humans will be, in some sense or other, superseded by other more complex entities. These entities will be the product of human technologies. One possibility might involve the fusing together human and machine, specifically the human brain (and the brain alone) and some sort of prosthetic body. Other possibilities would be the construction of computer systems that function, first, in ways equivalent to humans, but then go on to radically transcend those capabilities. Regardless of what shape such entities might take, they would mark the next stage in the history of complexification, the resisting of entropy, and the role of humans in the story would be over. One might retell Lyotard's history in such a way that it would sound more triumphant, like the hymns to progress found in the writings of transhumanists like Nick Bostrom (2005), but the version Lyotard himself tells utterly lacks any affect. Lyotard's fable is a strict chronology, eschewing the motifs of metanarratives. These nuances will become significant in the following chapter, but for now I will note important moments in the fable.

The most relevant moments mark transitions from one order of complexity to another. Specifically, these moments are the emergence of life, of humans, and of some sort of posthuman successor. Each of these moments involves the introduction of something fundamentally new into the universe. Life resists entropy through converting external resources into internal energy, allowing the organism to further transform its environment. Alongside the introduction of life, something else comes into play as well: death. Organisms are able to survive for periods of time, but, both at the level of the individual and the species, will eventually permanently cease to function. Before the advent of life, there was no death. These two concepts are bound up together with no precise analogue in the prelife universe. The next decisive moment is organisms developing tools, in particular language. While neither tools nor language are unique to humans (Shew 2017), one particular function of human language deserves special note. "Symbolic language, being self-referential, had moreover the capacity to provide its own memory and critique. Supported by these properties of language, material technique could refer to itself, build on itself, and improve its performance" (Lyotard 1997, 88). This capacity makes many things possible for humans including education, history, and politics. One particularly striking use is "fabulation." As he puts it:

> In the fable, linguistic energy is expended for imagining. It therefore does fabricate a reality, that of the story it tells, but this reality is left in suspense with respect to its cognitive and technical use. . . . Fabulation maintains this reality in reserve and *apart* from its exploitation within the system. This reality is called the imaginary. The existence of imaginary realities presupposes, in the system in which it appears, zones that are neutralized, so to speak, in relation to merely realist constraints of the system's performativity. (Lyotard 1997, 95. Emphasis original)

Many uses of linguistic energy require being constrained by reality. When producing a history or teaching students, one is expected to operate by the constraints imposed by the shared social and material world. Fables work differently. These are zones in which reality is held at bay. Their point is to create spaces in which reality does not operate as it does in the rest of the system. Fabulation produces linguistic objects that can imitate, if not appear like, reality, while not obeying "reality." These zones add something

Proliferating Realities 71

distinctly new to the world. Put simply, before the development of this sort of self-referential symbolic languages, the imaginary spaces of fables and other sorts of fiction could not possible exist. Once such languages are sufficiently developed, such zones become possible. Similar to the emergence of life (and death), the possibility of fabulation is something fundamentally new with no clear analogue in the universe before its advent.

While life and death and fabulation possess rather different functions, their introduction into the world both added something new. In Lyotard's story, these moments mark an increase of complexity in the universe. While entropy might still win out over energy given a long enough time frame, but in the short run, life and language are forms of energy that allow that energy to continue to be productive, to further complexify itself. Both are irreducible to the processes that existed before they came into play. In this sense, they add something fundamentally new to the world. Through chance, evolutionary processes, or deliberate activity, more is put into the world. Its contents take new forms. Dewey makes the point this way: "The distinction between physical, psycho-chemical, and mental is thus one of levels of increasing complexity and intimacy of interactions among natural events. The idea that matter, life and mind represent separate kinds of Being is a doctrine that springs, as so many philosophy errors have spring, from a substantiation of eventual functions. The fallacy converts consequences of interaction of events into causes of the occurrence of these consequences" (LW1.200). Dewey points to here to "the philosophical fallacy" in order to explain why so many take these three phases of Lyotard's forms of energy as fundamentally different comes about from taking the end point of processes as something substantial. Rather, each of these are terms for increasingly complicated processes. When there is a transition from one level to the next, something new enters the stage, but rather than being mysteriously different, it is an expansion of the possible interactions between events within the world. While a these points here will be useful later on, the primary reason I introduce this discussion is show how distinctly new levels can be added to the world while remaining part of that same world. This provides a foil to use again Borgmann's analysis of hypermodernism

## A VANISHING REALITY?

Early chapters presented Borgmann's argument about how the hyperreal comes to subvert and replace the "real" world. Borgmann finds hypermodern technologies subvert the real world by substituting elements of it with technologies. In his view, these are pale imitations of the majesty, contingency, and beauty of the real, especially the natural, world. That technology does this is why it poses such a danger. What Borgmann intends with his use of this term is not that the "real world" itself is disappearing, even though it might be changed (radically in some cases) by human technologies. Rather, its significance is being supplanted by hypermodern technologies. These technologies lead people away from establishing connections with nature and elements of the "real world." They come to prefer the ease, brightness, and malleability of the hyperreal. In choosing this path over that the "real world," people no longer participate in meaningful activities (or at least as meaningful activities) fitting for the robust capabilities of human beings. Borgmann is motivated by a neo-Heideggerian critique of technology, in which the danger of technology is that it prevents humans playing their proper role of "world-disclosures." Humans become nothing more than another "standing-reserve" to be drawn upon for the creation of more technology. Although Borgmann does not phrase his concerns in this way, Heidegger's Danger lurks within Borgmann's analysis of "replacement."

The claim that the "real world" is being subverted by the hyperreal echoes the "text-type determinism." This is the idea that one form of text is inherently superior to others, so books are inherently superior to video games (though as I noted in chapter 1, one should not obscure the ways in which different text, or objects, potentially possess different functions). Like with Borgmann's text-type determinism, his writing of "replacement" contains a fundamentally negative edge. The negative assessment arises because of the commitments Borgmann makes with respect to what counts as really "real." There is a fundamental reality to the natural world that human constructs can never match. Within human artifacts, there is also a clear hierarchy as well. Some creations, precisely because of their uniqueness, will always be better than others. One of Borgmann's most powerful examples of this is the Freiberg Minster. First built starting around 1200, it came to serve as an excellent example of Gothic architecture, even if its beginings were awkward because of the number of masons involved in designing it. It stood for centuries. The Minster came to acquire new, contingent, meanings in the wake of Allied bombing in World War II. Although much of the city nearby was leveled by bombs, the tower of the Minster survived. Mass-produced objects lack the capacity to take on anything like the rich meanings associated with the Minster (Borgmann 1999, 108–21). This hierarchy is part of the nature of things. While postmodern societies might emphasize technological devices at the expense of nature, this does not take away from the inherent value and superiority of the natural world, or even contingent, crafted things. Rather, to ignore the value of such things is a mistake on the part of the contemporary world. The assumption of this hierarchy helps makes sense of why he frames the rise of hypermodernism in terms of eclipsing "the real world." When humans act in ways that favor the hyperreal at the expense of natural world, or even the world of older technologies that still allow for the proper gathering of humans, they risk losing what is most significant about themselves. Instead of acting as "world-disclosers," they let themselves be consumed by hyperactive distractions, thus obscuring their own essence (Dreyfus and Spinosa 1997). This is Borgmann's reframing of the Danger Heidegger found in modern technology, which is explains much of why Borgmann is so critical of modern and hypermodern technology.

It is worth noting here how Borgmann uses the term "real" and its cognates. It functions, using Ian Hacking's terminology (Hacking 1999, 21–23), as "an elevator word," inasmuch it serves to raise up the importance of the other words it gets associated with. Reality here is primarily an honorific. In arguing that hyperreality eclipses the "real word," Borgmann highlights the ways in which that which is of more significance comes to be devalued. There are other strains of postmodern thought that are more radical, claiming that there is no such thing as reality. For Baudrillard, reality has been replaced, not simply in Borgmann's sense of misplaced priorities, by hyperreal simulations (Baudrillard 1994). This is not so much displacement as the destruction of reality. Perhaps in the very long term, the hyperreality that Borgmann fears might lead to such a complete replacement, but in the present and foreseeable future the natural world persists for Borgmann. A more radical possibility would be to propose that there is no such thing as reality, nor has there even been. Perhaps what is called "real" is nothing more than effect of society or power, as is sometimes claimed of social constructivists, or maybe one simply embraces a full-on metaphysical nihilism and holds that there is no reality. While this is not Borgmann's position, Best and Kellner (Best and Kellner 1991, 128–45) suggest that it might follow from Baudrillard.

The suggestion that I have drawn out from Lyotard's fable goes in a different direction. Rather than interpreting what Borgmann refers to as hyperreal as an inauthentic substitute for the really real, the hyperreal is better understood as a further addition to a complexifying universe. As Lyotard describes matters there, genuinely new phenomena can be added to the universe, beginning with the addition of life and death. So to with the hyperreal. Hyperreality, especially in the form of the Infosphere, is a technologically produced reality. For Lyotard, and most of the classical pragmatists, this reality does not exist apart from the rest of the "real world." To echo Lyotard's language, it is better thought of as a new zone within a larger reality. Each of the levels is itself real, but possess different properties. What is particularly distinctive about the hyperreal is the extent to which it is shot through with symbols, which opens up the possibility of more intensive fabulation.

The proposal taking shape here is that postmodernity involves an increased proliferation of these realities. Proliferation echoes aspects of these more radical positions, while avoiding their pitfalls. Borgmann heads in problematic direction by focusing primarily on hypermodern technologies, which then creates an impression that "reality" has fallen away. As he points out, such technologies are dazzling, creating a vertiginous experience (Borgmann 119, 82–97). But by situating the use of these technologies (better understood as an assemblage of techno-social objects) within a wider view that holds that reality is essentially pluralistic and capable of growth, one steps back from this edge to more stable ground because this account of "the real world" does not privilege the natural world over the social and technological world. They are all part of one dynamic universe. Elements of this idea are contained in many of the classic analyses of the postmodern like Jameson or Harvey. Both point to the ways in which different ontologies overlap, creating radical juxtaposition of worlds. Such situations appear to follow quite directly from what Harvey called "time-space compression." This implosion brings together, at least potentially, all the conceptual elements of the bounded infinite, allowing them to be sat alongside each other (Harvey 1990, especially 39–65). Especially within spaces like the infosphere, where social control does not operate through wholly traditional mechanisms, there are greater degrees of freedom to combine divergent elements. The limits typically found in the embodied world, either physical or social, need not hold, thus opening up the possibility for the simultaneous appearance of different realities. This marks not the demise of reality, as Borgmann might imply, but rather its complexification. Instead of these hyperreal technologies eclipsing the "real world," they add to it. There are new spaces, produced and sustained through human activity.

Classical pragmatism provides a set of tools making sense of this proliferation of realities, while avoiding the dangers described above. I now turn to following out the implications of this in light of their thought. Within pragmatism, there is no agreed-upon definition of "reality," but there are some commonalities that appear. For example, Peirce's classic definition of truth and reality is "The opinion which is fated to be ultimately agreed to by all who investigate, is what we mean by truth, and the object represented in this opinion is the real" (EP1.139). There is much that can be debated about the meaning and merits of this definition, and I will skip over such questions to cut to clue that he provided (Hookway 1985, 41–51; Misak 1991). The community of inquirers arrives at the fabled, fated end of inquiry when there are no more scientific questions to be asked. At least in the rather schematic theory of inquiry Peirce develops in the *Popular Science* series, one is aware (in some sense) that this point has been reached because inquirers are no longer cast into doubt, which prompts inquiry in the first place. The clue here is that the real is what stands up under inquiry. The "object represented" in beliefs after a line of inquiry is deserving the accolade "real." Rather than being a metaphysical term, "reality" is moved into the theory of inquiry. For

Peirce, especially in his early writings, the term was reserved for what inquirers finally arrive at. The later pragmatists will be less stingy in some respects with the application of the term, even if the spirit of its use remains similar. What James, Dewey, and Mead add to this discussion is an appreciation for the plurality of reality. This is most clear in James when states things like: "profusion, not economy, may after all be reality's key-note" (James 1987, 570). The world is fundamentally complex and irreducible to any sort of monism:

> For pluralism, all that we are required to admit as the constitution of reality is what we ourselves find empirically realized in every minimum finite life. Briefly it is this, that nothing real is absolutely simple, that every smallest bit of experience is a *mulitum in parvo* plurally related, that each relation is one aspect, character, or function, way of its being taken, or way of its taking something else; and that a bit of reality when actively engaged in one of those relations is not *by that very fact* engaged in all the other relations simultaneously. (James 1987, 776–77. Emphasis original)

While anything can potentially be related to other things, these connections must grow up within the world, since they are not found there at the outset.

This pluralistic space is one that pragmatism has operated within since its early history. Especially if one refuses, or at least puts off indefinitely, the possibility of Peirce's end of inquiry story, then the Jamesian pluralistic story becomes much more plausible. As James explores in *Pragmatism*, experience offers reasons to see the world as being both unified and divergent (James 1987, 541–57). It is all a matter of in what way. Certain parts of experience lend themselves to being interpreted monistically, while others, pluralistically, and where connections between parts of experience continue to grow up between things. Of course, this all lends itself to the claim that world is itself pluralistic, though not absolutely so. As James says of pluralism: "Provided you grant *some* separation among things, some tremor of independence, some free play of parts on one another, some real novelty or chance, however minute, . . . [pluralism] is amply satisfied and will allow you any amount, however great, of real union" (James 1987, 556. Emphasis original). The starting point is a multitude and connections are then built out of this. Also, contra more monistically minded philosophers, such a pluralism is in fact real inasmuch as it holds up under conditions of rigorous inquiry. In this way, it is not mere appearance, *a la* Parmenides. Instead, plurality is a genuine feature of the world. While Peirce's stance on pluralism is complicated (Misak 2005; Singer 1992), it plays a significant role within the work of James, Dewey, and Mead, although each took it in divergent directions. This is one significant reason that pragmatism functions effectively within a postmodern context: the pragmatists appreciated questions of pluralism since the movement's inception.

## TECHNO-SOCIAL OBJECTS

Given the emphasis of the previous chapters on ICTs, it is worth digging in further to see what is distinctive about the worlds that they sustain. Again, Lyotard provides a clue on this front: the centrality of language within contemporary science and technology. It is worth embedding this point within the wider postmodern conception of language mentioned in chapter 2. Under this conception of language, reference plays no role, but rather self-reflexivity. The meaning of words does not arise from reference to things in the world. Instead, words derive meaning from their relationship to other terms. Language is a field of differences. In the more radical formulations of this interpretation there is nothing outside of the text, in which case everything is reducible to language. Instead of words pointing to something beyond language, all there can be is an endless chain of references within the system of language. This understanding of language has had a profound influence on how postmodern theory describes a host of human systems, including informing the image of bound infinite. There is no outside to language, most radically stated with the idea that there is nothing outside of texts. While language might be infinitely malleable, it does not point to anything outside of language itself. It consists only in the infinite reconfiguration of its elements.

Information, understood in the sense of the code used by ICTs, is language, albeit of a peculiar sort. In the case of the information transmitted between ICTs, language (understood broadly) is translated into binary code, sent from transmitter to receiver and then decoded. What goes along with the expanded scope of information (understood in this technological sense) is the peculiar understanding of language that underwrites most of postmodern thought. While alien to some mainstream accounts of the philosophy of language, this idea of language as a self-reflexive network of differences can make sense of (technological) information. ICTs rely on information, which in turn consists of bits, binary code. Binary code can be interpreted as nothing more than difference, since it is comprised of two marks: 0 and 1, off and on, something and its negation. As difference is piled upon difference, messages in a more humanly intelligible sense arise (once it translated by a device). In this way, binary code can be understood as something of an illustration of the postmodern conception of language: a field of differences, with nothing to refer to outside of itself.

ICTs present a world composed of informational objects. When communication occurs through these devices, the sender's message is translated into a computing language and then translated back for the receiver. This use of computing languages operates as a metalanguage, at least in the sense that other languages are translated into and out of it, although no humans communicate directly through the language. As discussed in earlier chapters, certain sorts of meanings can be lost in this process of translation, even though new communicative modalities can emerge from such translation. Given the breadth of the usage of language both within postmodern thought and in this book, informational objects should be understood as doubly semiotic. The first sense is that these objects serve as signs, significant symbols, objects that bear meanings and allow for communication. The second is that, even though most users do not engage with them as such, these objects are fundamentally composed of language, in the sense of codes.

These informational objects constitute this latest layer of reality. Because of this, it is important to provide a fuller account of them. In order to do this, I return to Mead's concept of "social objects." These are objects that arise through the shared conduct of individuals. The object responds to the activity of each participant. Mead's principle example of this in "The Genesis of the Self and Social Control" is that of property, where an object is treated as property. In other circumstances, an object like a book will not be taken as property (it serves as a diversion, a doorstop, a repository of information). Yet, in the situation in which the buyer seeks to acquire it from the seller, the ways in which each responds to the others defines the book as property (as well as the human in their respective roles). Informational objects are social objects as well because of how these objects respond to the activity those who engage with them. Yet, there is a change from the objects that Mead discussed and ICTs. The technological dimension is much more prominent in ICTs. This is not to say that a book is not a technological object. It clearly is, if "technology" is understood in a broad sense along the lines of Hickman's definition discussed in chapter 1. But rather that ICT-based social objects are enmeshed in a different way in technical systems. In order to communicate with friends on Facebook, one requires some sort of ICT device, a program to run Facebook on, a power supply, access to the Internet, etc. Furthermore, many of the social objects engaged with through ICTs exist only through these ICTs. In order to distinguish these informational objects from those that Mead wrote on, I will refer to these as "techno-social objects" in order to designate the specifically technological character of these sorts of social objects.

Take as an example a "raid" in a Massively Multiplayer Online Roleplaying Game (MMORPG) like World of Warcraft. In a raid, a group of players gather their avatars together in order to explore a particular area of the virtual world, which usually involves fighting against different opponents, culminating in "boss fight" against a very powerful foe that requires contributions by all the players to successfully best. All of this from top to bottom is composed of social objects, because the opponents and the virtual space they are found in require that a player responds to both the objects and the other players in order for the experience to function as it should. These objects respond to the participants in the raid, allowing them to engage with both the objects and the other players. Meanings emerge through the practice of raiding, whether it be bonding among the participants of the raid or a chance to gather more loot or experience points. Yet, these objects require the sustenance of a large technical network in order to appear at all. There is something of a parallel, both historically and in practice, with table-top roleplaying games like Dungeons and Dragons (D&D), but this only goes so far. In a traditional D&D game, the action takes place through social interaction, perhaps augmented through the use of a map and miniatures or other aids (a whiteboard, sound-effects, handouts, etc.), and the participants' imaginations (Fine 1983). In a MMORPG, the computer graphics play an important role in creating the experience. The objects left largely up to the player's imagination in the traditional D&D game now become represented through pixels on the screen. It is in this sense that the social object is simultaneously a technological object (Nardi 2010).

I use the example of an MMORPG raid as a way to clearly illustrate the ways in which informational objects function as social objects. The participants in the raid engage with the other players through these techno-social objects. The same can be said of many of the uses of a social media platform like Facebook as discussed in chapter 3. The technology allows for (for all intents and purposes) instantaneous social action at a distance. Earlier I explored how friendships could be played out and sustained through ICTs. This is one use of techno-social objects. Using these objects as diversions, commerce or labor are other possibilities. Regardless of their use, because of their technological character these objects can call out different sorts of responses from their users, allowing for different social interactions. The possibility of acting at a distance allows for novel opportunities to interact more quickly with other individuals across the globe. Also, because ICTs can transmit more than words, distinct sorts of expressive behaviors open up. Communicating through GIFs and memes are options, in addition to the more conventional written word. What is instructive about a game like World of Warcraft is how the techno-social objects that comprise it allow for a certain sort of immersiveness. It involves two sensory modalities, vision and hearing, and the interface relies on a tactile engagement via a keyboard and mouse. The player can find themselves engrossed in the game, even opening up the possibility of addiction to it. This speaks to the depth of the symbols at work in techno-social objects.

Of course, there are constraints on this depth inasmuch as they are technological objects. Processor power or download and upload speed will impact objects. Consider the difference in graphics between computers and gaming consoles in the 1990s and the present. The technical specifications of the devices of one era shape the technical possibilities of these techno-social objects. As the processing power of ICTs increased, along with increased resolution and number of colors, the objects presented on such devices allow for greater detail, allowing for more "realism" or opening up new aesthetic opportunities (Egenfeldt-Nielsen, Smith, and Tosca 2016, especially 129–44). While such developments open up possibilities, given that much of this is subject to market pressures, older objects can fall by the wayside. Some of this is a result of "data rot" (the phenomenon of data actually decaying or lacking the proper equipment to access the data, for instance: like having video tapes and lacking a VCR). In other cases, this is because of changing trends. What appeared cutting edge in webpage design in 1999 seems so archaic two decades later (and it can be jarring to stumble across such "old" websites). On the other hand, because nostalgia remains a powerful force, there can be revitalization of older styles under the heading of "retro." A simple example of how these constraints play out is with Twitter. First launched in July 2006, the platform initially limited tweets to 140 characters. The choice of 140 characters was determined by what was the standard for text messages, which was also the result of the technical constraints of early cellular phones. These limits meant that individual tweets needed to be quite economical. The techno-social objects constituted through the platform take a distinctive shape, especially compared to those on Facebook where (while not the norm) much longer posts were possible (Hannan 2018). Although the number of characters per tweet was increased to 280 in November 2017, and the platform supports images (static and otherwise), these initial design decisions continue to encourage certain sorts of communication, which then shapes the techno-social objects possible (Isaac 2017). These technical points constrain techno-social objects inasmuch as these objects depend on and are part of large technical systems (Hughes 1987).

On the other hand, it is important to keep in mind that techno-social objects are not just technological objects (as if an object could be "just technological"). They are thoroughly social as well. These objects become meaningful through individuals responding to others and the object. On the one hand, because such objects are social, different users will respond to them differently. As Wiebe Bijker and Trevor Pinch document, there is a great deal of fluidity in this process (Pinch and Bijker 1987). As users engage with the object, the object's creators will retool the object based on the users' responses. Different groups of users can use objects in markedly distinct ways, requiring extensive negotiation as to the objects final form and meaning. This process of negotiation itself is a limit on techno-social objects. They do not simply appear, with individuals immediately using them as intended. Regardless of what the creator intends, others will play a role in the shaping of the techno-social object. Andrew Feenberg shows this in his analysis of "Teletel," a French videotex system "designed to bring France into the Information Age by giving telephone subscribers access to data bases" (Feenberg 1992, 308). This system went through two important transformations. The first was the design of its terminal, renamed "Minitel," "to look and feel like an adjunct to the domestic telephone" (Feenberg 1992, 308). This was meant to make the system approachable and not appear as something related to work. Once the Minitel was released to the public, they began to develop meanings for and habits around it that the designed did not necessarily anticipate, specifically: "Soon the Minitel underwent a further redefinition at the hands of these users, many of whom employed it primarily for anonymous on-line chatting with other users in the search for amusement, companionship, and sex" (Feenberg 1992, 308). On the other hand, negotiation is not itself limitless. First, the technical dimensions of objects matter as just discussed. Second, as Langdon Winner argues in his classic critique of social constructivism, "Upon Opening the Black Box and Finding It Empty," society itself is not an open, empty field. Instead, there are definite patterns in which society operates which Winner finds described by the likes of Karl Marx, Martin Heidegger, or the Frankfurt School (Winner 1993). Power is at work within society, which makes certain sorts of negotiations easier, others harder, and all but ruling out others. This can be understood in terms of Lyotard's network conception of the social bond, where the configuration of a network makes particular technological developments, implementations, and usages increasingly easier or difficult.[2]

These techno-social objects are also shaped by the very fact that they are postmodern. Since these techno-social objects operate within the bounded infinite, they are all, in effect, recycled from other objects. Nothing can be added to bounded infinite, only rearranged. The conceptual universe is bounded which prevents the addition of qualitatively new objects. Instead, all techno-social objects are composed by parts of from previously existing objects. Their arrangement can be quite novel or entertaining, as is illustrated by "mash ups" shared on SNSs, but this is not the same as creating something that goes beyond what already exists within the conceptual universe. Possible techno-social objects operate within limits, limits that prevent any and every conceivable object from being produced. The space of what is possible is quite large, and shifts as technical capabilities and societies change, which serves to forestall some of the "anything goes" postmodernism is sometimes accused of. Not every techno-social object will be feasible, because of technical grounds, social limitations, or both. Furthermore, the bounded infinite limits what is imaginable within the space of techno-social objects. In terms of aesthetics, this prevents the possibility of an avant-garde, which was crucial for modernism. In the realm of ethics and politics, it inhibits the moral imagination to the extent that reimaging situations is limited to simply rearranging rather than radical transformation. An important motif in modernism was revolution, the overturning of the old order and its replacement by the radically new. Even if the break between old and new was always less dramatic than claimed, this imagery remained decisive. The condition of existing within the bounded infinite prevents this sort of break altogether. The possibility of utopia, other than taking the present itself as a utopia, is excised because such a gesture depends on something outside of the present, which is what the bounded infinite eliminates.

## A WORLD OF TECHNO-SOCIAL OBJECTS

With the concept of a techno-social object in hand, I can now situate them alongside other sorts objects, social and otherwise. This will reconstruct the meaning of "hyperreal" in two ways. First, it provides grounds on which to push back against those who do not take this strand of postmodern thought seriously enough, whether this is Borgmann who treats the hyperreal as a pathology or others who find the whole thing to be a conceptual nightmare. Second, by developing this case on pragmatic grounds, it takes some of the air, or airiness, out of postmodernism, curtailing its excess and demonstrating the intellectual movement's continued relevance. The decisive move involves reconceiving the proliferation of techno-social objects as something occurring within a rather complicated world, rather than replacing such a world. This will show how the hyperreality of ICTs should be seen as an extension of, an addition to, the rest of the world, rather than the pathology that Borgmann takes it as or some sort of wholesale replacement as Baudrillard proposes.

Mead again proves useful as a way into making this case. Especially in his later writings, Mead is quite concerned at properly understanding the relationship between the natural and social worlds. He both takes the natural world as, in some sense, real and that the sciences provide an accurate description of this world. Like with the earlier discussion of levels, sciences like physics and chemistry provide descriptions of how physical objects operate inasmuch as they move or react with other compounds. Biology provides a description of a different level, the one at which a certain group of objects should be understood as psycho-chemical. Such objects, organisms, possess additional functions that include but go beyond the physical. For Mead, at least among some species of organisms, there is the possibility of sociality (whether social insects, herd animals or pack animals). Life is a more complicated arrangement of chemical and physical objects. What differentiates humans from these other social organisms is their capacity to possess not just consciousness, but self-consciousness. The mark of self-consciousness is not simply being able to take the attitude of the other, but also to take the attitude of the generalized other, discussed in chapter 3 (Aboulafia 2001). This is a further complexification of matter, though not reducible to such objects in any simple way. The social world extends out physical reality, built up out of the physical world, but going beyond it. To return to Mead's example, when purchased from the seller, the book becomes a particular social object, that is, property. Both the seller and I respond to the physical object in distinctive ways, given our roles as buyer and seller. These responses are what define the book as the social object "property." This sort of layering on of responses is typical of how social objects supervene on physical objects. In this respect, techno-social objects are quite similar to social objects. The book that is property is a physical object, whereas the raid in a MMORPG is presented through images on screens. Yet the status of the raid as a techno-social object functions much the same because it involves engaging with the informational objects and others in the process of raiding. Both objects supervene on some sort of base.

This is not to say that Mead's social objects and techno-social objects are exactly the same. There are several important differences that arise precisely because of the latter's technological nature. This first is that part of what makes techno-social objects distinctive is how the responses they call out can occur over great distances, while being (almost) instantaneous. While Mead does write about large-scale social objects involving nations like the World Court and the League of Nations (Mead 1964, 293), and the very idea of nation itself is also a social object, the technologies operative when he wrote did not allow the simultaneous responsive engagement of many individuals. This fosters a greater, and in some cases more intensive, degree of interactivity than social objects. What allows for this is the extent to which such social interaction becomes mediated through symbols. This sets up the second difference. Put stupidly, it is easier to transmit symbols (once translated into and then out of binary code) through networks than physical objects. Because significant symbols are such precisely through being part of a universe of discourse, the meaning of symbols is shared among participants in that universe of discourse. This property of being shared allows for symbols to be the basis of techno-social objects. The common meaning that terms (and other symbols) possess provides building blocks for these objects, because, regardless of distance, the same reaction is called out by the symbol. These symbols are assembled within these virtual spaces to create techno-social objects. They remain social precisely because they provide a shared center for different individuals to engage with one another, yet they are sustained through technological means. Lastly, the technology plays another important role here. ICTs support, to varying degrees, a complicated semiotics. The signs that underlie techno-social objects are not only words, but images, pictures, sounds, etc. So, when players of MMORPGs like World of Warcraft engage one another, the techno-social objects are not comprised simply of words and gestures, but also visual and aural components. Especially as the ICTs have become more powerful with respect to processing power and graphics, objects can then come to create representations that simulate the "real world" with increased accuracy and sophistication (or in the case of some video games and big budget movies, fantastic realities that appear more lifelike). These simulations remain signs and not the things signified.

It is this last point about semiotics that leads those like Borgmann and Baudrillard to declare that the hyperreal is un*real* (admitting that their reasoning and lessons drawn are quite different). Since these are only symbols, signs, and not "genuine" things, their existence is merely derived, secondary. The hyperreal is of a lower order of being than natural objects, or even other physical artifacts, especially those that are crafted. What they run together are two separate issues: how individuals engage with objects and their value.[3] Especially for Borgmann, this follows from his use of "real" as an elevator word. "Reality" simultaneously denotes both that something is natural (in the sense of not produced, at least wholly, by humans) and more valuable than nonnatural things. Running these two points together is something of a mistake. Even working with a rather simple-minded view of pragmatism ("look to the consequences"), such a move is problematic. Consequences inform answers to both questions of engagement and value, but such global assessments of whole classes of technologies are difficult to make in light of the inability to effectively to talk about technology *simpliciter* (Pitt 2000, 9–12). While the origins of something will shape its possible value, in the view of this pragmatic analysis, it cannot be the only, and rarely will it be the determining, factor. Instead, as I examine in chapter 6, a more well-rounded assessment involves understanding the examining the fitness of a tool for an end within a context, with the caveat that ends themselves are tools capable of assessment.

Even if the signs in question only refer to other signs and not Borgmann's "reality," they remain a part of a larger, complex world. The suggestion that drives this claim is to embed these objects within the process of inquiry and other activities. In order to defend this, consider one definition of pragmatism that Dewey provided: "the doctrine that reality possesses practical character and that this character is most efficaciously expressed in the function of intelligence" (MW4.128). In this article, "Does Reality Possess a Practical Character?" Dewey defends this interpretation of pragmatism against criticisms coming out of more traditional metaphysics and epistemologies. He works from the assumption "that the world itself is in transformation" (MW4.127) as opposed to the more static accounts of the world that underlie much of traditional philosophy. In such a world, it is paramount to determine how such transformations occur in order to find and produce stabilities. What allows humans to do this is intelligence, which Dewey defines as the "ability to size up matters with respect to the needs and possibilities of the various situations in which one is called to something; capacity to envisage things in terms of the adjustments and adaptations they make possible or hinder" (MW4.130). Given the practical nature of intelligence, what it seeks to manipulate is itself practical (and as Hickman reminds us, this can be considered "technology"). Even if they are not made of the same material as other objects of inquiry, techno-social objects can be examined, manipulated, and transformed using intelligence. This is why the claim of "weightless" needed to be criticized in the previous chapter. If social interactions carried out through ICTs were as ephemeral as Borgmann suggested, the would lack the necessary robustness to hold up under inquiry. They could be rightly regarded as mere epiphenomena. Yet, as I sought to demonstrate, such interactions, working through or with techno-social objects, do constitute part of an objective action-nexus.

All this points to support the pluralism introduced earlier in the chapter. Seen from one perspective, what the world contains grows, even if presently this might be understood at a material, but not conceptual, level. This is part of what the world being "itself . . . a transition" entails. It is not static, nor is it always reliably static. Even the conceptual world of bounded infinite involves the possibility of the rearrangement of its elements. As James noted, each element is capable of forming new relationships with others because of the possibility of "free play." This entails that techno-social objects need not be discreet entities. Rather, not unlike a fractal, they can be characterized as "*mulitum in parvo*." One of their defining characteristics is their capacity to build up these new relations in ways that go beyond other, more conventional, objects. Contra Borgmann, this does not take away from being a part of a wider world. It is simply noting different properties. Questions of the value of techno-social objects must be made *in media res*, based upon the context of particular inquiries, as I will discuss in chapter 6. Which is no different from social objects or material objects.

Techno-social objects operate as another layer of a complex world. They are part of the proliferation of reality. This then preserves some use to the term "reality" in contrast to more radical postmodern philosophers. The metaphysical commitments of Baudrillard on the nihilistic (Best and Kellner 1997, 95–110). Second, even for more somewhat modest versions (say merely solipsistic sorts of relativism), a different trouble arises. By relativizing reality in this way, it makes changing that reality impossible. If each individual determines the real, then when faced with issues that involve communities (which is to say, most serious issues), the way forward to transform those situations is unclear. For example, if reality is purely subjective, how can different individuals, or even communities, even agree that there is a problematic situation requiring reconstruction? The approach articulated here avoids this by treating the world as a locus of practical, social activity. Any part of the world will be capable of developing connections to other parts. This operates both at the different levels discussed above, Dewey's physical, psycho-chemical, and mental, the Infosphere, as well as between all of these different levels. Thus, social activity occurs in a complicated space, one buttressed by the growing connections between these different levels. It is this buttressing that prevents it from falling into relativism.

Finally, while I have been critical of Borgmann's talk of "replacement," this should not be taken as a blanket endorsement of hypermodern technologies. To simply do this merely inverts what Borgmann did. A more productive route involves making assessments of particular technological practices within the context of inquiry and in the light of particular goals (goals which themselves are open to criticism). This prevents global claims that all ICTs and other hypermodern technologies are inherently inferior (or superior) to other technologies. Given that the concern for pragmatists is to assess technologies based upon their function in context, the blanket critical claim that technology replaces the real world has difficulty getting off the ground (unless it can be shown that all hypermodern technologies are fundamentally destructive in all contexts). I develop a first sketch of how to pursue within a postmodern context in chapter 6 and the conclusion.

## SOCIAL CONTROL REVISITED

Thus far, I have largely been concerned with the playful, fluid, and heterogenous side of postmodernism. What has not been touched on is the dark underbelly of postmodern thought. Again, returning to Lyotard is instructive. Lyotard sometimes wallows in the postmodern metaphysical mud of relativism, but he is quite aware that the postmodern present is far from "anything goes." Terror can lurk anywhere, even in the seemingly constraintless realities of the Infosphere. As it turns out, Lyotard detects within ICTs a rather subtle danger. In his "Rewriting Modernity," first published in 1988, Lyotard chastises Baudrillard for misunderstanding the significance of ICTs:

> the noteworthy result of this is not . . . the constitution of an immense network of simulacra. It seems to be that what is really disturbing is much more the importance assumed by the concept of the *bit*, the unit of information. When we're dealing with bits, there's no longer any question of free forms given here and now to sensibility and the imagination. On the contrary, they are units of information conceived by computer engineering and definable at all linguistic

levels—lexical, syntactic, rhetorical and the rest. They are assembled into systems following a set of possibilities (a "menu") under the control of a programmer. So that the question posed by the new technologies to the idea of rewriting as expressed here could be: being admitted that working through is above all the business of free imagination and that it demands the deployment of time between "not yet," "no longer" and "now," what can the use of the new technologies preserve or conserve of that? (Lyotard 1991, 34–35. Emphasis original)

The chief danger here is that the computerization of communication is that every single level is structured by someone else. Lyotard privileges the free play of language as the primary way to resist the terror implicit within performativity. The structure built into information and communication technologies potentially limits the possible freedom and imagination of communication. Someone else is responsible for programming each level, determining the possibilities of how one engages with techno-social objects. There is something of Orwell's *1984* at work here, which is why Lyotard began to worry over whether the control inherent within these technologies feeds into to this sort of dystopia. ICTs allow for the sort of terror Oceana thrives on, while also making all but impossible to resist such terror because technologists (programmers, engineers, and so forth) build the means of communication in ways that the play necessary for this freedom is unavailable. While Lyotard never expresses it this way, in the present, the danger he points to links easily with debates of about the algorithms used by the likes of Google and Facebook. Given the sheer amount of data on the Web, some means of sorting it out is required, yet both the American Left and Right raise serious questions about the transparency of the methods used by Internet goliaths and the effects of the results on the public (Pariser 2011). This is one example of how the seemingly open-ended content of the Internet is in fact profoundly structured in ways that potentially inhibit the serious playfulness that Lyotard privileges.

In chapter 3, I discussed how social control plays a less overt role in ICT-based social interactions. Yet, in light of the passage from Lyotard quoted above, other sorts of control do not disappear when engaging with techno-social objects. Rather, social control becomes embedded within the technical specification of these objects. At this point, "social control" comes to be used in the more typical, negative way rather than in Mead's more agnostic sense of the degree to which an individual brings themselves into line with the group's attitudes. By embedding this negative sense of social control within these technologies, it becomes *possible* to bring the activity of individuals into line with those structuring the technologies. I qualify this as "possible" for two reasons. The first returns us to the other side of the tension I mentioned at the start of this chapter: playfulness. Lyotard calls for playfulness as a way to resist the corrosive logic of performativity. Others, like Derrida and Foucault, make plain how, despite every attempt to close systems off and make them unshakeable, play or resistance is always possible.[4] At the theoretical level, this leads to the conclusion that the dream, or Lyotard's nightmare, of establishing absolute control, especially over communication is likely overblown. Second, at least thus far, it appears that this theoretical claim is plausible empirically. Despite the proprietary nature of software and efforts by many groups to prevent interference with ICT networks, hackers continue to find ways around such restrictions. Yet, even if true at both these levels, remains a concern about the ways in which this sort of social control can inhibit creative, democratic intelligence (at least for those who lack the relevant expertise and energy to invest in resistance). In this way, the concern that Lyotard raises continues to be pressing.

## NOTES

1. In the different versions of this story Lyotard always says that this to will occur in four billion years, but more recent estimates put it at around seven billion (Appell 2008). Regardless of when this occurs, Lyotard sees the system beginning to prepare for it now, if for no other reason because of how daunting a task it appears (Lyotard 1997, 91). This is another reason he provides for why language and information come to play such a significant role in postmodernity.

2. There is also a great deal of affinity with Foucault's conception of power as well (Foucault 1978).

3. This is most clear for Borgmann, and to a large extent Dreyfus. Baudrillard position is much more complicated on this front.

4. Richard Bernstein makes clear the significance and subtlety of Derrida on this matter. See Bernstein 1992, 172–98. See Foucault (1978, especially 95–96) for his gloss on resistance.

*Chapter 5*
# How to Reconstruct "Timeless Time"

The very term "postmodern" belies a paradoxical experience of time. Upon first encounter, one might be tempted to ask "if 'modern' indicates the present or the contemporary, then how can one ever be 'postmodern?' How can one ever be *after* the present?" Without totally abandoning the paradox inherent in the term "postmodern," some sense can be made of it by considering the different role of the future in the time consciousness underlying modernity and postmodernity. The simplest way of describing this difference is that modernity is relentlessly future oriented, whereas within postmodernity there is no future. Crucial for "modernity" is a certain sense of historicity. As the "post" in the term implies, "postmodern" always refers to the "modern." This is the case with temporality as with everything else. Postmodernity carries within itself modernity's temporality, but like everything else, it becomes different, mutated, inverted.

To both make sense of this distinctive sense of temporality and show one way to work with it more productively, this chapter offers a critique of Castells's timeless time through an admittedly idiosyncratic reading of Mead. This phenomenon of timeless time is, to some extent, anticipated at a conceptual level in Mead's later writings. In published works like "The Nature of the Past" and in drafts, edited after his death, like *The Philosophy of the Present*, Mead seeks to articulate an understanding of temporality in which "reality exists in a present. The present of course implies a past and a future, and to these both we deny existence" (Mead 2002, 35). Common to both Castells and Mead is the claim that only the present exists. Inasmuch as the past and future have significance, it is because they exist in a present. As I explore later, Mead provides philosophical tools to explain how timeless time functions. Furthermore, Mead opens up possibilities for thinking about timeless time in a way that creates opportunities for the intentional, and possibly democratic, reconstruction of the future. While Castells provides a significant interpretation of the contemporary experience of time, his interpretation leaves little space for the meaningful transformation of societies governed by this experience of time because of (1) its supposed randomness in which present, past, and future are experienced without the necessary connection; and (2) that this randomness effectively eliminates the significance of a shapeable future (Wilkie 2011, 87–88). Mead's philosophy of temporality has a distinctive advantage on this front over Castells's because Mead's analysis of the present also incorporates what he refers to as "emergence" and "sociality," allowing me to avoid these troubles.

## THE GARDEN MYTH

Before turning to Castells and Mead, a few general comments about postmodern time-experience are in order. Once again, Lyotard provides a very clear overview of the historicity underlying modernity and how postmodernity differs from this. He identifies four major characteristics to this sort of historicity, most of which are significant here. The most vital is the eschatological structure of modern metanarratives. These narratives are, at base, salvation stories. As Lyotard puts it: "Eschatology recounts the experience of a subject affected by a lack, and prophesies that this experience will finish at the end of time with the remission of evil, the destruction of death, and *the return to the Father's house*, that is, to the full signifier" (Lyotard 1997, 96. Emphasis mine). Here we see the basic pattern of Fall, suffering, and redemption. For reasons which will be explored further in the following chapter, I refer to this a "the Garden myth." The subject enters the story possessing a lack, an absence that drives them forward in an attempt to fill it. In the core Garden myth, this begins with Adam and Eve being exiled from the Garden, and faced with suffering and mortality (a lack of the perfect existence within Eden, yet not lacking a memory of it). There is then the prophecy, the promise, of a return, though here a number of differences emerge between variations on the myth. Is it a return of a people to the Father's house, what I refer to as "the Garden?" Individual salvation? Does the subject await the return to the Garden or does the subject play an active role in the return? When one moves beyond the Christian tradition, these differences regarding the specifics of the prophecy multiply further. While Lyotard acknowledges that his framing of the metanarrative here is in Christian terms, he defends this by arguing that "over countless episodes, lay modernity maintains this temporal device . . . which *promises* at the end to reconcile the subject with itself and the overcoming of its separation" (Lyotard 1997, 97. Emphasis original). Throughout a variety of modern projects, such as the

Enlightenment, Romanticism, Marxism, etc., one finds that "an immemorial past is always what turns out to be promised by way of an ultimate end. It is essential for the modern imaginary to project its legitimacy forward while founding it in a lost origin" (Lyotard 1997, 97–98). Take as an example a rather unsophisticated interpretation of Marxism. Throughout the process of class struggle, culminating in the (apocalyptic?) conflict between the proletariat and the bourgeoisie, humanity finally achieves the Communist Utopia foretold by Marx and Engels. In resolving the contradictions of capitalism and overthrowing the bourgeoisie, the communists establish a perfect society where humans are emancipated from alienation and oppression. That is, the Garden, but recast in terms of labor. At a structural level, a simplistic reading of Francis Fukuyama's claim from 1989 that "the end of history" had arrived with the fall of communism follows this basic pattern as well. These cursory examples suggest this basic pattern of Fall, suffering and redemption underlies much of European philosophy. The details vary remarkably: the necessity of the Fall as a discrete phase (as opposed to beginning in a state of suffering), the degree of agency humans possess to achieve redemption (it is up to humans or are humans mere agents of historical forces?), and the sort of redemption dreamed of (too numerous to list). Even with this caveat, the fundamentals of the Garden myth persist.

Postmodernity breaks with modernity's historicity in the following ways. First, "history is in no way directed toward the horizon of an emancipation" (Lyotard 1997, 98). Rather, what Lyotard illustrates with his fable is a history of change that is not guided by liberation in any typical sense. What he charts in the fable is a physical history of different formations of energy in a constant struggle against entropy. While this is something of a goal, it is not a *telos* in any grand eschatological sense. Postmodernism is not predicated on emancipation. Instead, it merely involves a series of diachronic changes. In contrast to the metanarratives of modernism, postmodernism relies, or should only rely, on mere narratives. The prime motivation for the metanarratives is a return to fullness. Returning to the Christian version of the Garden myth, this restoration involves a return to the Father's house from which the subject had been exiled. The source of the subject's suffering is that they no longer live within the Garden, but they now exist in something outside of their fallen world. Postmodern narratives make no appeal to the Garden, at least in any affirmative way. Instead, everything within the narrative should be contained with the world itself. It is a bounded infinity after all. Hence, the reason Lyotard emphasizes physical histories of increasing complexity. This makes no appeal to some external concept or metric to determine progress. Complexity is only constrained by the physical parameters of the universe, and within some contexts, such as language, an almost infinite degree of complexity is achievable. This is in contrast to political emancipation (whether communist or liberal democrat) or the Return of Christ, which marks the achievement of history (better: History).

Second, the future "is not an object of hope. Hope is what belongs to a subject of history who promises him/herself—or to who has been promised—a final perfection" (Lyotard 1997, 99). This follows because the subject, knowing that a return to the Father's house is now impossible, the possibility of hope, understood here as a genuine expectation for redemption (e.g., in the Christian tradition, the Return of Christ and life everlasting), is impossible. Such hope is only made possible by God or some other metaphysical fiction. Yet, if God is abandoned, then the subject cannot be promised such a redemption. In the context of this fable, the universe is nothing more than a struggle between extropy (energy) and entropy, in which energy seeks to at least preserve itself (if not expand), while entropy seeks to prevent just this. Humans is no "final perfection" or "redemption" awaiting us. In light of this, Lyotard's fable appears rather pessimistic. Such an interpretation is problematic in part because if this essay is read in conjunction with his earlier "Answer to the Question: What is Postmodernism?" (Lyotard 1993a, 1–16) this dismalness shifts. Here he is concerned there with the distinction between modernism and postmodernism in the arts. He positions both as different ways are one, ultimately transitory, instantiation of this conflict. Humans should hope for nothing, because there to present the sublime, the unpresentable. What distinguishes the modern artist from the postmodern is their attitude toward the unpresentable. The modernist falls into melancholy, because the modern aesthetic "is nostalgic; it allows the unpresentable to be invoked only as an absent content" (Lyotard 1993a, 14). On the other hand, postmodern aesthetics revels in the unpresentable: "The postmodern . . . refuses the consolation of correct forms, refuses the consensus of taste permitting a common experience of nostalgia . . . and inquires into new presentations . . . to better produce the feeling that there is something unpresentable" (Lyotard 1993a, 15). The pull of the Garden myth is the longing for the Garden, while realizing its absence in a fallen world. The postmodern responds to this absence through playing with its unpresentability. It seeks not to present something beyond, but to experiment with demonstrating its very unpresentability.

At this point, we begin to see several different possible meanings to the end of history. The first comes from Francis Fukuyama (1992), where the end of history is the triumph of liberal capitalist democracy over possible rivals. Another comes from Jean Baudrillard (1994): a society of simulation built on the wreckage of metaphysics. Then there is Lyotard's own sense of playfulness at the end of history, which lacks the pessimism that can follow from Baudrillard. Regardless of which of these we follow, a time-consciousness quite different from modernism emerges. Modernist metanarratives require a future, because the Garden is what always awaits the subject at the end of history. Whether because history's end has been achieved or we have come to live in a truly nihilistic end times, one might say with Lyotard "the future is no longer an object of hope." In the case of the more optimistic option Fukuyama presented, the future cannot be hoped for because it is already here. On either Lyotard's or Baudrillard's account, there is no future because of the abandonment of the metanarratives that made the future necessary.

Clearly, this is all something of an overstatement, one that Fukuyama (2012) would agree with. The future is still an object of expectations, if not hope. As argued earlier, modernist narratives might not have the sway they once did, but something descended them remain potent. One can glimpse this in some writings on the posthuman and transhumanist arguments in favor of overcoming humanity (Best and Kellner 2001, 149–204; Hayles 1999; Pastor and Garcí 2014). While concerns with emancipation have been coopted by Lyotard's System, the future remains important as it allows for progress, specifically technological progress. Yet, technological progress is ambiguous in terms of its status as a metanarrative. There are definite aspects here of a narrative of emancipation, but without the metaphysical baggage of traditional modernist metanarratives. Rather at its base, technological progress relies on performativity for its legitimation that makes it a rather different creature, one more at home within postmodernity.

Now, it is tempting to write off "the end of history" as just ideological claptrap. And, as Lutz Niethammer (1992) shows, there is good reason to be highly critical of the concept. Yet, to dismiss this altogether is a definite mistake. Niethammer traces the concept of the end of history back to one of its sources, Hegel, whose philosophy profoundly shaped the contours of postmodern philosophy.[1] Beyond the philosophical origins, this end of history is also bound up with the deep-seated material changes I discussed in earlier chapters. While this is not wholly new, as the complex information disseminated through sub-Saharan African drumming illustrates (Gleick 2011, 13–27), the scale, speed, and complexity of communication in the present is increased compared to earlier information and communication technologies (ICTs). This is one part of what I referred to earlier as "time-space compression." A number of different technologies allow for distances to be covered increasingly quickly. I have emphasized ICTs throughout, but these are not the only relevant technologies. Transportation technologies play an important role as well. Over the course of centuries, humans could move more rapidly through animals, followed by railroads, cars, and airplanes. The capacity for some humans to travel greater distances at a faster rate effectively shrunk the world. It is this phenomenon that led Marx to declare: "Capital by its very nature drives beyond every spatial barrier. Thus the creation of the physical conditions of exchange—the means of communication and transport—the annihilation of space through time" (Marx 1973, 524). This insight led

Marxists like Harvey to emphasize how capitalism relies on sets of spatial fixes to keep ahead of the contradictions inherent within it (Harvey 1990). These same technologies cause time to undergo profound changes as well, including feeding into the claim that history has ended.

## DEFINING TIMELESS TIME

Manuel Castells builds upon many of Harvey's insights and, in doing so, presents a more radical version of them, which Castells calls "timeless time." He defines it as having "no past and no future. Not even the short-term past. It is the cancellation of sequence, thus of time, by the compression or blurring of sequence" (Castells 2013, 50). Because Castells offers one of the more sustained and empirically nuanced descriptions, an analysis of timeless time provides both a way of understanding contemporary experience of temporality and the problems posed by this experience. The blurring of past and future, through the elimination of sequencing of time that Castells describes, reflects a society in which deep-seated change becomes difficult to realize, especially if achieved through democratic means. What makes Castells's work preferable over more conventional postmodern theorists is his empirical approach. While there are important similarities between Castells's timeless time and the work of theorists like Baudrillard, Castells seeks to ground his analysis in empirical data which (a) prevents the occasional flights of fancy some postmodernists fall into and (b) makes it more difficult to simply dismiss.

The concept of "timeless time" plays a significant role in Manuel Castells's account of "the network society." The general drift of his three-volume work, *The Information Age*, is that "[n]etworks constitute the new social morphology of our societies, and the diffusion of networking logic substantially modifies the operation and outcomes in processes of production, experience, power, and culture" (Castells 2010a, 500). In the course of exploring how a networked society emerges from earlier social organization, he proposes that new forms of time emerge. On the one hand, there is "glacial time," which is "a slow-motion time that human perception assigns to the evolution of the planet. It is sequential time, but moving so slowly . . . that it seems to be eternal" (Castells 2010a, xlii). On the other hand, timeless time exists only in the immediate instant, with no necessary linkage to the past or future. This concept echoes a number of postmodern discussions of temporality, and Castells does make a few references to postmodern theorists (like Harvey's *The Condition of Postmodernity* [1990] and Jean Baudrillard's [1995] analysis of the Gulf War), but Castells largely seeks to build his analysis out of an empirical analysis of an investigation of social reality, rather than a metatheoretical discussion. As he puts it: "This is not a book about books. While relying on evidence of various sorts, and on analyses from multiple sources, it does not intend to discuss theories" (Castells 2010a, 25). This allows him to avoid some of the pitfalls of more traditional postmodern theorists. Many of the classic postmodern theorists (e.g., Baudrillard, Derrida, and to some extent Lyotard) tend to make scant references to material practices, and can fall into the excesses criticized earlier. Instead, these theorists tend to emphasis semiotics and textuality. Castells goes in a different direction, building his analysis of timeless time out of looking at the social transformations brought about by the use of technologies like information and communication technologies. The following discussion illustrates the difference between Castells and less materially oriented theorists:

> The relationship to time is defined by the use of information and communication technologies in a relentless effort to annihilate time by negating sequencing: on one hand, by compressing time (as in split-second global financial transactions or the generalized practice of multitasking, squeezing more activity into a given time); on the other hand, by blurring the sequence of social practices, including past, present, and future in a random order, like in the electronic hypertext of Web 2.0, or the blurring of life-cycle patterns in both work and parenting. (Castells 2013, 35)

Castells's emphasis on ICTs and other technologies at once provides a sociological account of many postmodern themes, like time-space compression, the end of history, and fragmentation while avoiding either the flights of fancy some postmodern theorists are accused of, or their sometimes nihilistic metaphysics. The movement toward timeless time is a direct consequence of the increased reliance on ICTs and other technologies like birth control and other pharmaceuticals.

At the core of timeless time is the "[e]limination of sequencing [which] creates undifferentiated timing, thus annihilating time" (Castells 2010b, 183). Within timeless time, the previously normal sequence of events can be disrupted, often in radical ways. For example, such eliminations "may take the form of compressing the occurrence of phenomena, aiming at instantaneity (as in 'instant wars,' or split-second financial transactions), or else by introducing random discontinuity in the sequence (as in the hypertext of integrated, electronic media communications)" (Castells 2010b, 183). This quotation hints at the important role technology plays, especially ICTs, in making time timeless. With respect to ICTs, two important features are noted. First, the effective instantaneity of contemporary ICTs feeds into the compression of time. Earlier communication technologies, like the various older forms of the written word, required greater amounts of time to convey messages over distance. This begins to change with the telegraph, telephone, radio, and television, where information could be transmitted more quickly over a given distance, and each technology marks an increase in the amount of information able to be easily transmitted, as well as the speed at which it is transmitted. Contemporary ICTs, like computers and smartphones, accelerate this trend to a greater extent, given the increased seamlessness of communication networks and the sheer amount of information available through platforms like the Internet. If time with respect to information networks is a function of distance, then referring to the increased speed of communication as "time-compression" is not far off the mark. Second, given the nonlinear interactions with content that ICTs foster, content no longer need be sequential in nature. Media like television, music, and film are profoundly changed. For example, the move toward online music platforms, be it iTunes or streaming music services, can transform the experience of listening to music. More traditional music media, whether live performances, LPs, or even the radio, possessed something of an intrinsic ordering (both chronologically between pieces and within a set of pieces) that the listener had less or no control over. Now, music can be consumed as the listener desires, without concern for ordering, like with the shuffle feature on a sufficiently large music library or the ability to download/stream only desired tracks instead of an entire album. Television exhibits some similar patterns, especially with the rise of DVRs and on-demand services. Instead of the viewer needing to be present at a specific, preordained time to watch a program, they are able to watch anything they have recorded (or have access to) in whatever order, at whatever time they desire. The phenomenon of "binge watching" does reintroduce a certain linearity into the experience, but such linearity is still imposed by the viewer on the program (it is their convenience or interest that determines what and when they watch, rather than the program enforcing the linearity on the viewer). Lastly, with the vast amount of information available on the Internet, combined with the use of hyperlinks, browser tabs, and search engines, the phenomenon of web surfing can be as linear or nonlinear as the user desires. A user might simply follow the links, usually linearly arranged, that websites provide, or instead hop from site to site to site with no necessary order. The latter is one of the more extreme forms of "random discontinuity in sequence" available at the present. These quick examples help to demonstrate both how timeless time arises from ICTs and the profound transformation that it exerts, in particular on popular culture.

Echoing Charles Baudelaire's definition of the modernity, Castells describes the network society as "*a culture at the same time of the eternal and the ephemeral.* It is eternal because it reaches back and forth to the whole sequence of cultural expressions. It is ephemeral because each arrangement, each specific sequencing, depends on the context and purpose under which any given cultural construct is solicited. We are not a culture of circularity, but a universe of undifferentiated temporality of cultural expressions" (Castells 2010a, 492. Emphasis original). ICTs allow for the (relatively) easy availability of the vast majority of human culture artifacts or reproductions of those artifacts. This provides the "eternal" dimension because these artifacts are all presented and without a necessary chronology. Yet, because there is no longer a necessary order to the artifacts, they can be re-presented anew each time. The ever-shifting context of these re-presentations prevents any sense of permanence, hence the ephemerality of culture. The example of cultural production illustrates the more general consequences of timeless time, that time is destroyed "by disordering the sequence of events and making them simultaneous in the communication networks, thus installing society in structural ephemerality: *being* cancels *becoming*" (Castells 2013, 35. Emphasis original). Castells's conclusion here, that being now cancels becoming, might seem counterintuitive, especially in light of so much postmodern theorizing. That noted, given the ways in which the network society dissolves time through simultaneity and the negation of sequencing, that being should trump becoming follows inasmuch as there is no space for "becoming" to open into. Rather, because timeless time is the time of what I referred to earlier as a "bounded infinite," there can only be a constant reshuffling of elements within being. While containing an infinite number of objects, the infinite is still of a fixed size. There is nothing beyond it. This precludes a sense of becoming, because there is no place for the change to occur, at least in the sense of genuine change which would reshape the fundamentals of society.

This is not to imply that time in the present is only experienced as timeless time. Although Castells devotes less space to exploring the matter, "clock time" and "biological time" remain significant. Depending on one's position in the network society, labor can be more or less structured by clocks and other schedules like the workweek. Inasmuch as humans continue to live as embodied beings, biological time also remains important. While birth control and in vitro fertilization allow women to exert more control when, or if, they reproduce, and other bio-medical technologies provide the possibility for some humans to increasingly forestall death, humans are still creatures that are born, live, die, and need to eat and sleep. Timeless time does not so much do away with these older forms of time, but rather restructures them. Certain aspects of human biological time remain unchanged, but the rhythms do not necessarily remain the same. Such transformations are not always seamless and can lead to dissonance when these different times overlap and interfere with each other. Yet, inasmuch as other experiences of time persist, Castells is unequivocal that timeless time now dominates biological and clock times. What we find, then, on the one hand is that an experience of time that is eternal and random. On the other, when considered at a material level, this is not a total triumph of desequenced time because other sorts of time persist (albeit in different forms), specifically biological and clock times. While timeless time has transformed aspects of the biological time of human life, that humans are organisms that grow, eat, and wear down remains.

## MEAD'S PRESENT

Before launching into my exploration of Mead's philosophy of time, I will give a brief explanation about my idiosyncratic reading of Mead. In his articles like "The Nature of the Past" and drafts like *The Philosophy of the Present*, Mead wrestles with developing a pragmatic interpretation of relativity and its significance for understanding temporality and history. In these works, he engages the philosophy of Alfred North Whitehead, Einsteinian relativity, and Minkowskian space-time. Two additional issues further muddy the general difficulty of this terrain. First, do the texts that we possess on the subject represent Mead's final work on it? Are these texts internally coherent? Such a question can be raised about the work of many philosophers, but here the question is particularly acute. Mead's most sustained treatment of the subject is *The Philosophy of The Present*, based on his 1930 Carus Lectures. According to Arthur Murphy, the book's editor, "the lectures were written hurriedly, in large part on the journey from Chicago to Berkeley" (Murphy in Mead 2002, 7). Unfortunately, Mead died shortly after giving the lectures, without having had the chance to revise them. Second, and beyond the issue of the texts themselves, is the adequacy of his interpretation of relativity (Cook 1993, 159; Joas 1997, 169–70). These are both serious issues. And I will ignore all of them. Rather than approaching Mead's philosophy of time as he intended it, my reconstruction will use Mead's texts as a way to reorient the contemporary experience of time. The concern here is not whether Mead adequately explains the underpinnings of the reality of time, but whether his philosophy can be used as a tool for reconstructing the present experience of time in a way that avoids the problems raised by timeless time. To do this, I will focus on three decisive concepts from Mead: the present, sociality, and emergence. With these concepts, a way out of the temporal cul-de-sac comes into view.

Mead started by pointing out that "reality exists in a present." From this, Mead develops his account of time-consciousness. Given this, it should be clear that everything will be oriented around the present, including the past and future. The first thing to note is that Mead's conception of the present is not as a "knife's edge," which is to say that the present does not exists as a single, nigh infinitesimally short moment. Rather, it is a "specious present," possessing duration. "Durations are a continual slide of presents into each other" (Mead 2002, 57). As Berit Brogaard explains: "Rather, the 'specious present' stands for a genuine passage as it becomes stabilized in experience and gives rise to a present that has duration and thus includes past and future parts" (Brogaard 1999, 578). This sense of passage is not that of a metronome ticking away a particular beat. According to Mead, both the knife's edge present and the "metronomic" understanding of passage of time are abstractions based upon the experience of passage of time. Rather, the present's "chief reference is to the emergent event, that is, to the occurrence of something which is more than the processes that have led up to it and which by its change, continuance, or disappearance, adds to later passages a content they would not have otherwise have possessed" (Mead 2002, 52). This quotation raises two vital points. First, it is not the bare tick-tock that determines the passage that defines the present. Instead, passage is marked by an *event*. Each event is a unique happening that involves some sort of change. This leads to the second point.

An event is shaped by the past, but what occurs through this passage is also different from the past. In this sense, the event is *emergent* inasmuch as the present involves something more or less than the past. For this reason, Mead states: "Everything that is taking place takes place under necessary conditions. . . . [Yet] these conditions while necessary do not determine in its full reality that which emerges" (Mead 2002, 47). In this way, the past sets the stage for the emergent event, but there is the possibility of genuine novelty, a present that differs from the past. What marks the present *qua* present for Mead is that it possesses novelty. The present is defined by its difference from the past. In this way, in order for the present to be, it must possess some duration through which what is novel in the present comes about. The past establishes the conditions out of which the present emerges, but because the present must differ from the past, such conditions are only necessary, never sufficient. Furthermore, all that exists for Mead is this duration in which the present continually emerges from the past. The past itself does not exist in a substantive sense.

This is not to say that one has no access to the past. It is simply that the past can only exist within the present. Mead describes how in the following way: "*first*, to the evident fact that all the apparatus of the past, memory images, historical moments, fossil remains and the like are in some present, and, *second*, to that portion of the past which is there in passage in experience as determined by the emergent event" (Mead 2002, 54. Emphasis original). Seen from one angle, this must be the case because if the past was more than these apparatuses, it would either create a more "real" sort of past than Mead argues for or effectively be the same event as present all over again (which is to say that it would not be an event at all). Instead of these options, Mead argues that how individuals reconstruct an account of the past is always done from a particular perspective, informed by the present. This is in contrast to the naive ideal of telling a perfectly objective version of what occurred, which is a goal forever out of our grasp. What occurs in the present shapes how the past is understood. What is said of the past applies to the future to some extent. Both in a fundamental sense are "unreal," except inasmuch as they exist in the present. Where the past is reconstruction of previous events, futures provide ways of thinking about how to reconstruct the present. Like the past, these futures are built out of what is found in the present, but they are aimed toward what is not yet here. Futures become possible ways that individuals can guide or direct passage. Fundamental to both is that: "The pasts and the futures are implications of what is being undertaken and carried out in our laboratories" (Mead 2002, 107). Mead's use of "laboratory" here is ambiguous. The narrow reading of the word indicates that he refers to sites where science is performed. Alternatively, a more broad reading is any site of experimentation. I adopt this reading for reasons that I will return to at the conclusion of this chapter.

## NOW, "THE NOW"

Now to how Mead's analysis of the present helps to make sense of both timeless time, and to engage it more productively. Although each presents his work at a different level, Mead addressing questions of science and ontology, and Castells working at the level of social phenomena, there is a great deal of commonality between them. While Castells does not frame timeless time in terms of ontology, the center of ontological gravity is the present in a sense very close to Mead. The horizon of timeless time is that of "the perpetual now" because of the fusing of the eternal and ephemeral in "the network society." The sequencing of events becomes random, disrupting older assumptions about the past and future. Yet, because "the whole sequence of cultural expressions" is immediately available, history becomes infinitely compressed. This results in the "perpetual now." Up to this point, despite their different emphases, Mead and Castells agree on what constitutes the present. Both Mead and Castells argue that reality exists in the present, and both hold that the present is self-contained. All that is, is contained within the present. Furthermore, Mead and Castells agree that there is continual movement from one present to another. It is here that they begin to diverge. For Mead, the transition from one present to the next contains the possibility for humans to shape what emerges. Castells appears to forestall this possibility. The present involves transition, but a transition only into further transitions, without a logical sequence. Since the present, past, and future can be presented "randomly" (whatever this phrase might mean now), we are left only with a self-constituting, undifferentiated, aimless present. It is at this point that Mead provides tools to move beyond the seeming randomness of Castells.

There are two points of divergence between Mead and Castells with respect to transition: (a) the duration of the present; and (b) the random connections between presents. The question of duration addresses whether the present is a knife's edge or is specious. As argued earlier, Mead holds that the present does possess some duration, a duration determined by the emergent event. Castells's rhetoric implies that the present is a knife's edge, especially in his discussions of financial transactions and "instant wars." Yet, for all the talk of instantaneity, a look beneath the surface makes clear that timeless time does in fact possess duration (albeit very short in some places). In terms of financial transactions, these are best regarded as nearly instantaneous, but not quite. The ICTs powering much of contemporary financial markets do allow for the transfer of information, and thus money, at mind-boggling speeds. Yet, this speed is limited, if by nothing else by the speed of light. This is not some mere quibble, but has important consequences for the U.S. Stock Market. ICTs can perform an incredible number of calculations per second, and then transmit orders to buy and sell based on those calculations at the speeds ICT-users are accustomed to. But because of the constraint of the speed of light, physical proximity to the trading floor matters so those orders can be received a fraction of a nanosecond before orders from one's competitors are received. Such differences are phenomenologically unimaginable for humans, but are not quite instantaneous. A close reading of Castells's "instant wars" reveals similar results. His principal example in *The Rise of the Network Society* is that of the U.S.-led Gulf War in 1990–1991 and relies in part on Baudrillard's (1995) analysis. While this conflict was not "instant" in a literal sense, the heart of the operation, according to Castells, took roughly 100 hours (Castells 2010a, 484–91). The U.S.-led Iraq War, begun in 2003, continuing until 2011, and with some U.S. troops still operating there at the time this work is published, is somewhat longer in terms of "major combat operations," but still bears many traits of "instant wars" at least inasmuch as it has become part of the perpetual now. Rather than being literally instantaneous, Castells uses the concept to explain the experience of war within network societies. Such wars are taken as instant, even though they are not for those fighting them or that must live with consequences of these conflicts.

What we find in these examples is the appearance of a knife's edge present, but beneath this veneer, a specious present operates. These examples discussed above show that the aim is toward everything happening on the bleeding edge of a knife, utterly cut off from past and future. While the orientation of network societies might be toward the knife's edge present, there is a measurable duration, however small. These persistent specious presents are marked by the features defined by Mead: events occur within these passages, and the present is defined by some change, which then feeds into the following present. In this way, Mead provides a tool for going beyond the implied knife's edge of Castells. Yet, Castells is largely on target with the claim that being now cancels becoming. Three things drive this. First, while instantaneity might be an illusion, taken as an aim, it clearly structures how network societies think about time. Second, the profound changes discussed earlier through which contemporary networks allow for the almost-immediate digital access to much of human production, remains. Third, given the scope of these networks, and the complex internal interrelationships defining any given network, the movement from one present to the next can appear to be random. In this way, the spirit of Castells's analysis remains, even if the specific point about instantaneity cannot be maintained.

The second divergence between Mead and Castells involves the supposed randomness of timeless time. Both agree that any experience of past or future will be built up around this eternal present. While Castells is a good bit more radical in his account of how the past is constituted within the present, there is a commonality here. For both, the material from which "history" is composed (memories, testimonies, documents, etc.) appears as part of the present. For Mead, any attempt to reconstruct the past will always reflect the present, so a certain degree of selectivity, and perhaps even arbitrariness should be expected in any reconstruction. Timeless time exacerbates this tendency, in particular because of the centrality of ICTs. The experience of past in the present becomes radically more open-ended and nonlinear because ICTs allow for immediate access to most of the entirety of cultural expression. The core motif of reconstructing the past from materials found in, and in light of the interest of, the present remains. What differs is the material available. While in principle, any material can be used for reconstruction of the past, in practice Mead anticipates that the order of events will be relatively constrained. ICTs complicate this reconstruction because of the ease in which connections can be made between a seemingly infinite variety of materials, which is why Castells argued that there is an inherent randomness within timeless time. This randomness is why being cancels becoming. As I will argue further down, this random element, along with how it privileges *being* over *becoming*, is a point of serious disagreement between Mead and Castells.

## THE SOCIALITY OF THE PRESENT

It is Mead's concept of sociality that permits an escape from some of the perils of randomness and returns to the concept of becoming. Castells's work lacks the concept of sociality in anything like the way Mead understood the term. This is not to say that Castells ignores the social dimensions of time, because he is well aware of the degree to which the experience of time and space are always shaped by society (Castells 2010a, 460–65). Castells is quite clear that there is no meaningful presocial conception of time, a point on which he and Mead agree (Joas 1997, 188–92). The addition of timeless time to biological and clock times is a result of deep-seated changes in society, particularly technological changes. In one sense, Castells clearly incorporates sociality into timeless time because society is necessary to structure the experience of time. What Castells's analysis of timeless time lacks is Mead's distinctive conception of sociality. This feeds into an additional qualification. The reason that Castells does not incorporate this into his account is because, inasmuch as his work is a description of society, the network society represses to some extent a prominent role for Mead's sociality. The earlier discussion of the randomness of timeless time helps to illustrate this point. Everything is potentially open to constant, ad hoc re-presentation. While this sort of re-presentation is a social activity, inasmuch as it involves appropriating elements from others and then disseminating them via ICTs, this can be described as a "ludic" sort of sociality, where ludic sociality is more aimed at playfulness than any sort of democratic social action (Ebert 1996).

The rather general definition of sociality Mead relies upon in *The Philosophy of the Present* is: "The social character of the universe we find in the situation in which the novel event is in both the old order and the new which its advent heralds. Sociality is the capacity of being several things at once" (Mead 2002, 75). At a very general level, Mead proposes that the mark of the social is being part of different systems simultaneously. He argues that this definition applies to not only human social activity but also that of animals, and even the basic constituents of matter. When something is social, it is involved in multiple systems. In the statement quoted above, an event is social inasmuch as it is both part of the system that it emerges out of, and the new system that it generates. He illustrates sociality in a very different way with reference to animals, where a predatory animal is stalks its prey. The jungle and the prey are all part of the predator's social relations. With these different examples, it becomes clear is that there are two dimensions to sociality. "A system can conceivably be taken at an instant, and the social character of the individual member would in that instant be what it is because of the mutual relationship of all members. On the other hand, an object can be a member of two divergent systems only in passage, in which its nature in one system leads to the transformation which its passing into another system carries with it. In the passage itself it can be in both" (Mead 2002, 98). This characteristic of something being a part of multiple systems at once, either synchronically or diachronically, reinforces Hans Joas's statement that Mead understands society as an inherently social objective action-nexus. I introduced this in the last chapter, but what is new here is that Mead extends out the possible participants of the action-nexus. The present, whether for humans, animals, or atomic particles, is an action-nexus.

With this account of sociality in hand, the reconstruction of timeless time can begin. I start with the past. As noted earlier, previous presents, and the aspects of them that continue on into the present present, will place constraints on how the past is reconstructed. The legacy of the past continues on through the present, whether in memory or records. Because only the present is reality, these fragments, although sometimes quite significant, provide the means for interpreting the past. It should be remembered that this reconstruction becomes a part of the present and will also flow into the future. The past involves Mead's "sociality." Given this broad definition of sociality, the other reason why there are constraints on how history is assembled becomes clear. The past, like the present for Mead, is thoroughly social inasmuch as it involves many different overlapping entities. Especially because history, in its discursive sense, relies both on the historian, as well as other humans and Mead's "apparatuses of the past" ("memory images, historical moments, fossil remains," etc.), the reconstruction of the past in the present must be socially negotiated. To provide a pragmatically adequate account of the past, the account must balance all of these different social entities.

To state the obvious, the future will be different from the past because it has not happened yet. Although the conditions for the future are contained within the present, there is the possibility for genuine novelty in the future. In this way, the future is not wholly determined by the present. One source for this novelty is human activity. Being self-conscious organisms, humans have a capacity to actively mold the future. That is, humans can take the elements found in the present, and use them to participate in the creation of a novel event. Whereas Castells describes the transition from present to future as random, this is not wholly accurate in light of Mead. The transition might appear random, but this is a result of the extraordinary volume of materials from which to shape the future. ICTs allow access to an incredibly wide range of means that humans can re-present in order to form different futures. Given this, and other social changes associated with timeless time, a wider possible selection of means can be used to fashion the future. Rather than being necessarily random, instead this opens new opportunities for possible futures. More artifacts, ideas, voices, etc., can be brought together in order to create futures out of the present. Castells obscures this in his discussions of timeless time because he fails to adequately incorporate human activity into sociality. These transitions result from human social activity. If one minimizes this activity, then the transitions between past, present, and future are effectively random. From Mead's perspective, these are the products of human sociality and within the sphere of human control.

## RECONSTRUCTING THE PRESENT

What is then necessary is to reconstruct the use of the technologies of timeless time in light of this new understanding of sociality. As discussed above, there are two troubling features about timeless time. First is the rather random ways in which the past, present, and future are experienced. Second, the future *qua* future becomes irrelevant because time is now undifferentiated. For reasons articulated by both Mead and a number of postmodern philosophers, returning to a more conventional conception of time and history is inadvisable, assuming such a thing is possible. Many postmodern philosophers will go further in criticizing modernist time-consciousness because of its problematic political implications (especially with respect to questions of difference). Mead does not propose the abandonment of past and future in favor of some sort of ludic present, which timeless time appears to reside. Rather, Mead's conception of the present as a social, durational passage is ideally suited for the particular fluidity of timeless time, while also incorporating into it the space for the construction of past and, more importantly, possible futures. Mead puts the point well when describing the virtues of his approach:

> This view then frees us from bondage to either the past or the future. We are neither creatures of the necessity of an irrevocable past, nor of any vision given in the Mount. Our history and our prognostications will be sympathetic with the undertakings within which we live and move and have our being. Our values lie in the present, and past and future give us only the schedule of the means, and the plans of campaign, for their realization. (Mead 2002, 108)

Timeless time follows from a complex set of social, particularly technological, changes. As I argue above, Mead's account of the present fits very well with timeless time inasmuch as both make the present the focus of reality. What Mead's writings on temporality add to this is a way to bring back in concepts of past and future. In particular, Mead moves beyond the rather thin conception of sociality at work in timeless time, society as mental (or electronic) presentations, toward a more robust vision of society as an action-nexus involving social individuals taking part in multiple systems. The future is necessary in order to transform the present, at least in a deliberate, and hopefully deliberative, way. By interpreting the future as part of the present, Mead makes plain that the future is shaped by social individuals through their social actions. Mead makes this plain is the conclusion of *The Philosophy of the Present*:

> We live always in a present whose past and whose future are the extension of the field within which its undertakings may be carried out. The present is the scene

of that emergence which gives always new heavens and a new other.... Since society has endowed use with self-consciousness, we can enter personally into the largest undertakings which the intercourse of rational selves extends before us. And because we can live with ourselves as well as with others, we can criticize ourselves, and make our own the values in which we are involved through those undertakings in which the community of all rational beings is engaged. (Mead 2002, 108–9)

The task from here is taking seriously the promise of Mead's philosophy of time and using it as a tool for the reconstruction of the technologies that foster timeless time. Rather than assuming these technologies produce a random, desequenced time, the first step in such a reconstruction involves foregrounding the role of human social activity in the constant construction of new presents. ICTs and other technologies that feed into timeless time appear to create a random eternal now, but only appears this way because of a misunderstanding. These technologies open up a new, and oftentimes bewildering, array of possibilities. Yet, in light of Mead's sociality, the linking of experiences need not be random. Instead, they are the result of humans' continual reconstruction of the present. By emphasizing the significance of human social activity, it becomes possible to reconstruct timeless time in a way that encourages the sort of creative and democratic intelligence Mead and other pragmatists value.

A theme raised earlier re-enters at this point. Castells falls into a trap because of his treatment of embodiment. Officially, Castells is well aware of the importance of embodiment, and includes technologies that reshape biology, like birth control, among those that create timeless time. Yet, his analyses of ICTs accept the standard disembodied image of these technologies. Given the centrality of ICTs to his account of the rise of the Network Society, both *The Information Age* trilogy and especially in more recent works like *Communication Power*, this leaves Castells in an awkward place. While contemporary technologies do challenge the experience of time that dominated most of human history, we remain embodied creatures, with requirements like eating, sleeping, and so on. And as shown in chapter 4, even when social interactions occur at a distance via ICTs, there are still embodied beings engaging in the interaction. Although these devices have properties that allow for distinctly different sorts of engagement, such as the nonlinearity Castells describes, these technologies are tools for facilitating communication and other actions of embodied creatures. By downplaying embodiment, the role of action becomes increasingly murky. Such accounts risk returning to the weightlessness of Borgmann and Dreyfus because it leads to an appearance that nothing more is occurring than the exchange of bits. In spite of Castells's attempts to address politics through the lens of timeless time (Castells 2012), it is unclear how this can meaningfully occur given the lightness of disembodied action and the aleotric nature of timeless time. His later work presents a way to avoid the former criticism by holding that "power relationships . . . are largely constructed in people's minds through communication processes" (Castells 2013, xix). The price of such a move is returning to the concept of sociality that Mead and other pragmatists argued against, and without having addressed the decisive role of randomness in timeless time.

Despite the excesses of Castells's thought, the broad outlines of timeless time captures the dominant experience of time within postmodernity. With qualifications, Castells is on the right track when he notes: "The time of history, and of historical identities, fades in a world in which only immediate gratification matters, and where the end of history is proclaimed by the bards of the victors" (Castells 2013, 50–51). The claim about "historical identities" fading is clearly shakier than the rest, given the persistence of nationalism and fundamentalism, though both Harvey and Lyotard provide explanations for this. Chapter 2 addressed how Lyotard's concepts explained the persistence of fundamentalism. In the context of criticizing the claims of postmodernism, Giles Lipovetsky points out that the past becomes an object of consumption through the "heritage industry." "From the museum of pancakes to the museum of the sardine, from the Elvis Presley museum to the museum of the Beatles, hypermodern society belongs to an age where everything is made into part of our heritage and duly commemorated" (Lipovetsky 2005, 57). In a different context, Harvey sees this as part and parcel of postmodernity, where the reentrenchment of the local is simply flipside of postmodern globalization, hence still part of postmodernity (Harvey 1990, 85–88). That Harvey is correct in this is supported by understanding postmodernity as being a bounded infinite where everything, including all of the apparatuses of the past are contained within it, and the possibility of turning to fundamentalism as a response to the collapse of metanarratives. The trajectory of my analysis here helps to illustrate the logic of the following statement from Jameson: "It is safest to grasp the concept of the postmodern as an attempt to think the present historically in an age that has forgotten how to think historically in the first place" (Jameson 1991, ix). Those living within postmodernity seek to make sense of it as part of the flow of history, but lacks the ability to because of how technology and other material practices make thinking historically increasingly difficult. This failure to be able to think historically follows directly from the account of postmodernity I presented, from the bounded infinite and the demise of metanarratives through technology to timeless time.

It is this experience of time that requires reconstruction. As hinted at throughout this chapter and the rest of this work, timeless time cannot be simply wished away. Like postmodernity more generally, it is the result of a lengthy history that must be worked through rather than pushed aside. The modernist desire for a radical break, the revolution where everything starts anew, is but a dream. Expecting that it might be possible to push aside the present experience of time in favor of some other possibility is a variation on this dream. Instead, what is necessary is transforming the situation through a reform of human activities. This is why I placed so much emphasis throughout on technology: it is one place where postmodern motifs become visible and are then open to inquiry. The starting point for reconstructing these technologies in light of such problems is to frame the matter in terms of habits. Framing matters as habits is important for three reasons. First, habits keep the dimensions of embodiment front and center because habits belong to embodied creatures. Habits do not exist in and of themselves, even mental habits. Second, habits are mutable. They are not hardwired, even though some might be rather challenging to change. Exactly how they can be changed depends on the habit in question, and how it is connected to things like human biology and society. There ultimately will be limits on how much a habit can be changed because of the constitution of the human body, even if these limits are not known in advance. Third, and most importantly for many pragmatists, because habits can be shaped, keeping in mind the possibility of limits, it possible to cultivate habits that foster particular values like what I referred to, following Hickman, as "creative intelligence." Finding ways to cultivate this intelligence will play a decisive role in the remaining chapters as a way to work through the postmodern condition.

## NOTE

1. Richard Bernstein also makes this case very clearly. See Bernstein 1992, especially 305–19.

*Chapter 6*
# Pragmatism and the Garden

In the introduction, I argued that postmodernity is best understood conceptually in terms of the bounded infinite. In chapter 2, I show how this image links up to Lyotard's description of the postmodern as the demise of metanarratives. While metanarratives have consistently faced criticism, both about the merit of particular metanarratives and their overall viability, once the metaphorical shift from an unbounded to bounded infinite occurred, reliance on these metanarratives becomes all but untenable, unless supported by "terror." From there, I sought to work out the consequences of these ideas by looking at technology. Through careful examination of how postmodern motifs work themselves out through technology, specifically information and communication technologies, I demonstrated why it is that that the concept of "postmodern" remains quite valuable. The assumption at work throughout is that the transition to the bounded infinite is not something that can be simply undone. For example, given the way that technology has reshaped lives, turning back the clock to modernity and all its associated assumptions is impossible. What Dewey wrote in the wake of the bombings of Hiroshima and Nagasaki holds true here as well: "The scientific and industrial revolutions are not the kind of revolutions that go backward. It is idle to suppose that exhortations, addressed chiefly to the emotions, will create subjection to abstract moral principles. The impotency of this method is evident; it has lost the support of the traditions, customs, and institutions which once gave it whatever efficacy it possessed" (LW15.201). If my appropriation of Dewey is correct here, then modernism is out of joint with the present because of the transition to postmodernity. In which case, instead of longing for an infinitely unbound world, it is necessary to turn instead toward figuring out how to live within a bounded infinite.

Of course, how to do this remains an open question, and a difficult one. As I have stated throughout, postmodern theorists have a tendency to fall into ludism: a cheerful, carefree playfulness. While Terry Eagleton (1996), Teresa Ebert (1996), and David Harvey (1990) might overstate their critiques of postmodernism on this front, and downplay or ignore altogether the ethical and political writings of postmodern thinkers, the rejection of grand narratives in favor of smaller-scale stories does make more traditional ethical and political discourse a problem, at the least. Yet, simply returning to the hallmarks of modernism as a way to avoid these difficulties of postmodernism amounts to ignoring the problem at best. At worst, it uses the concept of emancipation as a tool of terror.

This chapter seeks to address the question of how to work through the challenge of postmodernity without falling into difficulties of either traditional modernism or postmodernism. Lyotard remains useful here inasmuch as the Garden myth discussed in chapter 5 describes the basic logic of metanarratives. Given that both returning to modernity and embracing postmodern gestures of radically breaking with metanarratives will fail, it is necessary to find clues for how to work through this myth more effectively. I follow the leads of Richard Rorty and Donna Haraway, both of whom provide important insights about how to transform the Garden myth such that it avoids the traps of classical modernism. These clues provide the start of a pragmatic reconstruction of the Garden myth, one that preserves a place for emancipation, but without relying on the standard structure of a metanarrative. By appropriating James's meliorism and Dewey's democratic intelligence, I will be able to sketch a response to these serious problems inherent in postmodern ludism. The conclusion will then turn to post-postmodern theorists an argue that there attempts to shift terrain is at best premature and at worst falls into the troubles with either modernism or postmodernism.

## PLAYING IN THE GARDEN?

As previously mentioned, all of the basic elements of Enlightenment metanarratives can be found within Christianity. The myth can be summarized this way: God ejects humanity from the Garden of Eden with the promise of a return to it when certain conditions are met. While this might be implicit in his discussion of metanarratives in *The Postmodern Condition*, Lyotard is much clearer about it his "A Postmodern Fable" (Lyotard 1997, 83–102). He writes of the exile from the Father's House, what I refer to as the Garden, and the promise of a return. Now, if one is as thoroughgoing as possible in their postmodern skepticism, then this metanarrative, *and everything associated with it*, should be held at bay as well. Most importantly, this requires incredulity about the concept of God, since this concept plays the most crucial role within the metanarrative. Here then is the clue: if one is incredulous about God, then one should be incredulous about the Garden myth as well. It is God that ejects the subject from the Garden. If there is no God, then there cannot be a Garden either. Central to modernism is the expectation of the return to the Garden, the fulfillment of history. What Enlightenment modernism did was replace the concept of the Christian Heaven with some secular Garden, represented variously by Condorcet's vision of a rational society, Marx's communist utopia, or Fukuyama's liberal democratic capitalism. The structure of these stories is fundamentally the same; only the names have been changed. The core metanarrative at work in modernity, what I refer to as the Garden myth, depends on God, the Father, or some further variation on this concept. It is God that allows history to be a story of emancipation in which the subject can finally return to completeness. When God, regardless of guise, is abandoned, the possibility of the return to the Garden becomes impossible.

Lyotard is useful here if for no other reason than providing a reasonably clear way to frame this connection between God and the desire to return to the Garden, the Father's house. He is less useful on how to address the postmodern condition. We are left with a hopeless, yet endlessly playful, existence. His few normative hints in the conclusion of *The Postmodern Condition* leave few satisfied (Best and Kellner 1991, 171–80; Ebert 1996, 182–208; Harvey 1990, 357–58; Rorty 1991, 211–22). There he rejects appeals to consensus in favor of an undefined appeal to "justice." This is followed by opening up data banks so that everyone has access of information in order to proliferate language-games. Much like his quip about the then-president of France Giscard d'Estaing whose goal was to keep up with Germans: "it is not exactly a life goal" (Lyotard 1984, 15). While his other writings, in particular *The Differend* (1988), make such a vision more sophisticated and continues to accept the demise of Garden, for those who at once accept the Death of God and the necessity of addressing the ethical/political challenges of the present, Lyotard offers little that would transform the status quo. On the one hand, Lyotard is clearly correct in demonstrating the tie between the incredulity toward God and the necessity of the Garden myth, as well as the difficulties entailed by abandoning the Garden. On the other hand, Lyotard's own solution to this situation, playing with the absence rather than longing to fill in the absence, appears to do little to remedy the problem. It is thus necessary to look elsewhere for philosophical tools to reconstruct the postmodern condition.

## MURDERING THE FATHER

A different vision comes from Richard Rorty. From *Philosophy and the Mirror of Nature* (1979) on, he dealt with many of themes making up the postmodern constellation. One piece where he directly approaches something similar to the Garden myth is his "Pragmatism as Anti-Authoritarianism." He argues that one of pragmatism's greatest accomplishments is its extension of certain anti-authoritarian tendencies of the Enlightenment. The Enlightenment sought to develop morality, not as "a matter of correspondence to the will of a Divine Being" (Rorty 2006, 257), but in a secular way. Likewise, pragmatism rejects standard correspondence theories of truth, where knowledge-claims attempt to correctly represent an independently existing Nature or Reality. Much like the Enlightenment criticized the presumed authority of the Divine, so too does pragmatism reject the authority of Nature or Reality. Of the classical pragmatists, Dewey went the furthest down this path by claiming: "whole-hearted pursuit of the democratic ideal requires us to set aside *any* authority save that of a consensus of our fellow human beings" (Rorty 2006, 257. Emphasis original). In this way, the community should resist subjugation to any authority outside of the community itself. This removes the burden of the concept of Sin, which Rorty describes as "the paradigm of subjection to such authority" (Rorty 2006, 257). In Rorty's view, Sin comes about where individuals accept that they must live in accordance with each and every dictate of the Divine Will and feel deeply disturbed when they fall short of these prescriptions. Rorty is quick to note that Dewey does find acts of deception to be vicious, not because it is a Sin against the intrinsic nature of Reality, but because they interfere with the democratic community. So, on this interpretation, epistemic and ethical norms are justified not by appeals to some authoritarian Other that exists beyond the human, but by the democratic community itself.

For my purposes here, it is Rorty's concluding section of "Anti-Authoritarianism" that is most interesting. There he draws a curious parallel between pragmatic anti-authoritarianism and Sigmund Freud's (1967) final book *Moses and Monotheism*. In that work, Freud argues: "social cooperation emerges from parricide, from the murder of the primal father by the primal band of brothers" (Rorty 2006, 263). Summarizing Freud's story quickly: the brothers first work together in order to kill their father. In the aftermath, bickering ensues between them as they struggle for power. In time, the brothers realize the pointlessness of this conflict. So, in order to settle this dispute, they form what amounts to a social contract. At the heart of this contract is a substitute for the primal Father, a totem (like a feared animal). This totem is then worshiped as a guardian, but the murder of the father is ritually reenacted during regular festivals as a reminder of the brothers' accomplishment. In Freud's story, this totemism is the origin of religion and the gradual displacement of totems with other sorts of divinities (mother-goddesses, polytheisms, monotheisms, and so on) marks the history of religious developments. Yet, even though the totem has been displaced, "the murdered father was restored to his rightful role as one who demanded unconditional obedience, although he was now banished from the earth to the sky" (Rorty 2006, 263). Rorty extends Freud's account to philosophy by proposing that Platonism is another variation on the process of displacement. Plato's "Idea of the Good" is a depersonalized vision of the Father. Plato isolates what is admirable in the Father-figure, thus providing something to emulate, but without the dangerous and violent passions of the Father. Assuming, plausibly enough, that Heidegger is correct that "metaphysics is Platonism and Platonism metaphysics" (Rorty 2006, 264), then much of Western philosophy is at bottom variations on totemism.

While there are clear issues that should be raised with Rorty's interpretation of pragmatism in this piece, including the rather uncritically androcentric appropriation of Freud, his claim that Dewey and James straight-forwardly subscribe to utilitarianism, and his avoidance of the importance of the scientific method for pragmatism, he does raise several significant points. The first has nothing to do with pragmatism, but much to do with the Garden myth. His appropriation of Freud goes a fair distance in explaining, albeit in mythological terms, the origins of the Garden myth. Even though the band of brothers murders their primal father, their replacement of him with a totem preserves the Garden, the Father's house. What is at issue in Freud's story is simply the murder of the primal father. The other accouterments of the primal father remain intact, hence the reason that the Garden remains, even if as a crime scene. Rather than being exiled from the Garden by the father, the band of brothers exile themselves (since they all cannot live in the father's house). Regardless, the introduction of the totem preserves the dream of returning to Garden.

Additionally, by positioning pragmatism in relations to the story of totemism, Rorty foregrounds a novel aspect of the pragmatic attitude. While virtually all pragmatists do emphasize the significance of community, the story Rorty tells presents this in a different light. The use of Freud here brings into sharp relief the anti-authoritarian attitude of pragmatists, especially Dewey. Arguing that pragmatism has such a bent helps account for the resistance pragmatists have faced from other philosophical traditions (which on Rorty's view still relies on a rather meta-level authoritarianism). Unlike traditional Western philosophy, pragmatism has no role for the totem or any other substitute for the primal Father. Rorty claims that the bulk of philosophy is built around trying to isolate the best of the Father and enshrine that in abstract metaphysical systems. This allows for the continued significance of totemism, in particular the presence of something external to the society it governs, but in a more intellectual form. Instead, pragmatism maintains the solidarity of the band of brothers but without appealing to the totem to guarantee the peace. In this way, pragmatism allows for "fraternity freed from memory of paternal authority" (Rorty 2006, 265). This accounts for pragmatism's (and in Rorty's account, only that of Dewey's really) anti-authoritarianism. Pragmatism follows out the logic of murdering the father than others because it refuses to resurrect it in the totemic guise (the band of brothers murdered the father and the father should remain dead in everyway). Rather, pragmatism is content to see the band of brothers cooperate with each other in a democratic fashion without appeal to any authority beyond the community itself. One might refer to this pragmatic approach to authority as "post-totemic."

## DECONSTRUCTION OF THE FABLES

Although Rorty does not rely on ludic concepts like "play" in his posttotemic pragmatism, his approach to moving beyond the Garden is not without problems. On Rorty's interpretation, Dewey allows for no authority other than that of the community, that is, consensus. As mentioned above, Lyotard rejects appeals to consensus, instead proposing "war on totality . . . activate the differends" (Lyotard 1993a, 16). This entails a rejection of consensus because consensus risks relying on terror as a means to forge unity, doing irreparable damage to differences. This is why he claims "Consensus has become an outmoded and suspect value. . . . We must thus arrive at an idea and practice of justice that is not linked to that of consensus" (Lyotard 1984, 66). Lyotard's usual target for this criticism is Jürgen Habermas, but he also makes a similar case against Rorty directly in "A Bizarre Partner" (1997, 123–47). This criticism must be taken seriously because it exposes a serious concern for Rorty and, *potentially*, for others who rely on pragmatism. Clearly, the Rortyian vision of community entails open conversation between different participants, both in the sense of multiple members of the community and that the community is fundamentally heterogeneous. Yet, because Rorty explicitly denies any authority beyond the community, specifically God and other metaphysical concepts, he provides no obvious means for settling debate. To some extent this is not an issue for him, since what might well be more important is simply continuing certain conversations. Yet, the concern reappears with how to settle matters *within* a conversation. When what Lyotard refers to as a "differend" emerges, a disagreement between parties with no just way to adjudicate the disagreement within a conversation, Rorty only leaves open the options of: agreeing to disagree, using rhetoric to change one party's mind, or something less pleasant (terror, violence, etc.). None of these options are particularly appealing, particularly in the face of the rather serious challenges posed with respect to questions of difference and other sorts of politics.

There is something of a symmetry between the problems Rorty and Lyotard create for themselves. Lyotard rejects consensus in the name of justice and difference, but provides little in the way of guidance for transforming society. Rorty conflates justice with consensus, but runs the risk of being unable to adequately bridge differences and/or subsuming difference into a coercive homogeneity. That both Rorty and Lyotard end in a similar place should not be interpreted as either making utopian gestures. Rather, both accept a certain quietism. By this I mean that they accept, explicitly or not, the assumption that we now live at the end of history. Although the emphases are different, working within a liberal democratic framework is taken as a given, not to transform this framework, but at best to resolve the few remaining contradictions within it. As most critics of postmodernism argue, the conclusions of Rorty, Lyotard and many other postmodern theorists amount to little more than preservation of the status quo. For those who find that the status quo requires a more radical reconstruction, this is untenable. The difficulty is this: on the one hand, Lyotard and Rorty both make ultimately compelling cases about the necessity of moving beyond the Garden myth; on the other, both fail to provide an adequate solution for reconstructing contemporary communities in such a way as to move beyond the systemic problems inherent within those communities. This is a genuinely difficult problem, and one that many postmodern theorists stumble over. The easiest path involves a return to God and the Garden myth. However, this move is prohibited within the postmodern condition and rightly so. Yet, the alternative provided by the likes of Rorty and Lyotard is little more than a refinement to presently existing liberal democracy and/or mere ludism.

## SEND IN THE CYBORGS

While not beyond a similar criticism to Rorty and Lyotard (Ebert 1996, 72–126), Donna Haraway provides an alternative to both. What makes Haraway's writings particularly important is the ways she takes seriously many of the core motifs of postmodern thought, while retaining aspects of socialist feminism. The latter opens spaces for the radical reconstruction of society through reliance on a Post-Garden mythology. The most famous version of this approach can be found in her "A Cyborg Manifesto." I begin with the Manifesto, and then incorporate some of her later writings, specifically *Modest_Witness@Second_Millennium* and *Staying with the Trouble*. In "A Cyborg Manifesto," Haraway attempts to construct "a political myth" for the present, specifically the Cold War, Star Wars, and Reaganomics dominated 1980s, using the figure of the cyborg: "a cybernetic organism, a hybrid of machine and organism, a creature of social reality as well as a creature of fiction" (Haraway 1991, 149). In the context of the Manifesto, the cyborg is a slippery figure. Haraway discusses it both as a lived reality (quite literally humans have become this sort of hybrid) and as a metaphor (human identities are like hybrids, cyborgs, of science fact and fiction). The significance of Haraway here begins with the questions of origin stories and the Garden myth. Following Hilary Klein, and echoing a claim Lyotard mentioned earlier, even the radical politics of Marxism and Freud "depend on the plot of original unity out of which difference must be produced" (Haraway 1991, 151). The cyborg cannot fall back on this sort of origin story, since (emphasizing the science-fiction side) the cyborg is the illegitimate product of Western technoscience. Harawary usefully draws a contrast between the cyborg and Frankenstein's creature: "Unlike the hopes of [the creature], the cyborg does not expect its father to save it through a restoration of the garden; that is through the fabrication of a heterosexual mate, through its completion in a finished whole, a city and cosmos. . . . *The cyborg would not recognize the Garden of Eden."* (Haraway 1991, 151. Emphasis mine). For Haraway, the goal is not to attempt a return to some mythic origin. Individuals are always already heterogeneous and the dream of returning to organic unity is, ultimately, destructive. Rather than conceiving of traditional accounts of identity, where the individual either is or aims to be a consistent, coherent whole (a self that "longs for a return to the Father's house"), she argues in favor of a hybrid conception of identity in which the individual's self is fabricated out of numerous, heterogonous elements. In this way, to be a "hyphenated" individual marks not a failure to attain a proper identity but should be regarded as a proper sense of self. To make the self into a consistent, coherent whole amounts to either a deception (since all of those disparate elements constituting identity are vital) or a power-play (in claiming one's "marked" view as normal or "objective," one seeks to exclude other perspectives. See Haraway 1991, 183–201).

If Haraway is on target about cyborg identities, then appeals to the Garden are out of place here. Instead, cyborgs must chart their own course, forging alliances that might well be shot through with ironies. Rather than falling back on the Garden of Eden or its surrogates (the communist utopia, the fully realized Kingdom of Ends, Peirce's end of inquiry perhaps), cyborg socialist feminist politics will seek to reshape the contemporary sociopoliticoeconomic order from within, without the promise of redemption through returning to the Garden. What emerges out of Haraway's writings is a vision of *both* the individual *and* society as hybrids. Unlike Lyotard, who seems to lack a robust approach to the politics of the postmodern condition, or Rorty, who appears to lack any way to substantively change contemporary politics, Haraway reinterprets socialist and feminist politics, but through the myth of the cyborg. In contrast to more traditional approaches to politics that fetishize one-ness (claiming an identity of "proletariat," "American," or whatever to the exclusion of any other categories), Haraway emphasizes pluralism. For example: "I like to imagine the LAG, the Livermore Action Group, as a kind of cyborg society, dedicated to realistically converting the laboratories that most fiercely embody and spew out the tools of technological apocalypse, and committed to building a political form that actually manages to hold together witches, engineers, elders, perverts, Christians, mothers, and Leninists long enough to disarm the state" (Haraway 1991, 154–55). Here we find a tentative solidarity among fractured subjects. The goal of LAG, and any other "cyborg society," is what Dewey refers to as an "end-in-view," a practical, revisable target toward which the group aims (MW14.154-63; Hickman 1990, 12; Joas 1996, 154–56). It is not a pregiven *telos*, a fixed an immutable end, that all politics must aim. The goal is negotiated among the individuals that constitute the society, individuals without stable, integrated identities. In this way, both at the level of individual and society, Haraway preserves a more radical sense of difference that is closer to Lyotard than I have interpreted Rorty as arguing for. This approach provides a template for reconstructing the present without falling back on the Garden myth. Haraway's later writings, like *Modest_Witness* and *Staying with the Trouble*, both provide illustrations of this, with two added advantages over Rorty and Lyotard. First, while Haraway tells nothing like the typical logical positivist or empiricist story about the success of science, she in no way rejects science per se. Second, especially in her recent work, she effectively demonstrates the necessity of broadening out the community to include animals (Haraway 2016).

## BEYOND PLAY AND THE MURDERED FATHER

Rorty's presentation of pragmatism as a posttotemic approach to authority resonates in many ways with Lyotard and Haraway's deconstruction of the Garden of Eden. With Lyotard and Haraway, modernism's reliance on the Garden deeply structures both identity and politics. Haraway in particular provides a rather sophisticated vision of how to wrestle with the demise of the Garden through her cyborgs. The cyborg is the final result of the eschatology discussed above, but yet owes this fable no fealty. Instead, it must create itself and its own myths out the rubble of Lyotard's modernism. Yet, this puts the cyborg in a curious position. The motivation of Lyotard's modernism is the assumed lack, the general desire to return to the primal Father's house. If Haraway is correct, then the cyborg has no primal Father of the sort Freud discussed. In this case, the cyborg must wrestle with the results of societies structured around the primal Father, but without seeking to return to His house or to find a totem to fill the Father's void. Instead, the cyborg must construct itself and its community out of this rubble of modernity. As Haraway argues, this is shot through with contingency and irony, which

Rorty fully appreciates. Furthermore, both Haraway and Lyotard, by denying the power of metanarratives, demonstrate how dangerous such endeavors are because Haraway's cyborg cannot fall back on the hope promised to it by eschatological fables. Rather, any notion of hope must be constructed by the cyborg itself out of resources contained within the bounded infinite, in solidarity with other cyborgs.

Here one sees both the ties between Rorty's story and postmodernism, as well as why Lyotard (to some extent) and Haraway (to a greater extent) provide something important to pragmatism. All of these archetypal postmodernists seek not to find a better way of presenting the Garden myth, such that their problems evaporate. Rather, they seek to put the Garden myth to rest. While Rorty, and by extension the classical pragmatists, goes a significant distance in putting totemism and the Garden to rest, he fails to go far enough. While Rorty makes clear why this is an improvement on earlier versions of the Garden myth, it does not address what Haraway and Lyotard propose is the core problem: the Father, the Garden, and humanity's relationship to them. Instead of desiring a better Garden, they urge us to move beyond the desire for the Garden altogether. By framing pragmatism as the acceptance of the deed of the Father's murder by the band of brothers, but without an authoritarian totem, Rorty can still fall prey to the allure of the Garden. Instead of being the Father's house, the Garden might now be the product of the band of brothers, acting as a community. There is an additional danger here that pragmatists should be wary of. Rorty's presentation of anti-authoritarianism can be read in two ways. One reading takes anti-authoritarianism as an attitude: the other as a policy. The risk of taking anti-authoritarianism as a policy is that it becomes a sort of authoritarianism. Everything must succumb to anti-authoritarianism, except the community itself. If taken as a weaker attitude of skepticism toward authoritarianism, this can be avoided, *at least with diligence*, and leaves open the possibility of creating temporary, mobile, forms of authority in line with the cyborg politics discussed above.

While rarely wise to uncritically use Rorty as a way into classical pragmatism, his argument in "Pragmatism as Anti-Authoritarianism" is useful to get a sense of how classical pragmatists can be linked to these more mythical images. There are two things of note here. First, Rorty echoes Hickman's argument that pragmatism is not a species of modernist philosophy. Although I suggested above that Rorty is too quick to assimilate classical pragmatism into his understanding of postmodernism, he is right that classical pragmatism is clearly not a species of caricatured modernism. Second, it is instructive for pragmatists to follow the lead of postmodern philosophers in order to find ways to more effectively move beyond fables of the Garden and totemism. Rorty's work from the 1980s explored this in a variety of ways. Even if I quibble with his interpretations of both the classical pragmatists and postmodernism, he does show the deep similarities between them. Yet, as I have argued here, it is necessary to be mindful of the difference between them, even the small ones, because these potentially have significant ramifications for pragmatism, which I return to below.

Since I aim to remain closer to the classical pragmatists and hold that there is a break between them and postmodernism, establishing distance between myself and Rorty is necessary. As discussed above, Rorty takes pragmatists to endorse no other authority than that of the community. This is true, but misleading. In light of his other writings, Rorty ends up avoiding one of the sources that provides a potential guide for the community: science, in particular the scientific method. This absence is problematic. While the classical pragmatists, most obviously Dewey and Mead, give democracy a decisive role, they always wedded this to experimentalism. It is not simply the whim of the community that should settle questions. Instead, through a process of experimentation, the community sets its goals and answers questions. Answers arrived at in this way are taken as stable enough in routine circumstances, but being fallibilist means that all answers are open to criticism in light of further inquiry. Hence, the criticism earlier of Rorty's unqualified assimilation of Dewey and James into utilitarianism. The Deweyian critique of utilitarianism is that it treats happiness as a fixed end. Which is not to say that happiness is not reasonable goal, but that it can never be regarded as a final and unquestioned goal for all action. One cannot know in advance that happiness, or any other end, is itself stable enough to guide human action as an end (more technically "an end-in-view"). The case is even clearer with means. Means only appear as such in light of particular ends, yet the end selected will be shaped by the means available (MW14.27-9; Hickman 1990, 72). The two reciprocally inform each other. For classical pragmatists, the most reliable way to link together ends and means is through scientific inquiry. As Peirce argued, other methods like that of tenacity, authority, and *a priority*, fail to experimentally determine beliefs, which are rules for action (EP1.115-23). This ensures that the possessors of such beliefs are doomed to either fall into doubt or repress such doubts, which rarely ends well.

Unlike the caricature of many science studies scholars, Haraway does not deny the efficacy of science. Rather, it is precisely because of its power (epistemic, social, technological, political) that she engages its practices critically. Haraway's analysis of the gene in *Modest_Witness* illustrates this effectively. There she critiques the use of the gene concept as equivalent to "Life Itself." This is not a rejection of the gene concept, but rather an exemplification of the fetishism that underlies much of European thought. The gene comes to stand in for everything about living organisms. This at once obscures the complexity of organisms (because they cannot be reduced down to any single scientific concept) and the constructed-ness of the gene itself.

"The gene" exists at the intersection of scientific discourse, biotechnology, and capital investment. "A gene is not a thing, much less a 'master molecule' or a self-contained code. Instead, the term *gene* signifies a node of durable action where many actors, human and nonhuman, meet" (Haraway 1997, 142. Emphasis original). Various forces hold the gene together, leaving open the possibility that other configurations might be possible if the relationships between these forces shift. Clearly, Haraway is not a standard scientific realist, but this does not lead her to argue that anything goes in science or that science is "merely" constructed. Rather, science involves complex negotiations between innumerable entities, not all of them human, in order to create "durable nodes of action."

This illustrates the quip made earlier about the difference between anti-authoritarianism as policy as opposed to attitude. Sticking resolutely to anti-authoritarianism about everything except what is endorsed by the community results in the relativist aporias characterizing the most problematic aspects of postmodernism. To take his suggestion about anti-authoritarianism as far as Rorty appears to in his writings leads us to such places because it is unclear what allows for the settling of debates other than the authority of consensus. For example, it appears that in order to be anti-authoritarian, one must dramatically rethink the significance of science in a way that is much closer to Paul Feyerabend's "anything goes" proliferation, a position also endorsed by Lyotard (Rorty 1991, 40–41; Lyotard 1984, 60–64). For both the classical pragmatists and Haraway, this is as problematic as an uncritical acceptance of science. Many, including philosophers and scientists, fall into the trap of treating science as something like the God concepts discussed earlier. There are points where the classical pragmatists risk this as well, most clearly Peirce, but this can also be seen more technocratic interpretations of Dewey (Horkheimer 1947; Manicas 1998).

Some interpretations of classical pragmatism end up fetishizing science in ways that run afoul of what Rorty characterizes as pragmatism's anti-authoritarianism. This would involve privileging the results of science, usually understood in a rather narrow sense, in a way that excludes other discourses, in particular anything associated with religion or theology. To avoid this, constant vigilance is necessary. Rorty is correct that a certain skepticism about authority is always healthy, even about the cherished tools of pragmatism. Staying with the sort of open-ended, fallible scientific method that I have suggested is at the heart of classical pragmatism aids in cultivating an anti-authoritarian attitude. What is less important is the specific results of scientific inquiry, but rather the community's attempt to work together to find temporarily stable answers. Although the interpretation of Peirce's end of inquiry that reads it as some metaphysical terminus is ruled out for reasons clear enough at this point that the determination of what is "true" is a social affair is no doubt correct. The community assents to or dissents from possible answers. The importance of scientific inquiry is that, if pursued as Peirce and other classical pragmatists suggested, it prevents the community from sliding into the sort of relativism that I accuse Rorty of. There is the danger of fetishizing the results of science, which explains part of Rorty's reluctance to take science seriously in the way the classical pragmatists do.

Haraway provides clues as to how to achieve this balancing act. Although described in quite different language, Haraway agrees with the classical pragmatists that science is a process, an ever-shifting culture, rather than an accumulation of facts. While Peirce and Dewey embed their account of science within an evolutionary framework (with notable differences between them), Haraway consistently illustrates the relationship between science and other centers of social power, in particular the military and industry. Without discounting the power of science (quite the opposite: she takes this power quite seriously, which is why she tries to co-opt science), Haraway has an especially keen eye for the interrelationships between science and other cultures. For example, her dissections of advertisements for scientific instruments are serious jokes, because they at once speak, like other advertisements, to scientists' desires and self-conceptions, and demonstrate that science is big business (both in terms of the role of science in capitalism as well as scientists as consumers). When one comes to accept the degree to which science is not and never was socially autonomous, the naivety that allows science to function as a God-substitute becomes increasingly indefensible. Haraway's analyses contextualize science within patriarchal, racist, militarized capitalism, with the aim of opening up science to be more democratic, egalitarian, and, recently, anti-speciesist. This is simply anti-authoritarianism by another name: it is an unmasking of science's pretensions. Once these are stripped away, it becomes difficult to look at science as something that could be fetishized as another stand-in for God. Viewing science in this way allows for the necessary sort of anti-authoritarianism, and retains its capacity to avoid the fall into relativism.

## IN THE RUINS OF THE GARDEN

I now have several important pieces on the table about how to move beyond the Garden myth without falling into postmodern ludism. From Rorty, I take his anti-authoritarian attitude as a way to resist the lure of fetishism, the dream of returning to the Father's house. From Haraway, I borrowed the spirit of her cyborg mythology and her feminist analysis of scientific practice. What is necessary now is to fuse these with the classical pragmatist account of scientific inquiry and their concept of meliorism.

Unlike Peirce's characterization of Descartes and other modernists, pragmatist takes an anti-foundationalist approach to inquiry. They do not attempt to base knowledge on something "firm and lasting." Instead, inquiry begins *in media res*. The individual possesses beliefs that guide their actions via habits. Sometimes, these habits break down, leading to an undermining of the associated belief. This throws us into doubt. In order to reestablish the "calm and satisfactory state" (EP1. 114) of belief, individuals pursue inquiry. Through different methods, like that of science, a new belief is settled upon and return one to their previous state, hopefully with a more stable belief. The goal of inquiry is not the establishment of truth or certainty. All of the classical pragmatists have a story to tell at some point about how "truth" emerges out of inquiry, but (at least as usually understood) this is not the primary purpose of inquiry. Instead, the aim is to establish new beliefs. The aim of scientific inquiry is the establishment of beliefs that foster human action in an oft-times precarious world. The shift from talking about knowledge to inquiry helps to prevent the impulses that lead to the quest for certainty. The fallibilism inherent within this theory of inquiry requires that the inquirer accept that any belief is provisional, always open for criticism. At best, certainty arrives at the end of inquiry, as Peirce implies.

Even this tentative "at best" should be worrisome in light of the postmodern sensibilities articulated throughout this book. Something smells here of a metanarrative (and the same could be said of the appeal to naturalism). My response to this criticism is that the issue here is not so much what is essential to the theory of inquiry, but its interpretation. No doubt some interpretations of pragmatism do fall into the traps of metanarratives. C. S. Peirce is the most obvious offender. The later classical pragmatists have their moments of both resisting such temptations and giving in. Those inspired by pragmatism (like W. V. O. Quine, Wilfrid Sellars, or Rorty), and those who hew closer to the closer to the classical pragmatist tradition (like Larry Hickman, Richard Bernstein, and Charlene Haddock Seigfried) are more varied still in how they address this issue. While the metarnarrative lingering here might not be quite the traditional one discussed throughout this book, I propose it goes something like this:

> we find ourselves in a world both precarious and stable. Certain forms of inquiry, namely science, are better suited to navigating such a world, mitigating the precariousness and improving the stability. Given the success of science in this regard, it should possess an authority (i.e. legitimacy) superior to other forms of inquiry.

There are echoes here of legitimation by performativity, where knowledge is legitimated because of its effectiveness. But for Lyotard, this success is nothing more or less than providing the best possible solution to an input/output equation, which is not the interpretation of classical pragmatism presented here. This might appear when Rorty reads Dewey and James as unqualified utilitarians, inasmuch as there is some immanent, yet fixed, goal. There is some structural similarity between utilitarianism and performativity on this point, but given the unique status that some philosophers assign to happiness, it seems there is something of a muddled attempt at transcendence at work. Performativity officially eschews this. Part of the difference between classical pragmatism and performativity is the way in which pragmatism does argue in favor of definite goals, but these goals are also not above criticism. Performativity is beyond criticism, and those who dare to criticize it censure or worse. When pragmatists freeze goals, moving it from a Deweyian, living "end-in-view" to a fixed end, falling into this metanarrative about the authority of science follows rather easily.

In this way, pragmatists walk a knife's edge, which follows from the account I have developed throughout. As discussed throughout this book, pragmatism does anticipate a number of motifs of postmodern thought, but is better understood as a species of modernist philosophy. Given the pull of metanarratives within modernist thought, there is a persistent danger of these motifs appearing in pragmatist thought. As noted earlier, Peirce is the clear candidate for this worry because of the ambiguities in his end of inquiry. Dewey is clearly better on this, but even he had his moments that can be interpreted as embracing technocracy and scientism.[1] Given pragmatism's place between Enlightenment modernism and postmodernism, this vacillation is not surprising. The position they stake out is difficult to maintain. Postmodernists are correct that an unqualified embrace of modernism (at least as caricatured by foes and friends) is inadvisable. Yet, critics of postmodernism, including Hickman, and especially Marxists like Harvey and Ebert, are correct that the excesses of postmodernism are damning for totally different reasons. The difficulty here is structural. So long as pragmatism remains a post-Enlightenment, post-romantic modernist philosophical movement, it risks falling toward one side or another. In itself, this awkwardness might not be a bad thing. The question: how does one navigate a path between Charybdis and Scylla?

## CYBORG IDENTITIES

I can now demonstrate the significance of Haraway's myth of the cyborg for my purposes. Haraway provides a vocabulary for rigorously thinking about heterogeneous identities. Lyotard and other postmodern philosophers argue, modernism tends to fetishize the One, the Same, and the Totality. Postmodernists, on the other hand, seek to disrupt the appeal to any sort of "common denominator." Given the centrality of pluralism to pragmatism, the ways in which postmodern thought privileges the Different or the Other over the Same, there is common cause here. Yet pragmatists do run the risk of sliding into more problematic positions because it is a matter not just of the concepts, but the emphasis put on them. The myth of the cyborg helps to avoid this problem through emphasizing how the cyborg is an assemblage of parts that refuse to be made an organic whole, where these parts can exist in temporary relationships with each other. The first of these is vital because it disrupts the impulse toward totalization, either in terms of an individual's identity (that there must be a coherent self) or the social bond. As discussed in chapter 3, society is best understood presently as a network, and the cyborg is a monster of networks. Its ontology is that of contingent connection, and for this reason is ideally suited for circulating through communication networks. If nothing else, the imagery here is important because it gives a way of framing identity in such a way that reflects the "structure" of a network society. Identities need not be coherent, but instead a fusion of unlikely, if not contradictory, parts. This approach of identity through difference, both within an individual and between individuals, is necessary in order to respond effectively to the challenges of postmodernity. Postmodernity is a bounded infinite world with no recourse to transcendence. In order to reconstruct such a world, these various assemblages must conceive of themselves in a way that reflects the dynamism of the world. The functionalist block world does not account for the mobility of most things in the present. The modernist social bond relies on a rather static, holistic conception of identity, usually specified by one's position within a "block." Such conceptions no longer match the present world that is best analogized in terms of ICTs. Haraway's cyborgs were constructed against the backdrop of these technologies, the possibility of nuclear annihilation and globalized, just-in-time capitalism, which makes the myth valuable as a tool with which to reconceive identities.

Haraway implicitly provides a way to work with Lyotard's observation that "the course that the evolution of social interaction is currently taking: the temporary contract is in practice supplanting permanent institutions in the professional, emotional, sexual, cultural, family, and international domains, as well as in political affairs" (Lyotard 1984, 66). Chapter 5 dealt with Castells and a postmodern society that exists in a perpetual now, characterized by aleatoric changes. While I argued that this is an exaggeration, it certainly feels plausible. Even if time and space are not annihilated per se, David Harvey makes an excellent case for their compression (Harvey 1990, 284–323). In such a temporally mobile world, alliances need not always be long term. Where common interest appears, building solidarity around those is advisable, even if, as Haraway points out, it will lead to strange bedfellows. This does not rule out the possibility of long-term alliances, but simply does not require, or even assume, them. Yet, being able to foster such interconnections relies on important capacities that allow for the construction of more of them. That is to say, being open to seemingly divergent positions and then finding shared ends-in-view around which to build solidarity will foster those capacities that allow one to do this with others. This invokes the spirit of Dewey's writings on democracy, but in a way more attuned to our micrological times. Three further comments here. First, this points again to the need to eschew the relativism typically associated with postmodernism. It is not, nor can it be, anything goes. There might be someone out there with a wholly nonobjectionable set of positions, but I expect that they are few and far between. Putting these people aside, criticism of one's allies' other positions can, likely is, called for. And they should do the same for me. As Haraway argues (Haraway 1991, 191–92), this is about taking a stand, and stands cannot be taken from the nowhere of relativism. Second, we see again the failure of the modern social bond to account for the present. Within functionalism, the assumption at work emphasizes the relative permanence of blocks or organs. Once established, the contract remains in effect indefinitely. Within postmodern societies, this is neither realistic, nor necessary advisable. Lastly, there is something of a postmodern spin on the macrocosmos/microcosmos here. The same pattern plays out at every level: a heterogeneity of parts. The self is an assemblage, but so are the parts of the self and society itself.

## FABLES OF A RECONSTRUCTION

I am now in a position to recast the Garden myth. As presented above, the Garden was a gift from the Father, something He promised that humans would return to at the end of their struggle. Haraway makes plain why such mythology does not fit the cyborg, who is the end result, "an illegitimate child," of this modernist way of thinking. The dream of emancipation at the heart of modernism culminates in the production of such beings. Or at least the necessity of acknowledging the cyborg. Metanarratives relied on the imposition of a unity upon a multiplicity, inasmuch as humans tend to be diverse. With the demise of metanarratives, there is nothing, outside of terror or momentum, to hold together these unities. When the imposed unity falls away, what is left behind are heterogeneous cyborg subjects. Modernists never eliminated this heterogeneity, just obscured it. Without metanarratives to paper over differences, the cyborg makes its presence known. The cyborg stands upon the wreckage of modernism. This forces the question of what to do with the Garden myth. Does the cyborg find itself with the ruins of the Garden which it was never promised and does recognize? Or is the Garden more modernist clap-trap that should be relegated to intellectual historians?

It remains an open question as whether, in time, the very idea of the Garden should be rejected. There are twin dangers in simply jettisoning the myth *now*. On the one hand, merely replacing it with another myth is a utopian gesture, and one likely to recapitulate the Garden myth itself. The drift of the argument from Lyotard, and I largely agree with him on this, is that the fundamental structure of metanarratives is flawed. In terms of philosophy, part of the reason that we enter postmodernity is the growing acceptance that metanarratives are untenable and must be replaced. Many of the twentieth-century attempts to replace the Garden myth, like appeals to science, end up recapitulating it using different concepts in the same structure. Given that so many attempts to replace the myth end up falling into this trap, this option is a deeply problematic. Another option is simply to remain in the unreconstructed postmodern condition. This is the position taken by the caricature of postmodernism (which, of course, is connected to just enough actual postmodern theory to make it plausible). Such a position is unacceptable for many pragmatists (and I expect many self-styled postmodernists as well) given that there are serious problems in need of amelioration presently. To remain in a place in which relativism trumps all else prevents such labor. To take but one significant example, consider global warming. While it is not clear exactly how long it will be before we reach a point a no return (assuming we have not already), the necessity of action is clear based on the forecasts of the effects of global warming. Those who genuinely embrace a postmodern relativism about any truth claim would appear to have no grounds on which to argue against those who advocate against the hypothesis of anthropogenic climate change. That such genuine relativists are few and far between speaks to difficulty of this position, yet it can be difficult to see on what grounds certain postmodern theorists like Baudrillard, or even my relatively sympathetic interpretation of Lyotard might justify action based on scientific research. So to simply wallow in the ruins of the Garden is not acceptable either.

Before the time comes to determine whether the Garden is worth retaining, it is necessary first to reconstruct the Garden myth. It is a myth so long baked into European thought that to simply try to jump beyond it is impossible. While making such a break might have a certain seductive quality, it is difficult to achieve, especially with a myth that Lyotard traces back to early Christianity. The attempt to wipe this all away will prove ill-fated because of how thoroughly enmeshed the Garden myth is with philosophy and theology. This is a lesson that both certain postmodern theorists and pragmatists understand. Derrida's work of deconstruction proves necessary because, as he demonstrates, we exist in a region in which "there is a kind of question ... whose *conception, formation, gestation,* and *labor* we are only catching a glimpse of today" (Derrida 1978, 293. Emphasis original). As he shows again and again, such radical jumps only reinscribe what philosophers sought to break from, preventing what is glimpsed from being born. A similar concern motivates Haraway's cyborg mythology, inasmuch as it finds itself living in the wreckage of modernity and must build a world for itself out of this. The classical pragmatists appreciate this as well. From Peirce on, there is an acceptance that concepts are inherited and that one of the purposes of inquiry is to test the mettle of such an inheritance. Some concepts require clarification, others should be abandoned, and some Peirce and James could not see eye to eye on (like transubstantiation, reality, and truth). Much of this sensibility is captured in the word associated with Dewey: "reconstruction." The task of philosophy is not to create the world anew, but to rebuild it from within.

Given the necessity of reconstruction, the Garden myth requires transformation rather than wholesale replacement. Putting the matter in a rather mythical way, the reconstruction goes like this:

> The protagonist returns to the Garden, but this is not the end of the story. They find the Garden in ruins, the Father absent, with no sign of a possible return. The Garden is not the place promised, the protagonist will not find wholeness or comfort here. Yet, it is still what awaits them at the end of their exile. With no one else to tend the Garden, it is up to the protagonist to decide whether to tend it or not.

The crucial move is to see ourselves as inhabiting the ruins of the Garden. Instead of seeing the Garden as something promised to us by the Father, it is incumbent on us to see ourselves as living in the ruins of the Garden now. And in this sense, the Garden is *ours*, not God's, not the Father's, not whatever intellectualized surrogate one wants to introduce. For this reason, the Garden is the community's responsibility. One might choose to ignore this responsibility, but that remains one (troubling) use of their abilities.

The basic question then becomes "what sort of Garden shall we remake?" rather than putting faith in the Father to present to us with a place to dwell. Enlightenment modernism foists this responsibility on God or some surrogate, while Heidegger waits for a God who will save. Instead, this is the space that James put under the heading of "meliorism," which "treats salvation as neither inevitable nor impossible. It treats it as a possibility, which becomes more and more of a probability the more numerous the actual conditions of salvation become. . . . Some conditions of the world's salvation are actually extant, and she cannot possible close her eyes to this fact: and should the residual conditions come, salvation would become an accomplished reality" (James 1987, 612). In a twist that is somewhat similar to my earlier point, James finds that God made humanity responsible. James demands of us that we save ourselves without relying on the powers of God, other than to use the potentialities that God provided. Our ultimate fate is squarely within human hands. Although other classical pragmatists will phrase this in different, and usually less overtly religious, language, they endorse a similar conclusion (West 1989). In chapter 5, I showed how Mead explains humans' capacity to construct the future out of the present. This amounts to embedding this meliorist sensibility into the very operation of temporality. While less metaphysically grandiose than James, inasmuch as Mead accounts for the possibility of individuals actively shaping the future based on materials at hand via their values rather than the salvation of the entire universe, the insistence that there is space within the world for its reconstruction from within carries on James's legacy.

Given that both the classical pragmatists and postmodern theorists like Lyotard will accept the claim that there is no supreme authority as postulated by the metanarratives of traditional modernism, where does the difference between them lie? In this, Hickman makes the point quite succinctly: "I have trolled the works of Deleuze and Félix Guattari, Jacques Derrida, Roland Barthes, and even the master postmodernist Lyotard, in search of a comprehensive and coherent theory of inquiry. Nothing I have found approaches the treatment Dewey gave the subject" (Hickman 2007, 29). Whether one emphasizes Dewey's, as Hickman does, or Peirce's, or teases out the theory of James (Seigfried 1990) or Mead (1964, 171–211), this is a common thread that runs throughout. There is good reason for this. Inquiry offers not a foundation for knowledge, but rather an open-ended method of answering questions. The goal of inquiry is not certainty or something similar, but instead establishing reliable beliefs that enable the navigation of a precarious world. This goal at once acknowledges the contingency that so many postmodern theorists rightly mark as important, but pragmatists seek to address in a more constructive manner. On the other hand, inquiry is not the foundationalist enterprise that is definitive of traditional modernism. It is inherently fallible (Bernstein 1992, 326–29; 2010, 32–52).

## MELIORISM WITHOUT INNOCENCE

In order to meet the challenge posed by the postmodern condition, it is necessary for this reconstructive project to be thoroughly pluralist and democratic. As argued earlier, inquiry is a community endeavor. Individuals propose beliefs, but it is the community that criticizes and, potentially, endorses them. Given the need to scrutinize beliefs, the community must be, to some degree, pluralistic. If the community is too conceptually homogenous, then the distance between its members will be too small for criticism to emerge. This provides a reasonably technocratic justification for pluralism, inasmuch as pluralism is beneficial for knowledge generation. The pragmatic concern for pluralism goes deeper, ultimately being the ground out of which identity emerges. A later formulation of this came up in chapter 4 in discussing Mead's social genesis of the self. There I mentioned how it is the self that is produced only through social interactions with others and that the interaction comes before a conception of self. Peirce himself saw this, albeit in a much more schematic form when he wrote about the importance of the community as early as 1868 (EP1.52-5). Dewey highlights the significance of pluralism as well in his writings on democracy ("Creative Democracy" provides a very lucid statement LW14.224-30). Most radically, James in a certain sense ontologizes it with his *A Pluralistic Universe* (James 1987, 625–816).

The breakdown of metanarratives makes claims to monism much more problematic, because there is no "common denominator" to hold oneness together. The interpretation of classical pragmatism developed here appreciates the postmodern claims of the importance of "difference," "otherness," "alterity," etc. Fostering these, here under the guise of "pluralism," is an important part of the community of inquirers. Postmodernity forces a reckoning with the differences that exist within American and other societies. Such societies were always pluralistic, but this was repressed, sometimes violently. One important achievement of postmodern theory is the extent to which it makes plain the necessity of respecting and fostering such differences (Harvey 1991, 353–55; Bernstein 1992, 57–78). There is a definite affinity here between postmodernism and pragmatism, yet postmodern philosophers tend to embrace a more radical sense of pluralism. For example, Lyotard endorses "paganism" in a number of places (Lyotard 1993b, 148–58; Lyotard and Thébaud 1985). He defines this as the condition of there being an indefinite number of incommensurable language-games. This is his preferred situation because of the way in which totalization is prevented. Such radical, if not absolute, difference sits uneasily with pragmatists, Peirce most obviously given his concerns for continuity (e.g., EP2.1-3). Beyond the conceptual problems that can emerge from radical difference (if something is so radically different, then it cannot possibly be understood), there is an undercurrent of harmonization that appears in much pragmatic thought. Think back to chapter 3 and the ambiguity of Mead's claim that "Society is unity in diversity." Even if unity is not understood in the sense of Hegelian "*aufhebung*," this still requires some sort of integration of the individual into the wider society. The worry here is one of slipping from the more radical sense of pluralism into a pluralism that is only skin deep, that only preserves surface differences while enforcing a substantive unity (a "United Colors of Benetton" pluralism). This returns us to the problem of attitude, of how pragmatism should be interpreted. The classical pragmatists have resources to cultivate the more radical sense of difference that permeates so much postmodern thought. Yet, there is an undercurrent in their thought that stops many of them short of fully embracing the most radical sense because of a hope for a reconciliation without terror. This hope is in obvious tension with postmodern difference. One way to thread the needle between these is insisting on the mobility of relationships in the way Haraway does so that the lure of lasting unity can be disrupted.

There is a further caution that should be added here: there must be space left open for agonism, for conflict without recourse to terror. Again, incorporating this is more a matter of attitude for the pragmatist, rather than any change in philosophical orientation. Pluralism, after all, is a cornerstone of classical pragmatism, and when dealing with social pluralism there is no guarantee that the members of community will agree peaceably. The writings of Addams, Dewey, James, and Mead all testify to this, especially their less academic publications, though the more formal work of Dewey and others tends to downplay this possibility. One gets the feeling from them, and contemporary pragmatists as well, that with enough (for Rorty) conversation or (for others) inquiry, that even the deepest differences might be reconciled. Oversimplifying, the danger is that if this optimism about reconciliation is warranted, it cancels out a genuine pluralism in the long run because, at best, the differences do not make a difference when reconciled (they are only surface differences). On the other hand, if reconciliation is impossible, pluralism is retained, but at the expense of the community. In light of the considerations of Lyotard, and the general postmodern concern for difference, otherness, and incommensurability, differences must in fact matter. The solution to this challenge is taking Lyotard's work on differends seriously. One approach to this would be to see reconciliation as an end, a regulator ideal, while accepting that in the short run it might be impossible to attain such reconciliation, that there will be the risks of genuine loss and possibilities of terror. Again, this requires vigilance, a vigilance that must be incorporated into the process of inquiry in order to reassess the tentative settlement when there is cause.

Yet, it is conceivable to appreciate pluralism and not democracy, at least not in the sense that Dewey and others articulate. This is another variation on the criticism of postmodern ludism, the "political" response to the postmodern condition that encourages play and self-creation at the expense of coordinated social action. Dewey avoids this by holding that "the key-note of democracy as a way of life may be expressed . . . as the necessity for the participation of every mature human being in formation of the values that regulate the living of men together: which is necessary from the standpoint of both the general social welfare and the full development of human beings as individuals" (LW11.217-18). Balancing this Deweyian conception of democracy with the challenge of the postmodern is difficult. Going too far in one direction risks falling into totality; the other risks leaving unacceptable situations unreconstructed. Haraway again offers a few ways to walk this tightrope. One is through mobile solidarity. By keeping alliances flexible, produced as situations dictate, the calcification that can lead to terror can be prevented. The other is the Myth of the Cyborg, which is effectively a corollary of the first point. By accepting that identity is as heterogeneous and mobile as political solidarity, this also avoids the problem of falling back into a totality. From here, it is a matter of taking this cyborg politics and wedding it to Dewey's democratic pluralism. As should be clear at this stage, pluralism is inherent when Dewey states:

> is the belief in the ability of human experience to generate the aims and methods by which further experience will grow in ordered richness. Every other form of moral and social faith rests upon the idea that experience must be subjected at some point or other to some form of external control; to some "authority" alleged to exist outside the process of experience. Democracy is the faith that the process of experience is more important than any special result attained, so that special results achieved are of ultimate value only as they are used to enrich and order the ongoing process. (LW14.229)

The order Dewey refers to here cannot be imposed from outside, but must be fallibly determined within experience. Pluralism is required in order for the inquiry into such experience to be as robust as possible.

Recasting the Myth of the Garden as I sketched here provides a way to pursue the reconstruction of the postmodern present. So long as the bounded infinite provides the primary metaphor for understanding the world, the only resources available for its reconstruction must come from within that space. Postmodern philosophy continues to provide ways to understand the texture of the world, yet pragmatism is ideally suited for the positive task of working through postmodernity. First, although all the classical pragmatists made substantive claims about a wide range of philosophical matters, there is a sense in which pragmatism is always, first and foremost, a method. The advantage of a method is that it can be applied to numerous different situations (assuming there is enough continuity between contexts). Classical pragmatism grew up in modernity, yet its method can be transplanted to these postmodern times and thrive here as well. The method that lies at the core of pragmatism is open-ended enough to be of use in both eras. Where caution is required is with the application of the method. Some uses will turn pragmatism toward a more modernist, foundationalist interpretation that will likely only reproduce the very issues postmodernism problematized. Other interpretations fit more cleanly with postmodernity. For example, as James notes late in *Pragmatism*: "For pluralistic pragmatism, truth grows up inside of all finite experiences. They lean on each other, but the whole of them . . . leans on nothing. All 'homes' are in finite experience; finite experience as such is homeless. Nothing outside of the flux secures the issue of it. It can hope salvation only from its own intrinsic promises and potencies" (James 1987, 601). What he depicts here can be understood as the closed world of the bounded infinite. There is nothing outside of the infinite. It contains all that is. In this way, everything must grow up within experience. There is no possible appeal to anything outside of the infinite in order to guarantee certainty. Where James highlights something obscured in so much postmodern thought is that salvation only comes from within experience. It is not postmodern philosophers like Lyotard would disagree with this, because there is no beyond, so much as it tends to ignore issues of salvation or redemption because these tends to be part and parcel of metanarratives.

The reconstructed Myth of Garden provides a way to bring back in these concerns under the heading of meliorism. The radical transformation at heart of modern thought is abandoned in favor of relying on "promises and potencies" contained within the world. At present, there is no escaping the bounded infinite. Metanarratives in their full rationalistic glory remain defunct. This does not mean that the possibility of better world is dead as well. Although the present conceptual situation precludes adding more to the infinite, since it contains all that is, this does not entail that the objects it contains cannot be rearranged in better, or worse, ways. This is the project of pragmatic meliorism: working from within to improve the world. "Why may [our acts] not be the actual turning-places and growing-places which they seem to be, of the world—why not the workshop of being, where we catch fact in the making, so that nowhere may the world grow in any other kind of way than this?" (James 1987, 613). Unlike the modernist dreams, any reconstruction will be partial in two senses. First, it cannot be done from outside of the world. Rather, all reconstruction is done as part of the world. This requires abandoning the claim to omniscience in favor of partiality. Second, the fantasy of remaking the world whole cloth must be abandoned. The earlier discussion of inquiry is instructive here, since inquiry is a species of reconstruction. Inquiry always occurs within a context, addressing a particular problem. So, too, with pragmatic meliorism. Like knowledge for James, reconstruction "grows *in spots* . . . its growth may involve considerable modification. . . . But such modifications are apt to be gradual" (James 1987, 559. Emphasis original). In this way, any reconstruction will be partial, will take time, and requires constant reassessment. This partiality, in conjunction with Haraway's cyborg solidarity, allows pragmatism to meet the challenge of postmodernity. By making the once-hero of the narrative responsible for the cultivation of the Garden, that they are part of it and can expect no salvation beyond what they can provide through working with the rest of the Garden's inhabitants, pragmatism works within conceptual conditions of postmodernity, while going beyond much of postmodernism in providing, at least in theory, a more constructive response to finding the Garden in ruins.

## NOTE

1. As those familiar with Peirce can attest, the concept of the "end of inquiry" can be interpreted in a number of ways, including as regulative achieve, the actual achievement of beliefs impervious to doubt, or something metaphysical. Each interpretation raises different implications for the possibility of achieving certainty. See Wilkinson (2012, 127–31) for a discussion of why interpretations of Dewey can slide into technocracy.

# Conclusion

The concepts of the postmodern and postmodernity remain relevant and continue to help describe the present. This can be seen in the ways in which a sort of emancipation amenable to performativity comes to the fore while the reliance on metanarratives is undercut. The prominent place of difference and otherness in the contemporary lexicon, as well as its negation, does as well. Signs can be seen in the fluidity of identity and social relations, the undermining of traditional authorities (both modernist and premodernist), the increased demands for "performance," and so on. In this way, I suggest that the contemporary world continues to be accurately described as "postmodern" and that the epoch of "postmodernity" continues through the present moment. Yet, whether this is entirely plausible all this depends on how the terms are defined. I sought to provide a multidimensional definition of postmodernity that operates at both the conceptual and material levels. At the conceptual level, I emphasized Lyotard's "incredulity toward metanarratives." This allows me to draw together many strands of postmodern thought. Much of Lyotard's own work from the 1980s and 1990s goes back in one way or another to this concept. Lyotard helps to make sense of why Borgmann describes postmodernism as a critique of pillars of modern thought like realism and universalism (individualism, as always, remains more complicated), and why so many postmodern theorists assume the demise of objectivity and unity. By interpreting Lyotard's statement on metanarratives broadly and in the context of his writings on terror, many of the most important motifs of postmodernity can be accounted for. I introduced the image of the bounded infinite, which involves an infinite number of objects contained within a finite space, in order better describe conceptual life in postmodernity. I used this primarily to illustrate the way in which the conceptual universe of postmodernity is, at once, claustrophobic and vast. It contains, as Castells put it, "the whole sequence of cultural expressions" (Castells 2010a, 492), yet nothing more can be added to it. In this way, it is a "smaller" infinity than modernity presupposed. Anything "new" comes about through novel combinations of objects, rather than the creation of something that did not before exist within the bounded infinite. The avant-garde faded away with modernity. The bounded infinite illustrates the way in which there is no possible transcendence, no possible outside. While expressed in many different ways, this seems to be one of the primary lessons of postmodern philosophers, and one of the most significant challenges of postmodernity.

These conceptual changes did not occur in a vacuum, which is why the material dimension of postmodernity is so significant. While I only made passing references to changes with economics and society, like the emergence of the politics of difference, it is not because these are not important. There are two significant reasons for I did not explore this further. First, such issues have been discussed about extensively, effectively, and definitively by others.[1] Second, while technology has appeared here and there in analyses of the postmodern, rarely has technology been used as a way to thematize the postmodern. As I hoped to demonstrate in this work, highlighting the interconnections between technology and both postmodernism and postmodernity helps to demonstrate the continued salience of the concept of the postmodern. The technologies bound up with postmodernity, like ICTs, illustrate the ways in which Lyotard's concepts remain particularly fecund in making sense of contemporary society. I made a more limited case for Roland Barthes on this front and suggested the same is true for other classic postmodern theorists like Derrida, Deleuze and Guattari, and Baudrillard. These technologies embody many of the motifs central to postmodernism by fostering fluidity, heterogeneity, and hyperrealism.

Unlike the claims of many post-postmodern theorists, in particular Alan Kirby, instead of showing the staleness and limits of postmodern thought, these technologies show that there continues to be some life left in certain aspects of postmodernism. The most significant aspects of postmodernism at present are those that bear more society than aesthetics. When postmodern theorists are turned toward material practices, they continue to help explain how individuals engage with technologies, and how these engagements at once shape and is shaped by society. This suggests that there is a feedback loop between the material and conceptual levels, where each informs the other. For example, by discussing communication through ICTs and how technologies produce the dominate mode of temporal experience is that of "timeless time." It is a world without past or future, just the perpetual now. Standard conceptions of modernity depended on an openness to the future, a space in which the project of modernity could move into and prefect

(Habermas 1987, 1–22). The transition to postmodernity closes off both the future and the past, leaving only what Castells described as "the transformation is more profound: it is the mixing of tenses to create a forever universe, not self-expanding but self-maintaining, not cyclical but random, not recursive but incursive" (Castells 2010a, 464). Lyotard captures much of this sensibility in his writings on the system and where he describes the demise of the eschatological hopes of modernity, and I argued that this is recapitulated in the image of the bounded infinite.

## THE POSTMODERN CHALLENGE

In the introduction, I proposed that one way to conceive of postmodernity is as a challenge. The assumptions that drove modernism no longer hold, at least in some ways. On the one hand, the modernist dream of emancipation is far enough along to be coopted by "the system." This means that one of the ends of modernity has inched closer to being achieved (especially in a technocratic sort of performativity). On the other, the conceptual and material conditions of postmodernity make (the now traditional) appeals to some form of metanarrative increasingly difficult (i.e., now the use of metanarratives is primarily about a sort of terror, rather than rational legitimation). As a result, it becomes harder to forestall the claims of epistemic relativism or that society is some sort of unified, homogenous entity. In some respects, postmodernity marks the summation of modernism, the achievement of modernism's goals. In others, it marks the demise of modernism, its failure. The end of modernism, as both success *and* failure, creates the challenge of postmodernity: How does one live after modernity? The modernist means of answering this question is no longer viable because they merely recapitulate the problems that lead to this point. But serious problems, beginning with climate change, remain. How then does one respond to this situation?

What I argued throughout is that Hickman is correct. While Hickman fails to distinguish postmodernism and postmodernity, which leads him to too quickly to dismiss postmodernism, the punch line of his argument is entirely on target: pragmatism's voice remains vital in the present. Where I differ from Hickman is the extent to which this should be forged out of an engagement with postmodern theorists. When Hickman works with philosophers outside of the pragmatic tradition, he usually argues: (a) they misinterpret pragmatism or (b) how pragmatists (usually Dewey) anticipate that philosopher's thought and surpass their arguments.[2] On the one hand, Hickman has done an incredible service illustrating the depth and sophistication of Dewey's thought, never mind demonstrating Dewey's continued relevance to the contemporary world. On the other hand, there are certain distinctive trends and textures to postmodernity that postmodern thought is better attuned to because it grew up wrestling with this era. This is particularly true when it comes to describing contemporary phenomena. While pragmatism does have much to offer to the present, the approach I developed here relies on entering into more of an explicit dialogue with postmodern thought. Doing this allows me to preserve the most relevant aspects of postmodernism with respect to postmodernity, while demonstrating the relevance of pragmatism, in particular through critiques of the excesses of postmodernism.

Yet, when I write of the necessity of the concept of postmodernity, and hence aspects of postmodernism, this should not be interpreted as a slavish devotion to the concept. While I have defended its continued significance for understanding the present throughout, I have also sought to be sensitive to the fact that although the present should still be regarded as "postmodern," that this does not mean that the nature of the present is the same as when the term "postmodern" came into vogue in the 1980s. Obviously, this is not the case, especially for anyone who considers technology. Some broad outlines of how ICTs would develop were visible then, but it would have been quite difficult to exactly predict the specifics of how the Internet, computers and, first, cell phones and, later, smartphones would transformation social relations (Raines and Wellman 2012; Turkle 2011). Lyotard picks up on the general trajectory of these changes, but works at an abstract enough level that he did not address the details in ways like the uses I put Mead to. I use the term "postmodernity" as a way to describe the present in a broad sense, characterized by ephemerality, relativism, difference, heterogeneity, fluidity, and hyper-reality. The precise way that these traits have manifested themselves over the last fifty years has changed. And, if the drift of my argument is correct, these traits will remain relevant into the future, albeit in mutated ways. I propose this because of the technological forces bound up with postmodernity continue to be at work, if not intensifying it further.

Although the word "postmodern" is less fashionable now, the linkages mapped here between the postmodern and technology show how the challenge of postmodernity persists. Following Jameson, it is not appropriate to *reduce* postmodernity to technology, but by following how technology exemplifies motifs of postmodern thought it provides a rather valuable map of the contours of the present. Obviously, the term "postmodern technology" is quite broad. As discussed in chapter 1, it refers to a wide range of technologies including architecture, computers, running shoes, biotechnologies, food, and so. Then there is the notorious difficulty of defining the term "postmodern." Given this, the expectation of finding some precise essence of "postmodern technology" is clearly hopeless. Yet, the term is still of some use. Accepting that, much like the term "postmodern" itself, there will be blurriness at the edges which prevents precise use, "postmodern technology" does help discriminate between different sorts of technologies. There are more modernist technologies like the Hoover Dam, the Cold War Era Space Program, and the Fordist assembly line. And there are more postmodernist technologies like just-in time production (Harvey 1990), genetic engineering (Haraway 1991, 1997), and other posthumanizing technologies (Best and Kellner 2001, 149–204). I emphasized ICTs because of their pervasiveness and effectiveness in exemplifying postmodern motifs. As I show through discussing the transformations ICTs perform on listening to music, the listener can be free to select the music they would like, free from the intentions of artist. Although a trivial example, a similar logic plays out in many other places. Castells described general logic involved here when he discussed how (at least some) individuals have (relatively) easy access to the entirety of human cultural productions (that can be, and has been, reproduced electronically). Those with access to this repository are in a position in which they can re-present these in whatever manner they choose.

Running throughout all this is the issue of the loosening of social control. In these cases, when individuals use ICTs social control can appear less demanding, allowing for more open-ended responses. Overt social control does not disappear, but rather becomes much more dependent on the individual to internalize. This helps to explain why Lyotard describes this as "a moment of relaxation" (Lyotard 1993a, 1). At least at some levels, the expectations that dominated modernism recede. Within the arts, the necessity of an avant-garde seems like a relic of a bygone, perhaps sillier, day. The idea of expertise falls under relentless assault. The distinctions between high and low culture remains relegated to the sidelines. Identity continues to be something to be constructed. Each of these illustrates the ways in which the expectations of the modern have become frayed. Perhaps this is clearest in the case of identity, where, if modernity opened the door for individuals to explore whom they might be, postmodernity sees the self as something that can be wholly shaped by the individual (Giddens 1991). There is still some claim to social control, but the mechanisms of its operation have changed. In some cases, it becomes more a matter of individual decision to embrace or not. In others, as discussed briefly in chapter 4, it operates more covertly, built into the technologies themselves. Since each element of an ICT involves coding, usually designed by others, Lyotard worries that this can work to restrain or even prevent the openness and playfulness he argues for. This then reinscribes social control, often in a way that is more concealed, less open to scrutiny (if for no other reason than it is propriety software). As with so much of postmodernity, there is a double movement. At once social control is loosened and intensified.

## QUESTIONS CONCERNING TECHNOLOGY

This all points to the necessity of taking technology seriously in order to address this challenge, but not turn to technology alone as a means of salvation. Many analyses of how to respond to the present challenge, regardless of whether it is couched in postmodern terms or not, tend to treat technology as an afterthought. The full import of how technology is part of the challenge remains underappreciated. In light of the foregoing argument, this is problematic. Put perhaps too bluntly, the entire thrust of the foregoing analysis is that one must be attentive to the particularities of technologies, the general style of their use (Pitt 1988), in order to better appreciate the roles of technologies within postmodernity. Although trivial in the grand scheme of things, the analysis of music players in chapter 1 illustrates this effectively. The differences between listening to music via LP and CD as compared to a streaming service produce distinctive relationships to the music. The same lesson was shown in chapter 3 when considering the different possibilities created by different modes of electronic communication. In order to effectively reconstruct how of such technologies, it is necessary to first trace out their functions and operations, fully appreciating that such determinations cannot be made in the abstract. While they overstate the point, defenders of the position that technology is socially constructed are correct that the ends technologies are put to tend to be underdetermined and open to transformation by society.

There is a different danger associated with technology, one that pragmatism, at its best, avoids and is uniquely well placed to reform. It is the tendency to expect that technology will function as a secularized mode of salvation. Transhumanism can fall into this trap (Tirosh-Samuelson 2012). But it is also possible to have less grandiose variations on this theme like with the occasional declarations about how this or that technological development will allow for the creation of better societies, democracies, individuals, or schools. There is something of a metanarrative here, though it is important to note how its contemporary variation diverges from more traditional modernist ones. While this is something of a variation on the Garden myth, it is also fused to the logic of performativity. The mark of progress here is most clearly cashed out in terms of technical improvements. By this I mean improvements in the specifications of technology: increased efficiency, processing power, or number of pixels per square inch. Such technical progress is a variation on performativity inasmuch as it is a sort of "best solution to the 'input/output equation,'" that is, Lyotard's definition of performativity. There can also be shades of a shallow liberalism at work here, in which it is up to the individual what they do with this bounty, instead of the entire human race or some subsection of it. These changes indicate to which technology operates as a sort of "postmodern salvation," a pastiche of modern and postmodern motifs, dressing up the ghost of dead habits.

There are two worries worth noting about treating technology as a sort of salvation. The first is the extent to which it obscures the importance of human agency in the development of technology. This operates at two levels. The first is treating technology as if it was beyond human control; that it develops autonomously. A relatively clear defense of this position is offered by Jacques Ellul (1964), whom Hickman criticizes for being a grim inversion of scientific Marxism (Hickman 1990, 147–48). Second, it substitutes technological development for the transformation of society. Instead of approaching a problem as requiring solutions that rethink social organization, this salvation myth frames problems are requiring the introduction of further technologies (which might require readjustment on the part individuals using or otherwise impacted by the technologies, but this is best thought of as a negative externality). This second worry is the manner in which this salvation myth functions as a cover for late capitalism (Mandel 1978, 500–22). The implementation of technology is rarely done based on beneficence. Rather, these are commodities to be sold like any other. Hickman raises many important criticisms of technological determinism (Hickman 1990, 140–41) and takes Ellul and Heidegger to task for saying that we need to be saved from technology (Hickman 2001, 147–53). Although never phrasing the issue in this manner, Hickman correctly attempts to displace talk of "salvation" with that of "responsibility" (Hickman 2001, 153–56). Instead of expecting something to save humans from technology, or technology to save humans from their problems, the talk of "responsibility" relocates possible responses to the challenges posed by technology, or the challenge of postmodernity, within the sphere of human agency. Pragmatism requires that any salvation be built up by the democratic community, rather than outsourcing it to something external, whether the logic of a metanarrative, a god, or technology.

## THE SYSTEM REDUX

One complication for pragmatic meliorism is what Lyotard referred to as "the system." Society now functions as a self-regulating system, governed by a logic of performativity. This system possesses no "outside" per se, thus embodying the logic of bounded infinite. Rather, the system only serves to improve its own performance. In chapter 2, I described how liberal democracy is performatively defensible inasmuch as it is flexible enough to be able to respond to problems. For example, the continued expansion of rights was also explained part of this same development. Rights no longer serve a critical role, but rather ensure the proper functioning of postmodern societies (see also and compare to Marcuse 1964). The expansion of rights should not be seen as organic growth, but as the self-adjustment of a cybernetic system. Talcott Parsons in effect endorsed something like the concept of the system, though he understood this in terms of an organism instead of a network composed of heterogenous elements. Both the modern and postmodern bonds Lyotard considers hold that society is self-regulating, but the method of regulation is distinct. The inspiration for Lyotard's postmodern system is that of cybernetics and other sorts of feedback control systems. This imagery has three features of note. First, these systems can operate effectively instantaneously over large distances. They do not require the close proximity usually associated with organisms. Second, although organisms might be a part of a cybernetic system, the system is not itself an organism. Rather than relying on organic and holistic metaphors for making sense of society, using mechanical and, better still, electronic imagery is better for explain society's functioning and malfunctioning. Third, cybernetic systems can perform complicated activities, including ones that echo human intelligence, although these systems are not intentional agents themselves. These features help account for why the implication coming out of Lyotard's writings on the system is that the system is beyond human control. Given the size and self-adjusting nature of the system, it is outside beyond the power of any person to actually guide it. Rather, it guides itself with the goal of maximizing society's own performance (which, incidentally, should allow it to increase its complexity, thus forestalling the possibility of entropy).

On the one hand, the idea of the system is a fiction, and a dangerous one at that. To treat society as an autonomous, self-correcting network denies the important roles that human agency can play in shaping society. Even though it is not knowable in advance what affects humans might have on society, there are clearly places in which individuals can impact it (see and compare with Hickman 1990, 140–65). Without this tenet, pragmatic meliorism becomes vacuous because human endeavors cannot transform society, let alone improve the start of the world itself.[3] On the other hand, the appeal of this sort of system-thinking is clear enough. Human societies are obviously rather complex, without any one place in control (contra Parsons, the organism lacks a "brain." See Foucault 1978, 94–96). Yet, societies do seem to behave as if they were governed in some way, whether by notions of "progress," "tradition," capital accumulation, etc., even if all these ultimately boil down to performativity. So, there might not be any one center guiding the system, but it might not be wholly out of control.

The situation becomes more complicated, and more interesting, in light of contemporary technologies. ICTs in particular now execute decisions in lieu of humans. Two examples. First, much of the world of high finance is now handled by computers following algorithms. These are overseen by humans, but much of the trading done by large firms is performed by the computers (Lotti 2018). These algorithms take in information and execute orders based upon that and other priorities. While usually quite useful, there is concern that such algorithms can cause problems. One case of this was "flash crash" of the British pound in 2016, where "the currency nosedived by 9% against the dollar in Asian trading hours . . . caused by a combination of inexperienced traders, algorithmic trading and complex trading positions" (Treanor 2017). Second is the increased prominence of bots throughout the Infosphere. With an increased frequency, individuals engage with content that was produced by programs that was made to appear as it was produced by humans. These might be posts on Twitter, stories in newspapers, or chats to help with problems. The use of these bots can be more or less beneficial, more or less malevolent. Either way, bots illustrate the way in which human lives increasingly involve coordinating activities with technology. This goes beyond the ways in which humans have relied upon technologies throughout history. This coordination now operates at a level that goes back to Mead's significant symbols. The coordination does not just involve the actions of humans with technology, but also meanings and social objects, including sometimes maldeveloping such programs (Neff and Nagy 2016).

At this stage, computers do not meet Mead's criteria for self-consciousness, but it is possible that it is only a matter of time before this changes. If AIs can be created that should be regarded as self-consciousness in his sense, this further intensifies the issue here because it makes much more literal the concept of "autonomous technology." Even without going this far, these contemporary ICT-based entities can feed into the appearance that society is an autonomous, self-adjusting system, sustained by technology. The intersection of these technologies and social institutions appear to operate under their own logic. Lyotard describe the situation as "the needs for security, identity, and happiness springing from our immediate condition as living beings, as social beings, now seem irrelevant next to this sort of constraint to complexify, mediatize, quantify, synthesize, and modify the size of each and every object. We are like Gullivers in the world of technoscience: sometimes too big, sometimes too small, but never the right size" (Lyotard 1991, 78–79). The system seems to exist for its own ends and humans must, albeit awkwardly, be made to fit into it. While Lyotard's concept of the system is problematic for reasons touched on above, it is useful as a way of crystalize important dangers of the present, especially with the role of technologies.

## UNDER RECONSTRUCTION

The upshot: technology must be taken seriously in the work of reconstruction, but alongside other factors. To approach the challenge of postmodernity in largely cognitive terms fails to meet the challenge. The phenomenon of timeless time effectively shows this. The emergence of this distinctly postmodern time-consciousness is bound up with the development and widespread use of particular technologies. This time consciousness sets boundaries on possible ways for transforming the present condition as discussed in chapter 5. In order to work with, never mind potentially transform and move beyond, timeless time, the extent to which it is bound up with technology must be appreciated. Without such an appreciation of the particular roles that technology plays within the present, the extent to which problematic situations can be transformed is seriously hampered. Attention must be paid to specifically technological dimensions of the contemporary world in order to effectively understand and transform it.

The concepts derived from pragmatism brought forward here do just this by simultaneously bringing into focus both the social and technological dimensions of the postmodernity. Of decisive importance here is the idea of habit because habit functions at the intersection of thought and action. According to Peirce, the purpose of thought is reform beliefs in order to establish new habits that allow for successful action. As discussed in chapter 1, habits operate on and through technologies and, as suggested there, one way to understand what makes a particular period's technologies distinctive are the habits associated with those technologies. Dreyfus and Spinosa (1997) made a similar point through contrasting the different regimes involved with modern and postmodern libraries. So to with the habits associated with communication. In order to effectively communicate via Twitter requires a somewhat different, though not wholly unrelated, set of habits than writing a letter or face-to-face communication. The habits involved here bring together thought, action, and technology. Furthermore, given the current centrality of ICTs, such habits clearly underwrite elements of social relations as well.

Habit plays such a significant role in pragmatism because it serves an excellent site on which creative intelligence can operate. While not without limits, there are degrees of malleability to habits, allowing them to be transformed. Instead of the ephemerality that is sometimes associated with postmodernism, this pragmatic emphasis upon habit allows for a concrete place to focus attention in order to produce results. Habits are always embodied, which keeps things grounded as opposed to the sometimes overly playful, purely textual considerations of postmodern thought. Given the way that habit can operate at the boundary of the self and not-self, the adjustment of habit will transform both the individual and the world that they engage with. This is why pragmatists have written so much about the necessity of intelligently reforming habits. They play such an important role, that if one seeks to transform problematic situations, they will be vital since they involve both the individual and the world.

For these reasons, one site for reconstructing the postmodern condition will be the habits implicated in the usage of technologies. There are two things to consider here. First is the technology itself, then there are the habits involved with its use. Technology is neither a hero nor a villain here, though it is necessary to appreciate the challenges and opportunities posed by different technologies. Particular technologies can make the goals of reconstructions more or less difficult to achieve. A classic example of this comes from Langdon Winner (1989) where he contrasts the sorts of politics produced by nuclear and solar power. He suggests, not unplausibly, that between the security challenges and the risks of "mistakes," nuclear power requires the centralized authority of the state. On the other hand, generating power through solar and other "appropriate" technologies leads a more decentralized state because individuals or small communities can regulate these technologies as effectively. Winner might overstate the extent to which solar power sources encourages a decentralized state, but it seems reasonable enough that fostering such a state is easier with these technologies than with those associated with nuclear power.

Several points now follow. First, the way in which technologies make certain goals easier or harder. As Heidegger noted, one definition of technology is as a means to an end (1993, 312–13). This is correct, but misleading, for reasons different than Heidegger's. Instead, the trouble with interpreting technologies merely a means is that the choice of means shapes what ends can be taken up, can become Deweyian "ends-in-view." For example, the technical decisions of Twitter to limit tweets to either 140 or 280 characters encourages certain sorts of communication (with an emphasis on short, pithy statements) and discourages longer forms, like that of the essay (Hannan 2018). Second, this shows the necessity of choosing technologies wisely at the outset. This is at once important and very challenging. Important because the more technologies become relied upon, the more habits are built around their use, which makes dislodging the technology increasingly challenging (Hughes 1987). This speaks to the need to select technologies carefully, but doing so is hard. In part this is because of the reciprocal relationship between means and ends. Also it is difficult, if not impossible, to determine all of the consequences that follow from the adoption of technologies (Pitt 2000, 46–51). Although anticipating all the consequences is likely impossible, this should not be an excuse for avoiding such matters altogether. Rather, the matter calls for the use of creative intelligence, both when initially developing and implementing technologies, and after this, in order to provide course corrections for effective operation. It is also important to not just be attentive to the particularities of the technologies in present reconstructions, but also to be aware of spaces for reconstruction of the technologies themselves going forward. While not infinitely pliable, one important, though sometimes overstated, lesson from social constructivism is the malleability of technologies. The meanings associated with the technologies, how they function as "techno-social objects," is shaped by designers, manufacturers and users. Depending on the pressure brought by these relevant social groups, the meanings or habits can be reconstructed, or perhaps the artifact itself. One advantage of the pragmatic approach articulated here is the way in which, unlike much of the social constructivist literature, embodiment is foreground by beginning with habit.

Technologies must be reconstructed to be more "effective," but this term is rather troublesome. Left unchecked, the sheer momentum of contemporary world seems to be point toward more of the postmodern same like hyperindividualsim and hypercommodification, as illustrated through talk of "the system." This can qualify as "effective," but only understood in terms of effective for the current techno-social order. Especially within the context of the United States, there is a tendency to bury talk of "effectiveness" beneath a rhetoric of free markets. Such rhetoric serves to conceal the decisions that go into every stage of the usage of technologies. Of course, there is a tension here. On the one hand, all of the classical pragmatists, beginning with Peirce, were highly critical of the sociopolitical order of their day. Postmodernity mutated out of that order. While different from the modernity that the classical pragmatists criticized, the present remains quite open for criticism. On the other, central to democracy is the faith in individuals to work together in self-reflective manners. While not wholly untutored, this does involve trusting the community to make determinations for itself (LW2.235-372; Hickman 1990, 166–95). Philosophers and other intellectuals have roles in fostering the public, but the decisions must be made by the community itself via democratic institutions (which themselves are being reassessed and reconstructed by the democratic community).[4] There are many important tasks for such intellectuals including the attempting to describe the contours of the contemporary world and illuminating how they might be transformed. There is also the critical task of opening up concepts like "effective" in order to demonstrate the value judgments contained with them and exploring how these might be transformed to be better in line with other values.

The necessity of using creative, democratic intelligence can be seen with respect to the concept of the bounded infinite. I have attempted to be agnostic about the desirability of the bounded infinite. Given that it is a description of a conceptual universe, it is conceivable that it could be replaced by a different conceptual framework. I tried to avoid advocating for that, instead taking it as a given to be worked with. Even if is there is a conceptual universe radically different from the bounded infinite, the bounded infinite defines the present. Assuming that some conceptual universe beyond this is worth pursuing, it must be achieved through creative intelligences reconstructing the bounded infinite. And to the extent that creative intelligences can reconstruct conceptual universes, such reconstruction should be democratic in character. It is not simply the province of academics or others to pursue. Another reason for hesitancy here. Obviously, the larger the situation to be reconstructed, the more there is to be done. Simply because one starts to transform a situation does not guarantee that the situation's other elements remain static. In other words, only so much is under the control of a creative intelligence. Some elements can remain within the reach of intelligence, although which elements will likely change as a reconstruction proceeds. One element may be transformed intentionally, while others change because of inertia or evolution; when those others are addressed, further elements then do the same in turn. A certain humility is called for here since it is likely quite difficult to know ahead of time how this will work. After all, if one knew ahead of time how this would work, inquiry would not be necessary. Lastly, modernism set its own course, breaking from tradition (Habermas 1975, 1987). For a number of modernist philosophers, democracy was part of this project, though usually imperfectly by today's standards. What was taken as universal has been unmasked as representing the interests of a very particular, and peculiar, group. All of the classical pragmatists were aware of this problem, even if they only dealt with it indirectly. Dewey defines democracy in such a way that it discourages this sort of parochialism. The legacies of exclusion and elitism weigh heavily on postmodern philosophers, and rightly so. Contemporary pragmatists are rather aware of this as well and the concern for fostering democratic communities of difference.

The interpretation of pragmatism developed here does not seek to recreate the world a new. That was the dream of modernism. Rather, pragmatism flourishes when working in the midst of things in order to transform them. Initially, this is not a world of one's own making. Yet, there is space for improving the world from within. Hence, the reason that pragmatism is so ideally suited for operating within the bounded infinite. The conceptual space of postmodernity is comprised of innumerable elements and, while nothing new can be added, these elements can be rearranged, combined in novel ways. To do this is nothing less than a sort of reconstruction. Pragmatism provides tools for working within the bounded infinite in order to cultivate habits that will lay the groundwork for finding ways to operate more effectively within such a universe. Such reconstructions will necessarily need to involve technology, though technology should never possess sole responsibility in any possible salvation. Making technology play such a role either falls in the traps Lyotard diagnosed and proclaimed dead or into the traps of performativity. Instead, salvation can only be built up within the bounded infinite. The expectation that such salvation will be like the organic holism that Haraway finds in so much modernist thought should be abandoned. On this front, the postmodern emphasis on heterogeneity and difference should be taken as common sense. Of course, pragmatism can adjust itself to such concerns as demonstrated in the previous chapter.

Classical pragmatism was born in the later years of modernity. As a result, the classical pragmatists clearly incorporate a number of motifs of modern philosophy, like the embrace of science and democracy, a concept of progress, and the centrality of emancipation. Yet, they rejected other modernist motifs in unequivocal terms. All of them sought to embrace certain motifs of postmodern philosophy: anti-Cartesianism, anti-foundationalism, and anti-essentialism (Griffin 1993). Because pragmatism used the latter to reconstruct the former, pragmatism remains distinctly relevant to postmodernity (Stuhr 2003). The classical pragmatists eschewed the vices of modernism, while also avoiding the excesses of postmodernism that prevent that philosophy from being able to address the postmodern challenge effectively. Pragmatism can do this, though it is necessary for pragmatism to stay true to its pluralistic and democratic roots through an engagement with postmodern thought because of the latter's unique attunement to the present. In this way, pragmatism might have been born in modernity, but it has the opportunity to come of age in postmodernity.

## NOTES

1. David Harvey (1990) remains among the best on this front. Also indispensable are Best and Kellner (1997, 2001) and Jameson (1991). While note addressing postmodernity explicitly, Castells (2010a, 2010b) and Wilkie (2011) are also very illuminating for their analyses of related phenomena.

2. An example of the former is Hickman's (1990, 64–67) response to Max Horkheimer's critique of pragmatism. With the latter, Parts 2 and 3 of Hickman 2007 illustrate this tendency when he writes on philosophers like Borgmann, Feenberg, and Habermas.

3. Unless one takes the position that the uses of creative intelligence pragmatists advocate for are in fact part of the system.

4. Behind this point is a rather serious tension: that the community might endorse, even after reflective, democratic deliberations, conclusions that diverge from what might fit with the meloristic thrust of pragmatism. The seriousness of this challenge: (a) should not be understated; (b) goes well beyond the scope this work. It is not obvious to me how to effectively address this, besides returning to core pragmatic concepts like hope and seeking to resolve it experimentally.

# Bibliography

Aboulafia, Mitchell. 2001. *The Cosmopolitan Self: George Herbert Mead and Continental Philosophy*. Urbana: University of Illinois Press.
Adams, John. 2008. *Hallelujah Junction: Composing an American Life*. New York: Farrar, Straus and Giroux.
Adorno, Theodor. 2003. "Late Capitalism or Industrial Society? The Fundamental Question of the Present Structure of Society." In *Can One Live After Auschwitz? A Philosophical Reader*, edited Rolf Tiedemann, 111–25. Palo Alto, CA: Stanford University Press.
Akker, Robin van den, Alison Gibbons, and Timotheus Vermeulen (Editors). 2017. *Metamodernism: Historicity, Affect, and Depth after Postmodernism*. London: Rowman & Littlefield.
Appell, David. 2008. "A Solar Big Gulp." *Scientific American*. 299(3): 24–25.
Barthes, Roland. 1977. *Image/Music/Text*. Translated by Stephen Heath. New York: Noonday Press.
Baudrillard, Jean. 1994. *Simulacra and Simulation*. Translated by Sheila Faria Glaser. Ann Arbor: University of Michigan Press.
Baudrillard, Jean. 1995. *The Gulf War Did Not Take Place*. Translated by Paul Patton. Bloomington: Indiana University Press.
Bernstein, Richard J. 1992. *The New Constellation: The Ethical-Political Horizons of Modernity/Postmodernity*. Cambridge, MA: MIT Press.
Bernstein, Richard J. 2010. *The Pragmatic Turn*. Boston, MA: Polity.
Best, Steven and Douglas Kellner. 1991. *Postmodern Theory: Critical Interrogations*. New York: Guilford Press.
Best, Steven and Douglas Kellner. 1997. *The Postmodern Turn*. New York: Guilford Press.
Best, Steven and Douglas Kellner. 2001. *The Postmodern Adventure: Science, Technology and Cultural Studies at the Third Millennium*. New York: Guilford Press.

Biagioli, Mario. 1993. *Galileo Courtier: The Practice of Science in The Culture of Absolutism*. Chicago: University of Chicago Press.

Borgmann, Albert. 1984. *Technology and the Character of Contemporary Life: A Philosophical Inquiry*. Chicago: University of Chicago Press.

Borgmann, Albert. 1992. *Crossing the Postmodern Divide*. Chicago: University of Chicago Press.

Borgmann, Albert. 1999. *Holding on to Reality: The Nature of Information at the Turn of the Millennium*. Chicago: University of Chicago Press.

Bostrom, Nick. 2005. "In Defense of Posthuman Dignity." *Bioethics*. 19(3): 202–14. DOI: 10.1111/j.1467-8519.2005.00437.x.

Brogaard, Berit. 1999. "Mead's Temporal Realism." *Transactions of the Charles S. Peirce Society*. 35(1): 563–93.

Brubaker, Jed R., Gillian R. Hayes, and Paul Dourish. 2013. "Beyond the Grave: Facebook as a Site for the Expansion of Death and Mourning." *The Information Society*. 29(3): 152–63. DOI: 10.1080/01972243.2013.777300.

Bruce, Katherine McFarland. 2016. *Pride Parades: How a Parade Changed the World*. New York: New York University Press.

Burke, Tom. 2005. "The Role of Abstract Reference in Mead's Account of Human Origins." *Transactions of the Charles S. Peirce Society*. 41(3): 567–601.

Castells, Manuel. 2010a. *The Rise of the Network Society*, Second Edition. Malden, MA: Wiley-Blackwell.

Castells, Manuel. 2010b. *The Power of Identity*, Second Edition. Malden, MA: Wiley-Blackwell.

Castells, Manuel. 2012. *Networks of Outrage and Hope: Social Movements in the Internet Age*. Cambridge, UK: Polity Press.

Castells, Manuel. 2013. *Communication Power, 2013 Edition*. Oxford: Oxford University Press.

Chalmers, David. 1996. *The Conscious Mind: In Search of A Fundamental Theory*. New York: Oxford University Press.

Clegg, Stewart R. 1989. *Frameworks of Power*. London: Sage Publications.

Cook, Gary. 1993. *George Herbert Mead: The Making of a Social Pragmatist*. Chicago: University of Chicago Press.

Coxeter, H. S. M. 1979. "The Non-Euclidean Symmetry of Escher's Picture 'Circle Limit III'." *Leonardo*. 12(1): 19–25.

Craft, Ashley John. 2007. "Sin in Cyber-Eden: Understanding the Metaphysics and Morals of Virtual Worlds." *Ethics and Information Technologies*. 9(3): 205–17. DOI: 10.1007/s10676-007-9144-4.

Dempsey, Lorcan, Constance Malpas, and Brian Lavoie. 2014. "Collection Directions: The Evolution of Library Collections and Collecting." *Portal: Libraries and the Academy*. 14(3): 393–423. DOI: 10.1353/pla.2014.0013.

Derrida, Jacques. 1978. *Writing and Difference*. Translated by Alan Bass. Chicago: University of Chicago Press.

Derrida, Jacques. 1994. *Specters of Marx: The State of the Debt, the Work of Mourning, and the New International*. Translated by Peggy Kamuf. New York: Routledge.

Derrida, Jacques. 1998. *Of Grammatology: Corrected Edition*. Translated by Gayatri Spivak. Baltimore, MD: John Hopkins University Press.
Dewey, John. 1969–90. *The Collected Works of John Dewey 1882–1953 (Early Works, Middle Works, and Later Works)*. Carbondale: Southern Illinois University Press (*Middle Works* abbreviated: MW Volume. Page. *Later Works* abbreviated: LW Volume. Page).
Dreyfus, Hubert. 1999. "Anonymity versus Commitment: The Dangers of Education on the Internet." *Ethics and Information Technology*. 1(1): 15–21.
Dreyfus, Hubert and Charles Spinosa. 1997. "Highway Bridges and Feasts: Heidegger and Borgmann on How to Affirm Technology." *Man and World*. 30(2): 159–77.
Eagleton, Terry. 1996. *The Illusions of Postmodernism*. Malden: Blackwell Publishing.
Ebert, Teresa. 1996. *Ludic Feminism and After: Postmodernism, Desire, and Labor in Late Capitalism*. Ann Arbor: University of Michigan Press.
Egenfeldt-Nielsen, Simon, Jonas Heide Smith, and Susana Pajares Tosca. 2016. *Understanding Video Games: The Essential Introduction*, Third Edition. New York: Routledge.
Ellul, Jacques. 1964. *The Technological Society*. Translated by John Wilkinson. New York: Vintage Books.
Ermarth, Elizabeth Deeds. 1998. "Postmodernism (Version 1)." In *Routledge Encyclopedia of Philosophy*. Available at: https://www.rep.routledge.com/articles/thematic/postmodernism/v-1. DOI: 10.4324/9780415249126-N044-1.
Eshelman, Raoul. 2008. *Performatism: Or the End of Postmodernism*. Aurora, CO: Davies Group Publishing.
Floridi, Luciano. 2011. *The Philosophy of Information*. Oxford: Oxford University Press.
Floridi, Luciano. 2013. *The Ethics of Information*. Oxford: Oxford University Press.
Floridi, Luciano. 2014. *The 4th Revolution: How the Infosphere is Reshaping Human Reality*. Oxford: Oxford University Press.
Feenberg, Andrew. 1992. "Subversive Rationalization: Technology, Power, and Democracy." *Inquiry*. 35(3–4): 301–22. DOI: 10.1080/00201749208602296.
Fine, Gary Allen. 1983. *Shared Fantasy: Role-Playing Games as Social Worlds*. Chicago: University of Chicago Press.
Foucault, Michel. 1975. *Discipline and Punish: The Birth of the Prison*. Translated by Alan Sheridan. New York: Vintage Books.
Foucault, Michel. 1978. *The History of Sexuality: An Introduction, Volume 1*. Translated by Robert Hurley. New York: Vintage Books.
Foucault, Michel. 1983. "The Subject and Power." In *Beyond Structuralism and Hermeneutics*, Second Edition, edited by Hubert Dreyfus and Paul Rabinow, 208–28. Chicago: University of Chicago Press.
Freud, Sigmund. 1967. *Moses and Monotheism*. Translated by Katherine Jones. New York: Vintage.
Fukuyama, Francis. 1992. *The End of History and the Last Man*. New York: Free Press.
Fukuyama, Francis. 2012. "The Future of History: Can Liberal Democracy Survive the Decline of the Middle Class?" *Foreign Affairs*. 91(January/February): 53–61.

Garnar, Andrew Wells. 2009. "Must a Pragmatist Be a Historical Materialist?" *Contemporary Pragmatism*. 6(1): 67–86. DOI: 10.1163/18758185-90000105.
Garrison, Jim. 1997. *Dewey and Eros: Wisdom and Desire in the Art of Teaching*. New York: Teachers College Press.
Gibson, William. 1984. *Neuromancer*. New York: Ace Books.
Giddens, Anthony. 1991. *Modernity and Self-Identity: Self and Society in the Late Modern Age*. Palo Alto, CA: Stanford University Press.
Gleick, James. 2011. *The Information: A History, A Theory, A Flood*. New York: Pantheon.
Goodman, Dena. 1994. *The Republic of Letters: A Cultural History of the French Enlightenment*. Ithaca: Cornell University Press.
Griffin, David Ray (editor). 1993. *Founders of Constructive Postmodern Philosophy: Peirce, James, Bergson, Whitehead, and Harthshorne*. Albany: State University of New York Press.
Habermas, Jürgen. 1975. *Legitimation Crisis*. Translated by Thomas McCarthy. Boston: Beacon Press.
Habermas, Jürgen. 1987. *The Philosophical Discourse of Modernity: Twelve Lectures*. Translated by Frederick Lawrence. Cambridge, MA: MIT Press.
Hacking, Ian. 1999. *The Social Construction of What?* Cambridge, MA: Harvard University Press.
Hannan, Jason. 2018. "Trolling Ourselves to Death? Social Media and Post-Truth Politics." *European Journal of Communication*. 33(2): 214–26. DOI: 10.1177/0267323118760323.
Haraway, Donna. 1991. *Cyborgs, Simians, and Women: The Reinvention of Nature*. New York: Routledge.
Haraway, Donna. 1997. *Modest_Witness@Second_Millennium.FemaleMan©_Meets_ OncoMouse™*. New York: Routledge.
Haraway, Donna. 2016. *Staying with the Trouble: Making Kin in the Chthulucene*. Durham, NC: Duke University Press.
Harding, Sandra. 1994. "Is Science Multicultural? Challenges, Resources, Opportunities, Uncertainties." *Configurations*. 2(2): 301–30. DOI: 10.1353/con.1994.0019.
Harvey, David. 1990. *The Condition of Postmodernity: An Inquiry into the Origins of Cultural Change*. Cambridge, UK: Blackwell.
Harvey, David. 2011. *The Enigma of Capital and the Crises of Capitalism*. New York: Oxford University Press.
Hayles, N. Katherine. 1999. *How We Became Posthuman: Virtual Bodies in Cybernetics, Literature, and Informatics*. Chicago: University of Chicago Press.
Heidegger, Martin. 1993. *Basic Writings, Revised and Expanded Edition*. Edited by David Krell. San Francisco: Harper Collins.
Hessen, Boris. 1971. "The Social and Economic Roots of Newton's 'Principia'." In *Science at the Cross Roads*, edited by N. Bukharin, et al., 151–212. London: Frank Cass and Co. Ltd.
Hickman, Larry. 1990. *John Dewey's Pragmatic Technology*. Bloomington: Indiana University Press.

Hickman, Larry. 2001. *Philosophical Tools for a Technological Culture: Putting Pragmatism to Work*. Bloomington: Indiana University Press.
Hickman, Larry. 2007. *Pragmatism as Post-Postmodernism: Lessons from John Dewey*. New York: Fordham University Press.
Hookway, Christopher. 1985. *Peirce*. New York: Routledge.
Horkheimer, Max. 1947. *Eclipse of Reason*. New York: Continuum.
Hughes, Thomas P. 1987. "The Evolution of Large Technological Systems." In *The Social Construction of Technological Systems: New Directions in the Sociology and History of Technology*, edited by Wiebe E. Bijker, Thomas P. Hughes, and Trevor J. Pinch, 17–50. Cambridge, MA: MIT Press.
Hume, David. 1978. *A Treatise of Human Nature: Second Edition*. Oxford: Clarendon Press.
Hunt, Lynn. 2007. *Inventing Human Rights: A History*. New York: Norton.
Isaac, Mike. September 27, 2017. "This Isn't Enough Space To Tell You Twitter's Plan." *New York Times*. B3.
James, William. 1987. *Writings, 1902–1910*. Edited by Bruce Kuklick. New York: Library of America.
Jameson, Fredric. 1991. *Postmodernism, or, the Cultural Logic of Late Capitalism*. Durham, NC: Duke University Press.
Joas, Hans. 1996. *The Creativity of Action*. Translated by J. Gaines and P. Keast. Chicago: University of Chicago Press.
Joas, Hans. 1997. *G. H. Mead: A Contemporary Re-examination of His Thought*. Translated by Raymond Meyer. Cambridge, MA: MIT Press.
Judson, Horace Freeland. 1996. *The Eighth Day of Creation: Makers of the Revolution in Biology, Expanded Edition*. Plainview, NY: Cold Spring Harbor Laboratory Press.
Kaliarnta, Sofia. 2016. "Using Aristotle's Theory of Friendship to Classify Online Friendships: A Critical Counterview." *Ethics and Information Technology*. 18(2): 65–79. DOI: 10.1007/s10676-016-9384-2.
Kirby, Alan. 2006. "The Death of Postmodernism and Beyond." *Philosophy Now*. Issue 58. Available at: https://philosophynow.org/issues/58/The_Death_of_Postmodernism_And_Beyond.
Kirby, Alan. 2009. *Digimodernism: How New Technologies Dismantle the Postmodern and Reconfigure Our Culture*. New York: Continuum.
Koyré, Alexander. 1957. *From the Closed World to the Infinite Universe*. Baltimore, MD: John Hopkins University Press.
Krioukov, Dmitri, Fragkiskos Papadopoulos, Maksim Kitsak, Amin Vahdat, and Marián Boguñá. 2010. "Hyperbolic Geometry of Complex Networks." *Physical Review E*. 82(3): 036106-1-18. DOI: 10.1103/PhysRevE.82.036106.
Kuhn, Thomas S. 1996. *The Structure of Scientific Revolutions*, Third Edition. Chicago: University of Chicago Press.
Leitch, Vincent B. 2004. "Postmodern Theory of Technology: Agendas." *symplokē*. 12(1/2): 209–15.
Lindberg, David C. 1992. *The Beginnings of Western Science: The European Scientific Tradition in Philosophical, Religious, and Institutional Context, 600 B.C. to A.D. 1450*. Chicago: University of Chicago Press.

Lipovetsky, Gilles, with Sébastien Charles. 2005. *Hypermodern Times*. Translated by Andrew Brown. Boston, MA: Polity.
Lotti, Laura. 2018. "Fundamentals of Algorithmic Markets: Liquidity, Contingency, and the Incomputability of Exchange." *Philosophy and Technology*. 31(1): 43–58. DOI: 10.1007/s13347-016-0249-8.
Lovecraft, H. P. 1982. *The Best of H.P. Lovecraft: Bloodcurdling Tales of Horror and the Macabre*. New York: Del Rey Books.
Lyotard, Jean-François. 1984. *The Postmodern Condition: A Report on Knowledge*. Translated by Geoff Bennington and Brian Massumi. Minneapolis: University of Minnesota Press.
Lyotard, Jean-François. 1988. *The Differend: Phrases in Dispute*. Translated by Georges Van Den Abbelle. Minneapolis: University of Minnesota Press.
Lyotard, Jean-François. 1991. *The Inhuman*. Translated by Geoff Bennington and Rachel Bowlby. Palo Alto, CA: Stanford University Press.
Lyotard, Jean-François. 1993a. *The Postmodern Explained*. Edited by Julian Pefanis and Morgan Thomas. Minneapolis: University of Minnesota Press.
Lyotard, Jean-François. 1993b. *Political Writings*. Translated by Bill Readings and Kevin Paul Geiman. Minneapolis: University of Minnesota Press.
Lyotard, Jean-François. 1997. *Postmodern Fables*. Translated by Georges Van Den Abbelle. Minneapolis: University of Minnesota Press.
Lyotard, Jean-François and Jean-Loup Thébaud. 1985. *Just Gaming*. Translated by Wlad Godzich. Minneapolis: University of Minnesota Press.
Madzia, Roman. 2013. "The Concept of Rule-Following in the Philosophy of George Herbert Mead." In *George Herbert Mead in the Twenty-First Century*, edited by F. Thomas Burke and Krysztof Piotr Skowronski, 61–70. Lanham, MD: Lexington Books.
Mandel, Ernest. 1978. *Late Capitalism*. Translated by Joris De Bres. London: Verso.
Manicas, Peter T. 1988. "Pragmatic Philosophy of Science and the Charge of Scientism." *Transactions of the Charles S. Peirce Society*. 24(2): 179–222.
Marcuse, Herbert. 1964. *One-Dimensional Man: Studies in the Ideology of Advanced Industrial Society*. Boston: Beacon Press.
Marx, Karl. 1973. *Grundrisse: Foundations of the Critique of Political Economy (Rough Draft)*. Translated by Martin Nicolaus. London: Penguin Books.
McEvilley, Thomas. 2005. *The Triumph of Anti-Art: Conceptual and Performance Art in the Formation of Post-Modernism*. Kingston, NY: McPherson.
Mead, George Herbert. 1964. *Selected Writings*. Edited by Andrew J. Reck. Chicago: University of Chicago Press.
Mead, George Herbert. 2002. *The Philosophy of the Present*. Edited by Arthur Murphy. Amherst, MA: Prometheus Books.
Midgley, Mary. 2001. *Science and Poetry*. New York: Routledge.
Misak, Cheryl. 1991. *Truth and the End of Inquiry: A Peircean Account of Truth*. Oxford: Oxford University Press.
Misak, Cheryl. 2005. "Pragmatism and Pluralism." *Transactions of the Charles S. Peirce Society*. 41(1): 129–35.
Mooney, Chris. 2006. *The Republican War on Science*. New York: Basic Books.

Munn, Nicholas John. 2012. "The Reality of Friendship Within Immersive Virtual Worlds." *Ethics and Information Technology.* 14(1): 1–10. DOI: 10.1007/s10676-011-9274-6.

Nardi, Bonnie A. 2010. *My Life as a Night Elf Priest: An Anthropological Account of World of Warcraft.* Ann Arbor: University of Michigan Press.

Nealon, Jeffrey T. 2012. *Post-Postmodernism: Or, the Cultural Logic of Just-in-Time Capitalism.* Palo Alto, CA: Stanford University Press.

Neff, Gina and Peter Nagy. 2016. "Talking to Bots: Symbiotic Agency and the Case of Tay." *International Journal of Communication.* 10: 4915–31.

Niethammer, Lutz, with Dirk Van Laak. 1992. *Posthistoire: Has History Come to an End?* Translated by Patrick Camiller. London: Verso.

Ong, Walter J. 1982. *Orality and Literacy: The Technologizing of the Word.* New York: Routledge.

Pariser, Eli. 2011. *The Filter Bubble: What the Internet Is Hiding From You.* New York: Penguin Press.

Pastor, L. M. and Cuadrado Garcí. 2014. "Modernity and Postmodernity in the Genesis of Transhumanism-Posthumanism." *Cuadernos de Bioética.* 25(85): 335–50.

Peirce, Charles Sanders. 1992. *The Essential Peirce: Selected Philosophical Writings, Volume 1 (1867–1893).* Edited by Nathan Houser and Christian Kloesel. Bloomington: Indiana University Press. (Abbreviated: EP 1. page)

Peirce, Charles Sanders. 1998. *The Essential Peirce: Selected Philosophical Writings, Volume 2 (1893–1913).* Edited by the Peirce Edition Project. Bloomington: Indiana University Press. (Abbreviated: EP 2. page)

Pinch, Trevor J. and Wiebe E. Bijker. 1987. "The Social Construction of Facts and Artifacts: Or How the Sociology of Science and the Sociology of Technology Might Benefit Each Other." In *The Social Construction of Technological Systems: New Directions in the Sociology and History of Technology*, edited by Wiebe E. Bijker, Thomas P. Hughes, and Trevor J. Pinch, 17–50. Cambridge, MA: MIT Press.

Pitt, Joseph. 1988. "'Style' and Technology." *Technology in Society.* 10(4): 447–56.

Pitt, Joseph. 2000. *Thinking About Technology: Foundations of the Philosophy of Technology.* New York: Seven Bridges Press.

Poincaré, Henri. 1952. *Science and Hypothesis.* Translated by W. J. Greenstreet. New York: Dover Publications.

Poster, Mark. 1990. *The Mode of Information: Poststructuralism and Social Context.* Chicago: University of Chicago Press.

Raines, Lee and Barry Wellman. 2012. *Networked: The New Social Operating System.* Cambridge, MA: MIT Press.

Reed, S. Alexander. 2013. *Assimilate: A Critical History of Industrial Music.* Oxford: Oxford University Press.

Resnik, David B. 2007. *The Price of Truth: How Money Affects the Norms of Science.* Oxford: Oxford University Press.

Riordan, Michael, Lillian Hoddeson, and Adrienne W. Kolb. 2015. *Tunnel Visions: The Rise and Fall of the Superconducting Super Collider.* Chicago: University of Chicago Press.

Rorty, Richard. 1979. *Philosophy and the Mirror of Nature*. Princeton, NJ: Princeton University Press.
Rorty, Richard. 1991. *Objectivity, Relativism, and Truth*. Cambridge, UK: Cambridge University Press.
Rorty, Richard. 2006. "Pragmatism as Anti-Authoritarianism." In *A Companion to Pragmatism*, edited by John Shook and Joseph Margolis, 257–66. Malden: Blackwell.
Sætra, Henrik Skaug. 2018. "Science as a Vocation in the Era of Big Data: The Philosophy of Science behind Big Data and humanity's Continued Part in Science." *Integrated Psychological and Behavioral Science*. 52(4): 508–22. DOI: 10.1007/s12124-018-9447-5.
Seigfried, Charlene Haddock. 1990. *William James's Radical Reconstruction of Philosophy*. Albany: State University of New York Press.
Sellars, Wilfrid. 1991. *Science, Perception and Reality*. Atascadero, CA: Ridgeview Publishing Company.
Shew, Ashley. 2017. *Animal Constructions and Technological Knowledge*. Lanham, MD: Lexington Books.
Silva, Filipe Carreira da. 2010. *Mead and Modernity: Science, Selfhood, and Democratic Politics*. Lanham, MD: Lexington Books.
Singer, Beth J. 1992. "Pragmatism and Pluralism." *The Monist*. 75(4): 477–91.
Stuhr, John. 2003. *Pragmatism, Postmodernism and the Future of Philosophy*. New York: Routledge.
Taylor, Mark C. 2007. *After God*. Chicago: University of Chicago Press.
Tirosh-Samuelson, Hava. 2012. "Transhumanism as a Secular Faith." *Zygon*. 47(4): 710–34.
Toulmin, Stephan. 1990. *Cosmopolis: The Hidden Agenda of Modernity*. Chicago: University of Chicago Press.
Treanor, Jill. 2017. "Pound's Flash Crash 'was Amplified by Inexperienced Traders.'" *The Guardian*. January 13, 2017. Available at: https://www.theguardian.com/business/2017/jan/13/pound-flash-crash-traders-sterling-dollar (accessed February 14, 2020).
Trudeau, Richard. 1987. *The Non-Euclidean Revolution*. Boston: Birkhaüser.
Turkle, Sherry. 2011. *Alone Together: Why We Expect More From Technology and Less From Each Other*. New York: Basic Books.
Vallor, Shannon. 2012. "Flourishing on Facebook: Virtue Friendship and New Social Media." *Ethics and Information Technology*. 14(3): 185–99. DOI: 10.1007/s10676-010-9262-2.
Vermeulen, Timotheus and Robin van den Akker. 2010. "Notes on Metamodernism." *Journal of Aesthetics and Culture*. 2(1): 1–14. DOI: 10.3402/jac.v2i0.5677.
Voss, David F. and Daniel E. Koshland Jr. 1993. "Editorial: The Lessons of the Super Collider." *Science*. 262(5141): 1799.
Weber, Max. 1930. *The Protestant Ethic and the Spirit of Capitalism*. Translated by Talcott Parsons. New York: Routledge.
Weiss, Margot. 2018. "Queer Politics in Neoliberal Times (1970–2010s)." In *The Routledge History of Queer America*, edited by Don Romesburg, 107–19. New York: Routledge.

West, Cornel. 1989. *The American Evasion of Philosophy: A Genealogy of Pragmatism*. Madison: University of Wisconsin Press.
West, Cornel. 1993. *Keeping Faith: Philosophy and Race in America*. New York: Routledge.
Wiener, Norbert. 1961. *Cybernetics: or Control and Communication in the Animal and the Machine*, Second Edition. Cambridge, MA: MIT Press.
Wilkie, Rob. 2011. *The Digital Condition: Class and Culture in the Information Network*. New York: Fordham University Press.
Wilkinson, Michael A. 2012. "Dewey's 'Democracy without Politics': On the Failures of Liberalism and the Frustrations of Experimentalism." *Contemporary Pragmatism*. 9(2): 117–42.
Winner, Langdon. 1989. *The Whale and the Reactor: A Search for Limits in an Age of High Technology*. Chicago: University of Chicago Press.
Winner, Langdon. 1993. "Upon Opening the Black Box and Finding It Empty: Social Constructivism and the Philosophy of Technology." *Science, Technology, and Human Values*. 18(3): 362–78.
Wittkower, D. E. 2012. "'Friend' Is a Verb." *APA Newsletter on Philosophy and Computers*. 12(1): 22–26.
Wittkower, D. E. (editor). 2008. *iPod and Philosophy: iCon of an ePoch*. Chicago: Open Court Press.

# Index

Aboulafia, Mitchell, 82
Adams, John, 2
Addams, Jane, 130
Adorno, Theodor, 5
Agonism, 55, 130
Akker, Robin van den, xii
annihilation of space and time, 1, 38, 74, 93, 95, 124. *See also* timeless time
anti-authoritarianism, 46, 112–14, 117–28. *See also* Rorty, Richard
architecture, 2, 3, 9, 11, 17, 72, 138
atomized individuals, 48, 62. *See also* networked social self; social self
Augustine, 28
authority, 7, 28, 31–32, 34, 39, 135, 145. *See also* legitimation
avant-garde, xxi, 80, 136, 139

Bacon, Francis, 6–7, 29
Barthes, Roland, xxiv, 13–15, 21, 23n2, 25, 128, 136
Bauldrillard, Jean, 2, 6, 8, 15, 22, 48, 68, 73, 81, 83–85, 87, 92–95, 101, 126, 136
the Beatles, xxii, 15, 20, 107
Bernstein, Richard J., 87n4, 108n1, 122, 128, 129
Best, Steven, xiii, 2, 6, 14, 33, 73, 84, 93, 111, 139, 148n1

Bijker, Wiebe E., 79. *See also* social constructivism
binary code, 18, 44–45, 76, 82
Black Sabbath, xxii
Borgmann, Albert, xxiv, 2, 6–11, 13, 15, 18, 21–22, 23n1, 25, 44, 51–53, 55, 66, 68–69, 71–74, 81, 83–85, 87n3, 106, 135, 148n2
Bostrom, Nick, 70. *See also* transhumanism
bounded infinite, xviii–xxiii, xxv, 1, 36, 39–44, 74, 80–81, 84, 91, 97, 107, 109, 118, 124, 131–32, 135–37, 141, 146–48
Brogaard, Berit, 98–99

Cabaret Voltaire, 3
capitalism, xvi–xvii, xx, 1, 5, 7, 23n1, 26, 32, 34, 39–40, 68, 91–92, 94, 111, 121, 124, 141. *See also* neoliberalism
Castells, Manuel, xxii, xxiv, 58, 89–90, 94–97, 100–104, 106–7, 124, 135–37, 139, 148n1. *See also* network society; timeless time
complexification, 40, 69, 74, 82
Cook, Gary, 59, 98
Le Corbusier, 3
cybernetics, 40, 42, 115, 142

cyberspace, xii, xviii, 51–52. *See also* Gibson, William; Infosphere
cyborg, 6, 115–18, 121, 123–27, 131–32

Deleuze, Giles, 15–16, 128, 136
democracy, xvi, xxiv, 12, 17, 20, 23, 35–36, 41–42, 56, 68, 87, 89–90, 92, 94, 103, 106, 110, 111–12, 115, 119, 121, 125, 128–31, 140–41, 146–48. *See also* intelligence, democratic
Derrida, Jacques, 2, 15–16, 22, 25, 43, 58, 87, 95, 126, 128, 136
Descartes, René, xxi, 6, 29, 122
Dewey, John, xiii, xxiii–xxiv, 11–13, 16–18, 22, 71, 75, 83–85, 109–10, 112–14, 117, 119–21, 123, 125, 127–31, 133n1, 137, 145, 147. *See also* democracy; inquiry; intelligence, creative
digimodernism, xii, xiv–xvi, xxi–xxii, 22. *See also* Kirby, Alan; post-postmodernism
difference, 1, 32, 39, 63, 67–68, 76, 105, 114–17, 124, 129–30, 135–36, 138, 147–48
differend, 111, 114, 130
Dreyfus, Hubert, 4, 10–11, 13, 51–52, 55, 66, 68, 73, 87n3, 106, 144
Dungeons and Dragons, 78

Eagleton, Terry, 67, 110
Ebert, Teresa, 2, 5, 23, 67, 103, 110, 111, 115, 123
Ellul, Jacques, 12, 141
emancipation 110–11, 148; end of, 39–43, 91, 93, 125, 135; and modernity, xvii, 28–29, 32, 34–35, 39, 91, 125, 137. *See also* the system
embodiment, 4, 12, 22, 25, 47, 51–54, 56, 59, 63–66, 74, 97, 106, 108, 144, 146. *See also* habit; social self
Engels, Friedrich, 91
entropy, 40, 42, 49, 69–71, 91–92, 142
Ermarth, Elizabeth Deeds, 43
Escher, M. C., xxi, xxvn3

Eshelman, Raoul, xii

Facebook, xiv, 15, 52–54, 58–61, 77–79, 86
Feenberg, Andrew, 80, 148n2
flexible accumulation. *See* capitalism
Floridi, Luciano, xii, xx, 26, 47
Foucault, Michel, 2, 67–68, 87, 142
Freud, Sigmund, xx, 30, 112–13, 116, 117
Fukuyama, Francis, 35, 91–93, 111
functionalism, 48, 62, 124–25. *See also* Parsons, Talcott

Garden myth, 90–91, 110–18, 121, 125–27, 131–32
Garrison, Jim, 13
Gibbons, Alison, xii
Gibson, William, xii, xviii
Giddens, Anthony, 37, 139
globalization, 1, 32, 38, 39, 107
Guattari, Félix, 16, 128, 136

Habermas, Jürgen, xiv, xvii, 32, 114, 137, 147, 148n2
habit, 11–13, 16–22, 65, 80, 108, 122, 127, 132, 141, 144–47. *See also* embodiment; Peirce
Hacking, Ian, 73
Hannan, Jason, 79, 145
Haraway, Donna, xxi, 2, 6, 26, 110, 115–27, 130, 132, 139, 148. *See also* cyborg
Harvey, David, xxi, xxii, 1–3, 5, 8, 38, 67, 75, 94, 107, 110, 111, 123, 124, 129, 139, 148n1
Hayles, N. Katherine, 44, 93
Hegel, Georg Wilhelm Friedrich, 63, 93, 129
Heidegger, Martin, 10–12, 16, 30, 72–73, 80, 113, 127, 141, 145
heritage industry, 38, 107
Hessen, Boris, 26
Hickman, Larry, xiii, xxiv, 2, 5, 11–22, 23n3, 25–26, 39, 77, 84, 108, 117,

118, 119, 122, 123, 128, 137, 141–42, 146, 148n2
Hookway, Christopher, 74
Horkheimer, Max, 42, 120, 148n2
Hughes, Thomas P., 79, 145
Hume, David, 30
hypermodernism: Borgmann on 8–11, 22, 71–74, 85; Lipovetsky on, xii, 107
hyperreality, 6, 8–10, 21, 22, 25, 38, 51, 68–69, 71–74, 81, 83, 136

information, 10, 26, 31, 43–45, 47, 53, 60, 76–78, 85, 87n1, 93, 96, 101, 111, 143; as paradigm, 4, 26–27, 31, 43, 45
informational objects, 47, 76–78, 82. *See also* social object; techno-social object
information and communication technologies, xii, xxiii, 3–4, 8–9, 13, 21, 25, 32, 44–46, 47–48, 50–55, 57–61, 63, 65–66, 68, 76–87, 93, 95–97, 101–4, 106, 124, 136–39, 143–44
Infosphere, 47, 73–74, 85, 143
inquiry, xxiv, 17, 74–75, 83–85, 116, 119–23, 127–33, 147
intelligence: creative, 11, 17, 20, 84, 106, 108, 144, 146–47, 148n3; democratic, 87, 106, 110, 146; hyperintelligence, 9, 22, 142

James, William, xiii, xxiii–xxiv, 75, 84, 110, 113, 119, 123, 127–32. *See also* meliorism; pluralism
Jameson, Fredric, xii, xxii, 2, 4–6, 67, 74, 107, 138, 148n1
Joas, Hans, 51–52, 56, 62–64, 98, 103, 117
"just-in-time" capitalism. *See* capitalism

Kaliarnta, Sofia, 52, 54
Kant, Immanuel, xviii, xxi, 29
Kellner, Douglas, xiii, 2, 6, 14, 33, 73, 84, 93, 111, 139, 148n1

Kirby, Alan, xii–xvii, xxi–xxii, xxvn2, 3, 10, 13, 21–22, 26, 33, 37, 136. *See also* digimodernism; post-postmodernism
Koyré, Alexander, xx–xxi
Kuhn, Thomas S., 31
Kurzweil, Ray, 2. *See also* transhumanism

language, 26, 42–44, 59, 69–71, 73, 76–77, 86, 87n1, 91
language games, 28–31, 34–36, 48–50, 55, 64–66, 129
late capitalism. *See* capitalism
Latour, Bruno, 2
Led Zeppelin, xxii
legitimation, xvii, xxiii, xxiv, 27–46, 68, 91, 93, 122, 137; crisis, 32, 41; de-legitimation, 30–31; performativity as, 34–36; and science, xvii–xviii, xxiv, 28–31; through paralogy, 55, 68
libraries, 4, 144
Lipovetsky, Gilles, xii, 38, 107. *See also* hypermodernism; post-postmodernism
Lovecraft, H. P., xi–xii, xxivn1
ludism, postmodern, xiii, 37, 68, 103, 105, 110, 114–15, 121, 130
Lyotard, Jean-François, xxiii–xxiv, 2, 15, 25–50, 55, 61–66, 68–73, 76, 80, 85–87, 90–93, 95, 107, 109, 110–11, 114–18, 120, 122–24, 126, 128–30, 132, 135–43, 148

Mandel, Ernest, 141
Marcuse, Herbert, 142
Marx, Karl, 1, 36, 80, 93, 111
Marxism, xviii, 5, 12, 17, 20, 34, 67, 90–91, 94, 116, 123, 141
Mead, George Herbert, xxiii–xxiv, 13, 47, 56–66, 75, 77, 81–82, 86, 89–90, 98–107, 119, 128–30, 138, 143
meliorism, xxiv, 110, 121, 127–28, 132, 141

memes, 60, 78
metanarratives, xvi, xxiv, 26–47, 67, 70, 90–93, 107, 109–11, 118, 122–23, 125–29, 132, 135, 137, 140–41
Midgley, Mary, 29
Mies van der Rohe, Ludwig, 3
Misak, Cheryl, 74, 75
MMORPG (Massively Multiplayer Online Role-Playing Game), 77–78, 82–83. *See also* video games; World of Warcraft
modernism, xi–xiii, xvii, xx, xxiii, 6–7, 31–32, 37, 80, 91–92, 109–11, 117, 123, 125, 127–28, 137, 139, 147–48; Borgmann on 6–7
modernity, xii–xiv, xvii–xviii, xx–xxv, 1, 5, 28, 32, 37, 39, 43, 89–91, 96, 109–11, 117, 127, 131, 135–39, 146, 148; as project, xvii–xviii, 136, 147
modern social bond. *See* social bond
modern technology, 1, 6–7, 10–11, 19, 21, 73, 139
Munn, Nicholas John, 54

Nealon, Jeffrey T., xii, 35, 48
neoliberalism, xvi, 34, 38. *See also* capitalism
networked social self, 61–66. *See also* Atomized individuals; social self
networks, 3, 5, 9, 26, 34, 38, 42, 44–45, 47–50, 55, 61–66, 76, 78, 80, 82, 85, 87, 124. *See also* network society; social networking sites; technical networks
network society, 2, 38, 45, 94, 96–97, 101–3, 106, 124. *See also* Castells, Manuel; cybernetics; social bond; timeless time
Niethammer, Lutz, 93
Nietzsche, Friedrich, xxi, 30
the now, 100–102, 106, 124, 136. *See also* the present; relativity, theory of special

objective action-nexus, 55–62, 84, 103–6. *See also* sociality
Ong, Walter J., 58
online friendships, 52–54, 58–59, 77–78
Orwell, George, 86

paralogy, 55, 68. *See also* legitimation; ludism, postmodern; performativity
Parsons, Talcott, 48, 142
Paul of Tarsis, 28
Peirce, Charles Sanders, xiii, xxii, xxiv, 74–75, 116, 119–23, 127–29, 133n1, 144, 146
performativity, 34–37, 40–42, 44, 45, 70, 86–87, 93, 122–23, 135, 137, 140–42, 148. *See also* legitimation; paralogy
Pinch, Trevor J., 79. *See also* social construction
Pitt, Joseph, 83, 140, 145
Plato and Platonism, 113
pluralism: postmodern, 37, 43, 116; pragmatic, 74–76, 84, 124, 128–31, 148. *See also* relativism
Poincaré, Henri, xviii–xix, xxi
Poster, Mark, 6, 15,
postmodernism, xii–xvi, xxii, xxiv, 2, 4–10, 13, 20–23, 25–26, 32, 36–37, 45, 50, 67–68, 80–81, 85, 91–92, 107, 110, 115, 118–20, 123, 125–26, 129, 131–32, 131–38, 148
postmodernity, xi–xviii, xx–xxiv, 1–6, 10, 12, 21, 25, 27, 32–43, 46, 47–48, 54, 67–69, 73, 87, 89–94, 107, 109–10, 124, 126, 129, 131–32, 135–41, 144–48; as challenge, xvii–xviii, xxiii, 111, 124, 128, 132, 136, 137–48
postmodern social bond. *See* social bond
postmodern technology, 2–10, 12–16, 19–22, 43–46, 65, 138–41
post-postmodernism, xii–xvii, 13, 21–23, 110, 136. *See also* digimodernism

the present, 98–108. *See also* the now; timeless time

Quine, Willard Van Orman, 122

Radiohead, xxi–xxii
Raines, Lee, 65, 138
reconstruction, 12, 17–19, 23, 47, 81, 85, 90, 98–100, 102, 104–8, 111, 115, 117, 124–29, 131–32, 140, 144–48. *See also* intelligence, creative
relativism, xiii, xxiii, 32, 36, 39, 42–43, 45, 67, 84–85, 120–21, 125–26, 137–38. *See also* pluralism, postmodern
relativity, theory of special, 31, 98
Resnik, David B., 26, 48
Rolling Stones, xxii
Rorty, Richard, 110–23, 130

science, xvii–xviii, xx, xxiv, 26–32, 34–37, 39, 43–46, 68, 76, 81, 100, 117, 119–23, 126, 148
Seigfried, Charlene Haddock, 122, 128
Sellars, Wilfrid, 50, 122
semiotics, 50, 77, 82–83, 95. *See also* significant symbols
Shew, Ashley, 70
significant symbols, xxiv, 56, 58–60, 64–66, 70–71, 73, 77, 82, 143. *See also* semiotics; social act; social object
Silva, Filipe Carreira da, 56
social act, 53–66, 68, 77–78, 85, 103–8
social bond, 47–52, 61–65, 68, 80, 124–25, 142
social constructivism, xv, 12, 73, 80, 103, 120, 140, 146
social control, 57, 60–61, 65–66, 74, 85–87, 139. *See also* social act; social object
sociality, 47, 51–52, 58–61, 65, 81, 90, 98, 102–7

social networking sites, xiv, 15, 22, 52–61, 65, 80. *See also* Facebook; networks; Twitter
social object, 57–61, 77–80, 82, 143. *See also* informational object; social act; social control; techno-social object
social self, xxiv, 13, 56–64, 66, 81, 86, 104, 106, 129. *See also* atomized individuals; networked social self; taking the attitude of the other
Spengler, Otto, 30
Spinosa, Charles, 4, 10–11, 13, 73, 144
Stuhr, John, 148
Suzuki, Koji, xxiv–xxvn1
the system, 35–37, 39–43, 68, 70, 93, 137, 141–43, 146, 148n3

taking the attitude of the other, 57–61, 65, 82, 86. *See also* Mead, George Herbert; social self
technical system, 77, 79
technological determinism, 5, 11–12, 17–21, 72, 141
technological essentialism, 5, 11–12, 16, 19–20, 36, 74, 91, 122, 148
technology: Borgmann on, 6–11, 18, 21–23, 44, 51–53, 55, 68, 72–74, 83–85; and embodiment, 4, 16, 22, 51–54, 59, 63–66; and flexibility, xxiii, 13, 25; Hickman's definition of, 16–19; and music, xiv, xxi–xxii, 3–4, 14–15, 18–21, 25, 96, 139–40; and salvation, 93, 140–41, 148
techno-social object, 68, 74, 76–86, 146. *See also* informational object; social object
temporality, xxiii–xxiv, 89–90, 128, 136; Castells on, 94–97; Mead on, 98–107; postmodern 90–94
terror, 32, 36–39, 42, 46, 55, 63, 65, 85–86, 109–10, 114, 125, 130–31, 135, 137. *See also* legitimation; Lyotard, Jean-François

Throbbing Gristle, 3
timeless time, 89, 94–98, 100–107, 136–37, 144
time-space compression. *See* annihilation of space and time
Toulmin, Stephan, 29
transhumanism, 2, 70, 93, 140
Trudeau, Richard, xviii–xix, xxv
Turkle, Sherry, 55, 138
Twitter, 15, 79, 143–45. *See also* social networking sites

Vallor, Shannon, 53–54
Vermeulen, Timotheus, xii

video games, xii, xiv–xv, 8–9, 11, 21, 72, 83. *See also* MMORPGs

Weber, Max, 1, 30, 36
Wellman, Barry, 42
West, Cornel, 1, 128
Wiener, Norbert, 40. *See also* cybernetics
Wilkie, Rob, 27, 90, 148n1
Winner, Langdon, 80, 145
Wittgenstein, Ludwig, 28, 49
Wittkower, D. E., 23n4, 53–54
World of Warcraft, 54, 77–78, 83. *See also* MMORPGs; video games

# About the Author

**Andrew Wells Garnar** earned his PhD from Virginia Tech and primarily works with the tools of American pragmatism to understand the social implications of technology. He also dabbles in the philosophy of science. He coedited with Ashley Shew *Feedback Loops: Pragmatism about Science and Technology* (Lexington Books). Presently living in Tucson, he has been known to teach at the University of Arizona.

www.ingramcontent.com/pod-product-compliance
Lightning Source LLC
Chambersburg PA
CBHW050907300426
44111CB00010B/1419